Late in the Third
Observations from Both Sides of the Glass

Joe Bertagna

Late in the Third
Observations from Both Sides of the Glass

Printed by Daily Printing in Beverly Farms, MA

Front Cover Photo: Joe Bertagna and Bill Ranford
(Courtesy of Boston Bruins)
Back Cover Photo: Joe Bertagna
(USA Hockey Photo)

Cover Design: Alicia Zampitella, Zampitella Creative

ISBN 978-0-578-94893-5

"Late in the Third" website:
www.lateinthethird.com

Dedication

To my mentors.

Inside the Glass: Eddie, Billy and Timmy
Outside the Glass: Scotty and Clayt

Table of Contents

Introduction

"Studies show that most people have four or five jobs in their lifetimes. Today's guest speaker has five jobs right now."
— The author's introduction at a high school career day

I don't recall the year of that career day referenced above, but I would place it somewhere in the 1990s. And the five jobs were all in ice hockey: conference commissioner, coaches association administrator, goalie coach, freelance writer and freelance broadcaster.

Having been blessed to hold all of those positions — in the 1990s and for decades on either side of that period — I have enjoyed a front row seat for a half century of hockey. I have played, coached and administered the game for most of those years, and when the opportunity arose, was paid to write about it and talk about it.

In deciding to chronicle this journey, I had to deal with one basic question that was offered freely by many friends and acquaintances: "Who do you think will read your book?"

Good question.

That could just as easily have been, "Who are YOU to write a memoir?" To write a personal memoir is inherently self-serving. And when your life story is not one of historic consequence, that basic question looms over the undertaking. Early on I decided to get over this concern. The short answer is that I really don't know who will buy it. Maybe it will just be close friends and relatives. But to be candid, I actually believe there is an audience out there for the stories and observations from this lifetime in hockey.

During the writing process, my copy editor, John Veneziano, asked me if there would be an introduction. He said, "You should let people know who you are and what you have done." At the time, my response was, "Why would I have to do that? The only people who will be buying this book will be people who already know who I am." I have since come around to thinking that might not be the case.

While you will get to know who I am and what I have done through these pages, I can provide a little background and, in the process, perhaps explain why I felt I could pull this off.

I am going to use my personal history on Causeway Street in Boston to provide a condensed résumé. Causeway Street, of course, is where the TD Garden can be found. It is home to the Boston Bruins and the Boston Celtics. I have been a participant in events on Causeway Street, either at the old "Gahden" or the Fleet Center or the current incarnation for six decades.

In the 1960s, I was a goalie on high school teams that won a pair of championships there. In the 1970s, I played college hockey there. In the 1980s, I broadcast games from there and began a stretch of 38 years directing college tournaments there, starting with one league and ending with another.

In the 1980s and 1990s, I was also an NHL goalie coach there. In the 2000s and 2010s and falling just shy of a seventh decade, I directed more of those college tournaments.

The Causeway Street part of my history provides a convenient yet incomplete summary of my hockey life. Maybe a scrapbook of images could do a better job of revealing the variety of experiences I have enjoyed. There I am playing in college hockey's Beanpot Tournament. There is an article on me in the *Harvard Crimson* written by my friend, Benazir Bhutto, the future Prime Minister of Pakistan. This photo was taken of me on the set of *Love Story*. Oh, look, there is a photo of me in goal when we won the Italian National Championship.

I'm in street clothes in these next pictures. In this one, I am on the bench at Harvard coaching its first women's hockey team. Here's one of me broadcasting a Hartford Whalers game alongside play-by-play announcer John Forslund. Oh, in this one I am the sideline reporter at the Beanpot for ESPN. I didn't remember this picture of me representing Team USA at the final Olympic press conference in Lillehammer. Is that a picture of me at Ken Dryden's house when he helped me with my first book on goaltending?

As I bring you from the playing days of my youth to my adult years as an administrator, you will see how simple the game was when I began in the 1960s. Hockey was important to us, but we played other sports as well. For our hockey games, two on-ice officials were enough to control our game. We got by without video replay, and in college, we got to the NCAA Tournament without a computer ranking. Games on TV? I'm old enough that none of the photos of me in the scrapbook my mother kept are in color!

In planning and executing this book, I had many friends and peers to contact for guidance and two of them, both established authors, were uniquely helpful. One was particularly interested in the stories. He would steer me toward the behind-the-scenes stories, and my guess is that if he had the final word, he might have kept more of the sensitive accounts in the finished product.

The other, while certainly supportive of my storytelling, saw greater value in the historical observations and comparisons and suggested that if done properly, this book could be of value to professors who teach classes on sports administration.

While I was likely to arrive at this place on my own, these friends helped me identify my primary charge: I had to find a way to share the stories of this hockey life in a way that wasn't just a string of anecdotes but, when put in some chosen order, revealed how the game has changed through this half century.

When famed NHL general manager Brian Burke wrote his memoir, he commented that he owed his former employers a "level of confidentiality." That resonated with me as I went through various situations that I felt could be of interest to a reader. First drafts allowed me to get everything out there. Upon reflection, some stories simply could not be shared. Or, at least, not shared the way I first told them.

Still, I am confident that college hockey fans, beyond "close friends and family," will enjoy what made the final cut. It has been a treat to relive this hockey life and put it all down for the record. I hope you enjoy the journey.

Joe Bertagna,
Gloucester, MA — July 2021

iv - Late in the Third

Chapter One —
Arlington, Massachusetts

"The Atlantic Ocean was somethin' then. Yes, you should have seen
the Atlantic Ocean in those days."
              Burt Lancaster as Lou Pascal in "Atlantic City"

Everything was better in the old days for Lou Pascal, Burt Lancaster's character in the 1980 film *Atlantic City*. The food, the weather, the Atlantic Ocean. I don't want to be Lou Pascal. However ...

Arlington, Massachusetts. Six miles northwest of Boston, Arlington was a great place to grow up, and it was there that my lifelong interest in athletics took root. This was nurtured by two parents and two siblings who supported my various pursuits.

Ah, parents. Parents were somethin' then. You should have seen parents in those days. My parents signed us up for what we wanted and then stayed out of it. No going to practices or questioning our coaches' decisions. My sister, Carol, was the first person to bring me to a pond to learn how to skate. My brother, Bob, played high school hockey before me and was my inspiration.

But before there were organized games, there was time alone. The youngest of three children, I was more than four years younger than my brother and nine years younger than my sister.

This was a time when we played as many sports as we could. The Big Three were football, hockey and baseball, and there was a season for each. We were just as likely to find a game on a local playground as we were to do something formal for which we had to sign up.

Sure, we signed up for Little League in the spring and organized youth hockey in the winter. But back then, those pursuits didn't occupy too much of one's time. We had hours of free time. Time at the playground with friends. Time alone. I have always had the ability to keep myself occupied and amused. Still do. Give me a set of steps and a ball that bounced. I could play forever, making up games and broadcasting them to myself.

My favorite spot was the next door neighbor's driveway. They had a three-car garage and a funnel-shaped driveway leading from the street to those car stalls. It was enclosed with concrete walls that were great for targeting rubber-coated baseballs. Throw straight and the ball bounced right to you. Throw to your left, and the ball would deflect further to your left so you had to hurry. Throw to your right and you learned how to make a nice backhanded catch.

The driveway also had a small lip to it, with about a six-inch dropoff to dirt. I would deliberately stand behind that lip, forcing me to react quickly to changes of direction the end of the concrete caused. I wasn't thinking about this at the time, but I'm sure it was good practice for the goaltending I would take up as a teen.

More meaningful were the hours spent playing games with friends. These games could take place anywhere. A playground, an open field, a frozen pond or maybe in someone's backyard. To this day, when I first visit someone's house, I take note of the backyard to see how a good Wiffle Ball game could be laid out.

That same neighbor's driveway was a great locale for street hockey. The neighbors were the the Shaws. So I called the large driveway Shawcago Stadium. I can still feel a frozen tennis ball hitting some part of my body, followed immediately by a mixture of sand and salt left behind by winter plows.

Playing games without adult supervision had so many benefits. We got to make up our own rules. We learned how to settle differences. We had to pick teams. We could include which kids we wanted and get rid of the jerks. And we could play without worrying about making mistakes. We could be creative. In our play. In our language.

In good weather, baseball of some sort dominated our play. Two people? No problem. Narrow the field and hit out of your hand. Three people? Hitter, pitcher, fielder. More than three, the possibilities were endless.

In the winter, Arlington had three surfaces that might freeze and allow for skating. Maybe that's why hockey was so important to the town. There was Hills Pond, about 100+ yards from my house. There was Spy Pond, so big that it never froze completely.

Not only had Arlington High School played games on Spy Pond, hence the Spy Ponders nickname, but so did Harvard University. Actually, Harvard hosted Brown University in a game of ice polo on Spy Pond in February 1896, two years before they met in an ice hockey game in Boston's Franklin Park. Ice polo was played with a hard rubber ball and without borders or offsides. For the record, Brown won that ice polo game, 5-4.

And there was a small body of water called Meadowbrook toward the Medford town line. I can still feel the thrill when, at the end of the school day, messages over the PA system would include, "Safe skating at Hills Pond and Meadowbrook."

That would be followed by a quick sprint home to get skates, gloves and a stick and look for a pick-up hockey game. At Hills Pond, skaters had one side and hockey players the other. Two duffle bags would serve as goal posts, snow banks defined "out-of-bounds" and quickly our game was on. Any number of groups would carve out space for games, their pucks crossing invisible borders, retrieved carefully. It was a great place to hone skills. Stickhandling in close quarters was a necessity. Making a crisp short pass was also desirable, to avoid having to enter another group's territory in search of a wayward disc.

It's likely that the actual number of days that I skated on a pond were far fewer than in my memory. But the impact of those days was strong. And like summer baseball games, we were free to play without adults, make up rules, start and end games as we saw fit and, when it was too dark to see the puck against the black ice, take off the skates, rub the numb toes and go home for dinner.

For many of us, the first taste of organized sports was either Little League baseball or youth hockey. I don't know if this is true, but two stories circulated a number of years ago, anecdotes intended to show how times had changed. In one, a Little League team showed up for a game only to find that its opponent had the wrong date and did not appear. Coaches told the players to make up teams on their own and play among themselves. The kids looked at each other and weren't sure how to do that.

In the other story, a hockey opponent showed up without enough players for an official game. While one adult suggested that one team loan a player or two to the under-manned team, the other coach declined the offer, stating that since it wouldn't count as an official game, why would they play it? There was a time when kids on a playground, without adults, would have known what to do in both of these situations.

While I have often acknowledged how good hockey has been to me, both in my youth and as an adult, I have always, at my core, been a baseball guy. Nothing has ever matched the pure joy of opening up a wax pack of baseball cards in the mid-to-late 1960s and finding a Red Sox player among the cards and stale gum. And it didn't have to be Ted Williams. Ted Lepcio or Ted Bowsfield would do just as well.

My family still reminds me that on the hottest summer days of my youth, while everyone else was on a beach or in a boat, I would be parked in front of the television, in suffocating indoor heat, pounding the pocket of a well-oiled baseball glove, as I watched my beloved Red Sox. I still recall, with some detail, watching the 1961 All-Star Game held at Fenway on a small, likely black and white, television in our summer home in Gloucester. I remember the annual summer trip, by train, to a Red Sox game with my mother. I recently went on line to see if my memory of Johnny Blanchard hitting two home runs for the Yankees was accurate. It was.

And so you can imagine the glee when one of my first jobs, at the age of 15, was as a vendor at Fenway Park. It was the glorious summer of 1967. From ninth to first. The summer of Yaz. And there I was, rarely missing a game, selling soda and hot dogs and "tree-flavuhd ice cream." To this day, after working an Olympics (1994) and two Stanley Cup finals (1988 and 1990) and multiple college championships, the most exciting day of sports in my memory was the last day of the 1967 baseball season.

The Sox needed success at home against the Minnesota Twins and some help from others, and by late Sunday afternoon, the Impossible Dream regular season was successfully in the books. The game also began my own Zelig-like existence that would find me as a minor participant at a series of great sports moments.

Think of being a 15-year-old in that summer. What a great first job! Work for 10 days, get 10 days off. Work mostly nights and weekends, enjoy the rest of summer. No summer ice hockey showcases on my schedule to market myself to college coaches, as teens must do today.

Oh sure, as a rookie vendor I had to sell ice cream on April night games when the temperature was in the mid-40s. But later, when you established yourself, you would sell Coca Cola on a hot July Saturday, selling so many so fast that the concessionaire (Harry M. Stevens) couldn't keep up.

The hot dogs cost more, so your 10% commission grew faster, when that was what you were selling. Two things about the hot dogs I recall. First, when the price went from fifty cents to sixty-five cents, those vendors who struggled with math had a hell of a time making change.

Second, the machine that sealed the dogs in cellophane would occasionally mangle the odd puppy. You would wait for that family of five to order hot dogs for everyone, and you'd bury the one mutant dog in the middle of four good ones. Invariably, I'd look back and see the father giving the damaged dog to his youngest child.

I also got an education from the city kids who dominated the vendor workforce. In those days, as hard it is to believe now, you were not allowed to bring beer to your seats. I was taught a way to make some extra coin from the city kids. You would stand near one of the ramps going up to the seats from the concession concourse, and watch a beer holder denied access to his seat. As the disgruntled fan trudged below, I would approach him, having moved all my hot dogs to one side of the aluminum box I carried around, and having blown out the Sterno flame that had kept those dogs warm.

"Hey, give me your beer. I can carry it to your seat in here," I'd say, showing him the empty compartment. They almost always agreed. Arriving at their seat, I'd wait for the tip that usually came. If it didn't, I would put my hand out, and that would free a quarter or two from the patron.

Of course, if that didn't work, I'd go down below, get an usher, and direct him to the cheap beer-drinking SOB who was about to learn a lesson. I liked to follow the usher up the aisle, and as he directed the fan back down below, I'd make sure to catch his eye.

The 1967 World Series against the Bob Gibson-led Cardinals was a high point. I remember getting autographs from Roger Maris and his Cardinals teammates. In fact, that job provided so many unique autograph opportunities in those years. Red Sox owner Tom Yawkey. NBC commentator Sandy Koufax. Oakland hitting coach Joe DiMaggio.

I remember Jim Lonborg's one-hitter in Game Two, with the lone single coming in the eighth inning from Julian Javier, a .257 lifetime hitter. And then seeing the homemade sign at the next home game, declaring, "Julian Javier is a Herk."

I almost missed much of the World Series experience because my beloved mother wasn't sure I should skip school for the afternoon games that are now a thing of the past. She made me accompany her to the office of Dr. Bert Roens, the Arlington Superintendent of Schools. I have to give him credit that he listened to my mother while maintaining a straight face. At one point, he got up and said he needed to confer with one of his colleagues. I have no doubt that he went into the next room and said to someone, "Do you believe this mother is considering denying her son a chance to attend, let alone work, a World Series game at Fenway Park?"

He returned to us, maintaining a level of seriousness that kind of scared me, but allowed that this was not missing school to simply watch a baseball game but was a chance to maintain my work relationship with the Red Sox. So I got the pass.

Sadly, my love of the game did not translate into much of a playing career. I played Little League ball and briefly at the next level but that was where one of my more embarrassing youth sports memories resides.

One of our decent players was screwing around before a game and the coach benched him. I was inserted in his place, batting sixth. As it turns out, I got up sixth ... with two outs and the bases loaded. The coach assessed the situation, turned to the punished player and said, "Are you sorry for what you did?" He said, "Yes. Very sorry." With very little additional thought, the coach said, "OK. Go bat for Bertagna." Taken out for a pinch-hitter in the top of the first inning! The worst part was that I had the whole game ahead of me knowing I couldn't go back in.

When it came time for me to sign up for organized hockey, I had a choice: the Arlington program, that, at the time, consisted of just playing games on Saturday mornings, or the preferred program in Belmont. This program, organized by Scott Parrot, took place at the Belmont Hill School and had the benefit of weeks of drills and training before any games would be played. I don't have any memory of advocating for this so my parents must have done some research.

Scott Parrot was the heart and soul of this program. A Dartmouth graduate who was injured in World War II, Parrot was a dynamo, moving quickly around the perimeter of the rink, aided by his cane. He made sure that qualified coaches were on hand to teach the game properly before we started keeping score. His son, Kent, was one of the better skaters of the era and went on to a solid career at Harvard. Scott also ran the hockey school of Harvard coach Cooney Weiland at the Boston Skating Club that many of us attended while in middle school.

I recently converted some of my father's old 16-millimeter films to DVD and was pleasantly surprised to find some footage of a Saturday morning game at Belmont Hill.

Stocking cap stuffed under a leather helmet, exterior mouthguard over my lips, I actually looked like a competent, if slow, defenseman. I would end up playing defense for the Belmont Bantams and another season with the North Cambridge Bantams. It was with the latter that I first put on goalie pads when our regular goalie got sick on the way to a game. More on that later.

While these youth hockey experiences set the stage for our budding athletic careers, the individual who took many of us to a greater heights was Edward P. Burns.

A native of Arlington, Eddie Burns was a three-sport star at AHS, serving as captain of the football team as a senior in the fall of 1939. He played football at Fordham Prep for another gravel-voiced coaching legend, a young Vince Lombardi. He went on to a Hall of Fame career at Boston College, again playing three sports and once scoring five goals in a game for the Eagles. He was assigned to a Marine Artillery Unit in 1943, interrupting his Boston College education while he served in Guam with his Marine Division, until his return to school in 1946.

By the time I entered high school in the fall of 1965, Burns was finishing his second decade at AHS. He established a culture of athletic excellence in Arlington, carrying out his magic through 21 seasons as the high school football coach and 50 seasons as its hockey coach. In all, Burns won 805 games in those combined 71 seasons. In addition to numerous league and state titles, he won a phenomenal 75% of the 1,108 games he coached.

Burns' success made young Arlington athletes want to play for him.

Even kids who could have started on the basketball team wanted to give hockey a try. It drove the basketball coaches crazy.

I have been asked, from time to time, how I got into a sports career as an adult and, more specifically, how or when exactly did it begin. I have identified two possible "start dates," to borrow a phrase from the NCAA.

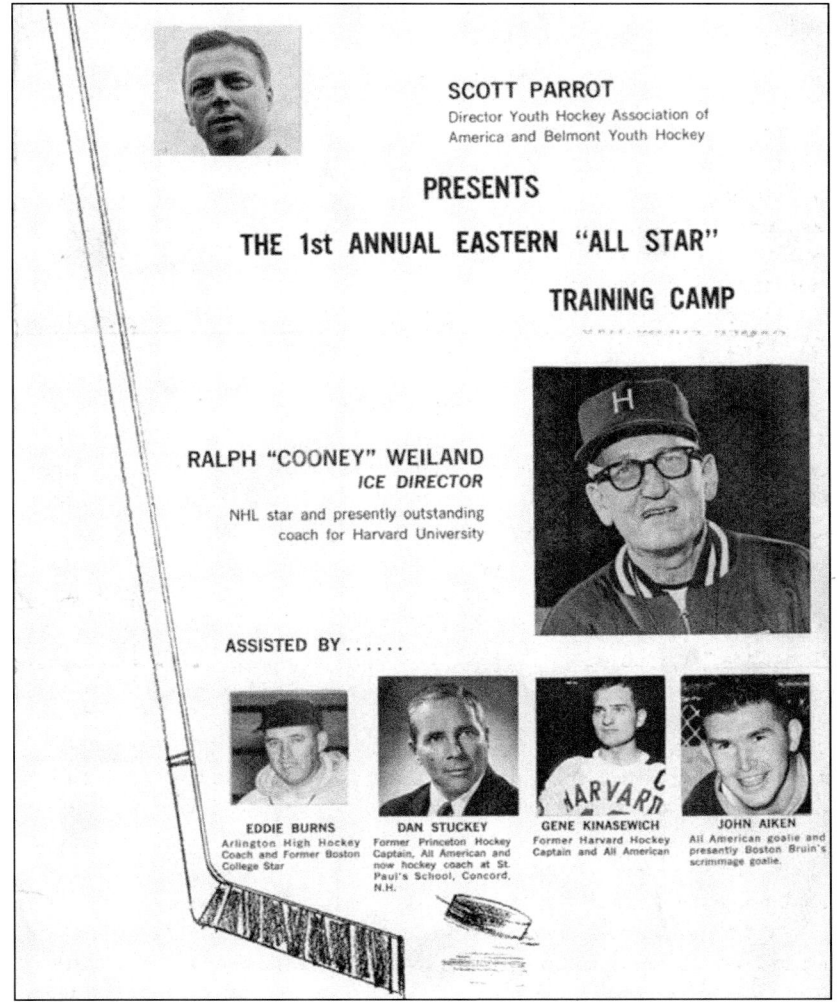

SCOTT PARROT
Director Youth Hockey Association of America and Belmont Youth Hockey

PRESENTS

THE 1st ANNUAL EASTERN "ALL STAR"

TRAINING CAMP

RALPH "COONEY" WEILAND
ICE DIRECTOR

NHL star and presently outstanding coach for Harvard University

ASSISTED BY . . . . . .

EDDIE BURNS
Arlington High Hockey Coach and Former Boston College Star

DAN STUCKEY
Former Princeton Hockey Captain, All American and now hockey coach at St. Paul's School, Concord, N.H.

GENE KINASEWICH
Former Harvard Hockey Captain and All American

JOHN AIKEN
All American goalie and presently Boston Bruin's scrimmage goalie.

This is the brochure from the first hockey school I ever attended. A middle school defenseman at the time, I would play goal for two of the coaches (Burns and Weiland) and play adult hockey with another (Kinasewich.) And, yes, I have saved a lot of stuff over the years.

First, and this may be a stretch, was that Christmas when my brother and I received a table hockey game. This was the kind that used a marble and whose thin metal players, in Original Six uniforms, did not move up and down the ice but rotated in place. I cite this moment because I started to make schedules and keep stats and sometimes, despite the NHL players on the board, we were college teams in our minds.

But a more appropriate starting point would be my four years as a football manager for Coach Burns at the high school. Burns made it known that he wanted his hockey players to play football. He said it would toughen us up for the winter, but I think he really wanted to be able to keep his eye on us in those months leading up to hockey season.

This was a time when a young athlete took great pride in playing for his hometown. This was well before the days when athletes and parents were constantly on the lookout for something better. Leave the town youth program for an independent team. Leave the local high school for the private school. Attend a "hockey academy" with on-line learning. Delay college for a junior team. Leave that junior team for another junior team.

There was still a great respect for tradition. There was the attractiveness of being a hometown hero. I wanted to play hockey for Arlington because my brother did. Later on, when I married Kathy Leonard, I was part of an extended Burns Family, as Kathy's father and two uncles had also played for Eddie. It was a big deal for us.

When I entered high school in the fall of 1965, I wanted to keep in the coach's good graces, but I had no desire to play football. Another defenseman, Bob Bartholomew, was two years older than me and found a solution to this dilemma: He became a manager.

Bob and Tom Peters, who was a year older than "Barts," went this route. Both would go on to play hockey at the University of Massachusetts and both would remain in athletics for decades. Bob returned to Arlington High School to teach and coach through five decades, while Tom would enjoy a long and successful administrative career, first at the Boston Garden, and then in a series of college stops, including Rutgers, Tulane, Virginia and, for 26 years, Boston College.

So, I decided to become a football manager, working for Director of Athletics Bill Lowder. "Lefty," as he was known, was gruff on the outside but a great guy for whom to work. That, in all reality, was my first exposure to the organizational side of athletics. While our jobs were, at first, pretty low level — filling cups with water, making sure the bag of footballs was brought out, cleaning cleats during timeouts on muddy game days — we got the chance to see an "AD" and all that was part of his world.

He ordered equipment, which we helped store and inventory. He took care of scheduling. He confirmed that buses had been arranged. He made sure the games had officials and that they got paid. He lined up the sideline crew, who moved the chains. He made sure the coaches could film the games and that the film was properly shared with opponents, and that the scores of the games were called into the appropriate media outlets. That last responsibility was where the managers enjoyed one of their perks.

In those days, before cell phones and the internet, reporting scores meant finding a pay phone and calling a newspaper or a television station with the results. This was also a time when the high schools and colleges enjoyed far greater coverage than now, when the pros dominate the media.

So, technically, my first paying job in sports entailed calling one of those TV stations and recording a brief recap of the game. "It was a rainy day at Pierce Field in Arlington where the host Spy Ponders rallied for 14 fourth-quarter points to defeat a stubborn Waltham team, 20-19, and remain undefeated. This is Joe Bertagna reporting for Action Sports." A week later, I would receive a check for $10 in the mail. A career was born.

It wasn't always glamorous or so rewarding. The first assignment on game days was to be ready to run out into the team huddle during timeouts. We would carry these trays of tiny paper cups, maybe eight to a tray, water splashing everywhere as we ran on uneven surfaces. I can't say how much water remained for the players when we actually got there. And as referenced earlier, on rainy days, the job of taking a large nail and scraping mud off of cleats (attached to high top black shoes) always fell to the freshmen as part of the "class system."

But with time, our responsibilities changed, and we moved up the managerial ladder. We had keys to the equipment room. We spent more time with Bill Lowder. We learned how to tape ankles. Well, some of us did. And some even did so without cutting off circulation in the players' feet. We earned a varsity letter and got a reversible AHS football jacket. Some managers had "ST" embroidered where the athletes had their position listed. We might tell people that it stood for "Strongside Tackle," when, in fact, it was for "Student Trainer."

Yes, this was the start of a life in athletics. Years later, in my adult work life, I would be scheduling games, making sure scores were publicized, exchanging video, keeping team stats and assigning game officials. In all, I spent four years in a college sports information office and 38 years as a conference administrator. On top of this, I have been a goalie coach for nearly 50 years, as I write. So who knows what I have been able to apply from being a disciple of Eddie Burns in that part of my life?

The 1966 AHS football team went 9-0 and won the state championship. That launched a phenomenal year where those who played football, hockey and baseball did not lose a game until the first game of the baseball state tournament in the spring. The streak reached 46 before anyone tasted defeat. Many of the athletes on these teams went on to play college athletics in one sport or another, including some at the Division I level.

One of my assignments on game day was to throw footballs to receivers where they would start with their backs to me and I would throw the ball and immediately clap my hands. Their response, in theory, was to hear the "clap," turn around quickly and the ball would be there waiting to be caught. As one might envision, there were some malfunctions where I might get distracted and either clap too late or, perhaps, not at all, the point of the football smacking into the back of their heads. One of these receivers, Denis Sullivan, would go on to Harvard and play varsity football and junior varsity hockey.

There were other standouts. Quarterback Mark Driscoll would play both football and baseball at the University of Arizona. He was also the goalie on the undefeated hockey team, one who frequently faced fewer than 10 shots a game and often played without a chest protector, guarding himself with the quick and skilled hands regularly on display in his other sports.

Halfback George Gill played football at Boston College and running back Bob Havern set a state record for scoring in ice hockey before going on to Harvard where we would be teammates. He later had an exemplary career as a Massachusetts state senator. Paul Boudreau attended Boston

The Arlington High School football staff. From left, Ralph "Ike" Bevins (an All-American goalie at BU), Eddie Burns and "Red" Hill.

College before launching a coaching career, where he served as offensive line coach for eight different NFL teams. Center Paul Traverse also went to BC, along with backup QB Joe Pandolfo.

Kevin McNeeley played at Weber State. McNeeley's older brother, Tom, had played football at Michigan State but was better known as a heavyweight boxer. He was on the cover of *Sports Illustrated* in 1961, the year he fought Floyd Patterson for the heavyweight championship. Bringing a 23-0 record to champ Patterson's 37-2 career mark, McNeeley didn't get through the fourth round, knocked down nine times before the fight was stopped.

I provide this list of peers who went on to college or professional sports to show the culture in which we grew up. It was easy to set goals for ourselves when so many who preceded us enjoyed success at higher levels, many doing so straight out of our public high school.

The success of those who came before us, who went from our high school to college, dulled any instincts we might have had for leaving the public school. My father spoke with me, briefly, about whether or not I should consider Belmont Hill School, a private school with a great hockey tradition. I would have nothing of it. I didn't want to leave Arlington.

Is there anything wrong with this? I have heard arguments that the more experiences, the richer the learning. Maybe. But there is something to be said for putting down roots in one place, becoming a leader and earning greater responsibility. When you are constantly moving around, always the "new kid," you are not often the beneficiary of special duties and responsibilities.

Many of my generation who played high school hockey in the 1960s, whether in the Iron Range of Minnesota, at a Connecticut prep school or in the handful of indoor rinks in Greater Boston, have undoubtedly maintained vivid memories of the experience. For me, it was Saturday afternoons at the Boston Arena (now Northeastern University's Matthews Arena). French fries in the lobby. A slight cloud of cigarette smoke hovering over center ice, perhaps. The scoreboard on the far wall, much like the one we watched at the old Boston Garden, had those small penalty "clocks," where a hand was set at the length of the penalty and it would move up as play went on, lit up during the action and the light extinguished at each whistle.

The seasons were short compared to how much hockey kids play today. When I entered high school, we only played 10-minute periods and 14 games. Think of that. The entire regular season consisted of just seven hours of competition.

In those days, two games were played intermittently. That is, Arlington might play its first period against Brookline, followed by the first period of Newton vs. Waltham. Then we would play our second period and then the ice was resurfaced. After fresh ice, their second period, our third, and their third would close it out. Four cheering sections in the building, each in its own corner. And after this, four more schools entered the building and they did it again.

This meant that one intermission would be extremely long, consisting of a re-surfacing and the other game's next period. During one of these sessions, it appeared that my back-up goalie was bleeding through his white game jersey. It turned out to be ketchup, as his younger brother had brought some French fries to him during the break and he sloppily hid them under his shirt.

My older brother, Bob, was a scrappy forward who lived and died with each day of his high school hockey experience. I watched up close how much this meant to him and how much this legendary coach influenced his life and his moods. In so many ways, I wanted to be like my brother and I particularly wanted to wear the maroon and gray AHS uniform.

The problem was that I would not likely reach my goal as a defenseman. And I had only played goal once, in that bantam game referenced earlier. Then I caught a lucky break.

The star goalie in our class, Ed Walsh, transferred to a local private school. (He would become an All-American at Boston University and later played for the Montreal Canadiens.) With suspiciously abundant encouragement from virtually every adult with whom I spoke, I decided to abandon my career as a defenseman and a week before varsity tryouts my sophomore year, I assembled an odd collection of goalie gear and made a life-changing decision. I would become a goalie.

The Arlington hockey experience was about kids identifying a goal, working to get there and then having this incredible experience molded by one man. He was larger than life to all of us, a strong father figure even for those of us who already enjoyed a strong father figure at home. We got a bonus: a second male influence to help shape our lives.

As already noted, he was hugely successful by the time our group got to him, so our respect for him came easily. We knew he had created something special and not only did we want to be part of it, we wanted to continue it and pass it along to the next group. I think we realized that even while we were in the midst of it.

He had us believing we always had an edge. We felt that we were always more prepared than our opponent. We knew we put in more time than the other guys did. We believed in his system. We believed in him. He was ahead of his time. He was our Belichick.

Burns was very structured. We met in a classroom every afternoon. ("To stay away from the dames.") And we had to maintain notebooks. We had a variety of breakout plays with designated names ("Flip Out," "Deep Flip,"

"Post"). His theory was that in games whose periods were only 10 minutes long, if you could get out of your zone, you could almost guarantee that you would be in every game, regardless of the opponent.

Not only did the breakouts have names, so did the defensemen on the points. The guy along the boards was always "Pete" and the guy at mid-point was "Mike." If the mid-point was open, for example, he — or some-one else — would yell, "Mike! Mike!," encouraging a pass to the mid-point. It worked well, except for the occasional slow-witted teammate who, not quite grasping the system, would yell indiscriminately, "Pete! Mike! Pete! Mike!"

Of course, much of this was a direct result of Burns' football coaching. Set plays. Naming plays. Delegating specific duties to his assistant coaches.

No one was allowed to take slap shots. The Arena was shaped very much like an oval. There were hardly any corners to speak of and hard shots that missed the net could quickly exit the zone on the far side. "And some lazy guy not backchecking gets a breakaway," we were told.

Wings religiously stayed on their side of the ice. It was not uncommon to see an Arlington wing race for a loose puck and then, suddenly, pull up as if there was an invisible wall splitting the ice surface from goal to goal. Forget that with another stride or two they would have their quarry. Their responsibility was to stay on their side of the ice. Period.

Left: Ed Burns poses at the what is now the Edward P. Burns Rink in Arlington. Right: A work in progress by one of my old AHS students, Rich Sullivan. The finished work resides at Arlington's Menotomy Grill, another at the Burns Rink.

If there was one legitimate criticism of the system, it was that individual potential was suffocated. Arlington players who went on to college hockey would prove to be well schooled and disciplined, but those with special gifts needed a little more time to develop them, as that opportunity was denied them at AHS.

Opposing players and coaches frequently mocked all of this. "Oh, you play for Eddie Burns? How many breakouts do you guys have now, twenty?" Affectations aside, Burns won. And he won often.

He wasn't perfect. And we had fun with that. He might start a story with, "Ninety-nine times out of ten …" The capacity crowd of 13,909 at the old Boston Garden might come out as, "Thirteen thousand nine-oh-thousand." Before taking on a major rival, his pregame talk frequently included some politically incorrect motivation. "Nervous? Why there are fifty million Chinamen who don't even know you're playing."

His wardrobe made even me look like a GQ model. And we all tried to mimic that gravelly voice. But never in front of him.

I can still see him, more than five decades later, walking into one of those Boston Arena locker rooms, reaching high to leave his cigar on top of a make-shift wall and getting set to deliver his pregame remarks. We would play the period, he would return and reach for that cigar, and then go outside the room to discuss the period with his assistants.

Once, to the astonishment of the rest of us, a teammate stood up and, just as Eddie left the room ahead of us, moved the cigar about two feet to the left. At the end of the period, we all watched Eddie reach in vain for that cigar for several uncomfortable seconds. Given our respect for him, such moments were rare.

One of my teammates once observed that Eddie accomplished all of this by rarely raising his voice and never, to our collective memories, using a bad word. (As one alum said, "He sometimes used the wrong word but never a bad word!")

He was competitive. We never thought he placed too much emphasis on winning, but he wasn't afraid to make it clear how important it was. Once, after winning a state tournament game, he crossed the ice to shake the hand of the opposing coach. When he extended his hand, his vanquished foe ungraciously said, "Well, you're one up on me," and then turned and walked away.

As fate would have it, the two teams met in the following year's championship game. Same result. As the postgame handshake was about to unfold and the losing coach feebly extended his hand, Eddie didn't wait. "Now I'm two up on you," he said with a smile.

He was an innovator, something in which he took great pride. "We were the first ones to skate four lines," he said, something he started as high school periods went from 10 minutes long to 12 and then 15. "Four lines and 20-second shifts, and we backchecked. That really tired out the other teams."

The shifts were never quite that short, but he made a good point. He believed in rolling out fresh guys who were taught to go hard for a short amount of time and get off. He had the benefit of a deep talent pool for so many years so he could pull this off. Others said he was lucky to have this talent. "Lucky?" He was the one who made it so important to want to play hockey in Arlington for those many years. He was responsible for that deep talent pool. And he derived the benefits.

In the fall of 1967, I was looking forward to the high school hockey season. I would be starting my second full season as a goaltender and with the previous year's starter having graduated, I was one of a handful of goalies with a chance to take over the position.

The previous year's team had gone 19-0-0 , making us the defending state champions, so we were feeling pretty good about things. There were plenty of solid returning players, no one more important than senior center Billy Corkery, who had scored the winning goal in Arlington's 2-1 state final win over Norwood. When my college career ended, I had won only two overtime games in my combined careers, one in high school and one in college. Bill Corkery scored the game-winner in both.

Coach Burns lights up a cigar after winning the 1967 state championship. From left Denis Sullivan, Bill Corkery and Mark Driscoll. All three players went on to shine in college, Corkery in hockey and the other two in football.

When the games began, I was battling with Herbie Richardson for the starting job. Herbie was a year or two behind me, a small "lefty" who was capable of beating me out for the job.

A few observations on the season are important to set up the rest of the story.

• We finished second to Brookline, ending a streak of five straight seasons in which Arlington had won the Greater Boston Interscholastic league (GBI.)

• We lost only two regular-season games, which sounds pretty good. However, the previous four years featured a total of only one league loss. In fact, when we lost on the third weekend of the year, 2-1 to Medford, it ended a 49-game unbeaten streak in the GBI.

• Herbie and I alternated games throughout season, and the job was still up for grabs when we entered the postseason tournament in March.

All of this is meant to show that when the tournament began, the defending champions were not among the favorites. One Boston paper covered itself when it ran a small article suggesting that despite the second-place finish, Arlington should not be discounted.

That year, the traditional statewide tournament was scrapped and replaced by the first Eastern Massachusetts Tournament, along with a smaller event for teams in Central and Western Massachusetts. The winners of the two events would meet in a single-game showdown.

The event now has different divisions based on school enrollments and geographical breakdowns, perhaps 8-10 different mini-tournaments. So, you might make the tournament and play in the Division 2 North bracket, which means you are likely to play a school from your own league early in the tournament. Part of the excitement for us was playing schools we had never played before. People weren't worried about mismatches and maybe the 12-minute periods (bumped up from 10) mitigated that.

Our draw for the opening game of the EMass Tournament was Xavier High School, a small and now defunct private Catholic school out of Concord. Xavier was coached by former Boston College player Jack Cusack, and his roster contained a number of talented Arlington players. Among them, Jay and Kevin Connors, with whom many of us had played growing up. They also had Sandy Milley from Winchester, with whom I played at Harvard. (He is the older brother of General Mark Milley, Chairman of the Joint Chiefs of Staff, as I write. More on Mark later.)

The goaltending competition remained so tight that both Herbie and I played in the 9-3 win over Xavier, all three of their goals, as I recall, coming from Jay Connors. Next up would be Christopher Columbus High School from Boston, coached at that time by Kevin Walsh, who was also a sportswriter at *The Boston Globe*. (His by-line appeared in tournament coverage.)

We had a strong group of defensemen, most notably Dave Brine, Mark

Noonan, Charlie Harrington and Ed Burns Jr. Noonan and I would play together at Harvard while Charlie Harrington, co-captain of the football team, would go on to play football at Wichita State. Harrington was on the ill-fated team that was decimated by a plane crash in October 1970. Two planes were used by the team, the one that crashed killing 31 players. Charlie did not make the trip due to a football injury.

We played a nearly flawless game against Christopher Columbus, winning 4-0. Coach Burns kept me in the entire game, and the job was mine from that point on. Those first two wins came at the Boston Arena and earned us a date with arch-rival Melrose on Wednesday, March 13, at the Boston Garden.

Arlington and Melrose were two of the traditional super powers of high school hockey. The last three times the two schools had met in the tournament, Arlington prevailed by scores of 1-0, 2-1 and 2-1. This time, however, Melrose was favored.

The Arlington-Melrose match-up brought us together with opponents we knew as friends. The coaches, Eddie Burns and Henry Hughes, ran a summer hockey school together and that relationship led to frequent in-season scrimmages between the two programs. We probably scrimmaged Melrose six or more times during the 1967-68 season.

The Middlesex League champions took a 1-0 lead in the first period of our quarterfinal game when I got beat from 15-feet out by Steve Dolloff, a future Boston University All-American. (It was Dolloff who would beat me in double overtime a year later and end my high school career.)

This is the Eddie Burns I remember.

That was the last goal Melrose would score. We responded with goals from Charlie Harrington, Tony Lyons and Billy Corkery and took a 3-1 upset win to advance.

The semifinal match-ups on Saturday, March 16, at the Boston Garden would be Arlington playing Bay State League co-champion Needham and Hingham playing the other Bay State co-champ Norwood. The game program lists the two game times as 1:00 and 1:20. That's because the two games continued to alternate periods as in the regular season.

The fans got their money's worth as they witnessed two 1-0 games, shutouts provided by Norwood's Neil Higgins and myself. In our game, our first shot on goal came with seconds left in the first period and it turned out to be all we needed. Kent Davison, who went on to play at Brown, got the goal. Higgins, who was pretty much the gold standard for public high school goalies in Massachusetts, went on to play at Boston College. The Higgins name was made famous not only by Neil's talent but also because his father, Ernie, was a legend in the mask-making business. The Boston Bruins goalies, most notably Gerry Cheevers, helped make the Higgins mask popular and easily identifiable with the two triangles on each cheek.

Now let me say up front that I do not know if this is true, but I have been told that our 1-0 win over Needham was the only game in his high school career in which Robbie Ftorek, future head coach of the Boston Bruins, did not register a point. I cannot confirm this, but that's my story and I am sticking to it.

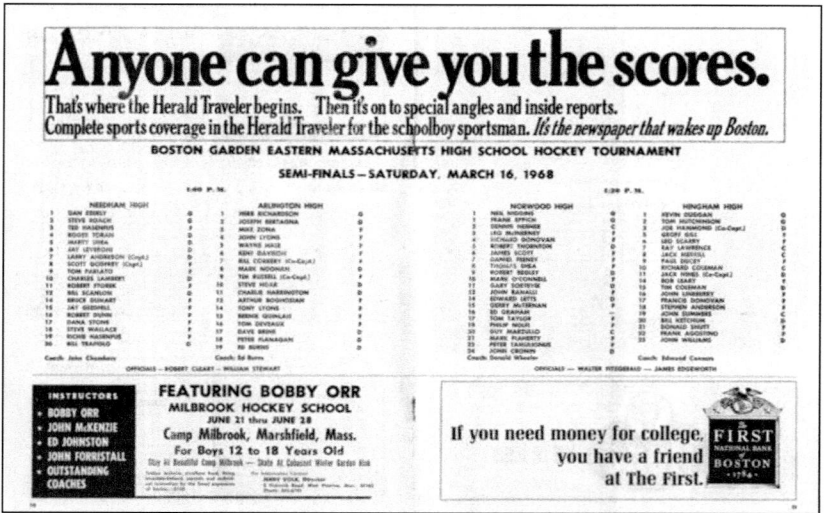

This is the centerspread of the 1968 EMass Tournament semifinal round played at the Boston Garden. (Program courtesy of TD Garden)

The Needham roster was loaded. They would go on to win the next two state titles behind Ftorek and company. The 1968 squad had future Boston College players Chuck Lambert on defense and Scott Godfrey and Tom Parlato up front. Larry Anderson was a strong defenseman who played at Williams. Dan Eberly was in goal and not only would he go on to Northeastern, but the Beanpot Tournament's top goalie receives the Eberly Award, named after Dan and his brother Glen, who played at Boston University.

That set up the first-ever Eastern Massachusetts Championship Final between underdog Arlington and heavy favorite Norwood, the same two teams that met in the state final the year before. In that one, undefeated Arlington notched a 2-1 win.

Arlington's magic ride seemed to be on cruise control when it held a 3-1 lead in the third period. Norwood received a gift when defenseman Mark Noonan, attempting to clear a puck behind the net, accidentally shot it on goal, off my pants and in, to make it 3-2. (Coach Burns told a subsequent team that I "should have had the short side covered.")

Just seconds before the end of regulation, Dennis Hebner, brother of NHS grad and future baseball major leaguer Richie, took a shot that broke off the end of my catching glove and into the net to tie the game at 3-3.

I recall an unusual moment, unusual for me, as I look back on things. The team was walking from the locker room to the ice for the start of over-time. We had fans lining the way because the old Garden did not have much separation between participants and the public in those days. As I walked by my brother Bob, I winked at him. I say this is "unusual" because I was plagued by nerves for much of my playing career. But that night, I think all of us believed in ourselves and believed in Arlington Hockey.

That belief was tested when Bernie Quinlan took a minor penalty in overtime. But that only created another moment for Billy Corkery. In the 1967 State Tournament, Arlington enjoyed victories of 10-0, 6-0 and 5-0, sandwiched around two tough 2-1 wins over Gloucester and Norwood. In both of those close wins, Billy Corkery scored the game-winner.

Killing the penalty, Corkery took possession of the puck in our zone and worked his way through the neutral zone. As he approached the far blue line, another odd thing happened. First of all, he took a slapshot, something the coach actively discouraged.

The shot ended up bouncing. And as Neil Higgins dropped, the puck bounced over his pad and into the net. The underdogs had completed the improbable sweep of Melrose, Needham and Norwood, three of the tourna-ment's top four seeded teams.

Out of respect for my friends in the town of Auburn, I can't finish the story here. There was the matter of the East-West game between two champions. And, alas, on Saturday, March 23, 1968, the Auburn Dandies prevailed, 3-2 in overtime, taking just a little shine off the 1967-68 season.

So why am I devoting all of this time to one week of a 50-year hockey life? This might be where Paul Harvey would tell you "the rest of the story."

The referee for many of those tournament games was Billy Cleary. In our time, when some of the best college players didn't have much of an avenue to the NHL, we got many of them as referees. I think of BU great Jack Garrity. Dartmouth legend Bill Riley Sr. My future father-in-law, Bob Leonard, was another referee in those days, as was his BC teammate, Ned Bunyon. The officials listed in the semifinal program shown on these pages: Veterans Walter Fitzgerald (an American Football League referee) and Jim Edgeworth did one semifinal; Bill Stewart (father of Hall of Fame referee Paul) and Bobby Cleary, Billy's brother and fellow Harvard and Olympic star, did the other.

I still remember tying up or catching pucks and handing them over to Billy after a whistle in the championship game. He was a talker, and we had some back and forth during breaks in the action. Within weeks of the tournament, Billy was on the phone, calling me to see if I might be interested in applying to Harvard. Eventually, I would start every game in Billy's first two seasons as head coach.

It was a simpler time. As I said earlier, there were no summer showcase tournaments. No family advisors. My high school team's success gave me a chance to perform on a big stage, I played well and, as a result, I was recruited out of high school. And I entered college as a raw 17-year-old, with just three years as a goalie.

It helped that high school sports got great media coverage back then. Each league had its own story in the Sunday sports sections, with lineups and box scores from each game, and the tournament was covered as a major event.

Looking at our 1968 team photo, with the exception of a few guys who may have spent a "PG" year in prep school, we sent plenty of guys directly into college athletics. When it was all done, 10 players on that team played hockey in college, one played football and one signed a professional baseball contract.

Some 53 years after his high school graduation, Bob Bartholomew still lives in the Arlington house in which he grew up. "Barts" returned to AHS after graduating from UMass where he played on championship teams in the early 1970s. A proud UMass alum, he returns to Amherst frequently and maintains some great historical memorabilia from high school and college.

"Mr. Barts," as younger generations know him, has spent a half century teaching and coaching and keeping alive decades of Arlington sports accomplishments and memories. Every community needs a "Barts," and Arlington is certainly blessed to have him.

Arlington Wins Title in Overtime

Tips Norwood, 4-3
On Corkery's Goal

By KEVIN WALSH
Staff Reporter

Co-captain Bill Corkery scored a short-handed goal at 1:06 of sudden death to earn Arlington a 4-3 victory over Norwood in the Eastern Mass Hockey Championship final Monday night before 8063 at Boston Garden.

The roar of the crowd was deafening when Corkery scored his second goal of the game to give the defending state champions a chance to win the state-wide crown once again.

"We just have a bunch of kids who caught the tournament fever," is the way veteran coach Eddie Burns described the victory.

Arlington finished second in the G.B.I. competition and arrived in the tournament unseeded. They pulled off another Impossible Dream, eliminating Melrose, Needham and Norwood to win the title.

Once the puck was dropped, Arlington went right to work. They had built their lead to 3-1 with less than three minutes to play and then had to pick themselves off the ice in the overtime.

LOW CURVE—Arlington goalie Joe Bertagna appears set to bat puck away while Norwood's Dennis Hebner closes in.   Arlington defenseman is Dave Brine. (Danny Goshtigian Photo)

WORTH A SMILE—Arlington goalie Joe Bertagna, Coach Eddie Burns and Bill Corkery express victors' pleasure after Corkery's goal beat Norwood. (Danny Goshtigian Photo)

No Day Off for King Corkery

By DON WHITELEY
Staff Correspondent

The king of Arlington's

houses. I don't know which one yet, but that doesn't really matter anyway."

poor center, the line goes nowhere."

Corkery was named the

The Arlington crowd h been silenced when Den Hebner tied it up late in third period. When Cork

The Boston papers gave high school hockey great coverage in the 1960s.

On an unusually warm November afternoon in 2020, I met up with Tom Peters and Barts at Robbins Farm in Arlington. The three of us, at one time, lived within a mile of the spot. Tom and I actually lived on the same street. On this afternoon, we looked at old team pictures going back as far as Little League. And the stories came out from our managing careers.

Top: The 1968 Eastern Massachusetts champions celebrate on the Boston Garden ice. Bottom: These six dapper guys made up the 1968 All-Tournament Team. That's future Boston Bruins head coach Robbie Ftorek front row right.

We reminisced about the change of seasons that football covered. You would start in late August heat, practicing on a dusty field behind the field's stands. You would end at Thanksgiving, possibly in freezing temperatures, maybe with snow. In between, there were glorious New England fall Saturdays, the excitement of "Game Day" in perfect weather, the town turning out to support the players and cheerleaders and their public high school.

I recall junior varsity games, played on midweek afternoons. I would work the sideline chains. And I remember a specific afternoon when, at halftime, I shagged punts from one of the referees. He was Chet Stone, later the legendary equipment manager at Harvard University.

At the time, Chet worked up the street from the high school at Holovak and Coughlin's, a sporting goods store founded by Mike Holovak, the former BC star and head coach of the Boston (later New England) Patriots, and Art Coughlin, a local businessman and a school committee member.

The Spy Ponders were well-represented at Frozen Fenway 2012 when we had a private hour of hockey. From left: Donnie Murphy, Rick Rigazio, brother Bob, Tony Lyons, Bob Bartholomew and Bernie Quinlan. I think the fact that Bernie could fit into his high school game jersey 43 years after graduation was the most impressive thing any of us did that night. (Photo courtesy of the Boston Red Sox)

Chet became Harvard's equipment manager in January 1972 and performed the job well and with great fondness from generations of Harvard athletes.

I shared the start of this piece with Tom Peters, and he called me, somewhat amazed at the timing. "I can't believe this story arrived when it did," said Peters. "I was just asked by the UMass people to come back to the 50th anniversary of the graduate school I attended and talk about how I got involved in athletics. I had never thought of it in this way."

Tom was part of the first class of the University of Massachusetts' graduate program on sports management, one of the first in a field that is now quite crowded. There was a time that athletic directors followed a typical path: player, coach, administrator. Today, many have played, but fewer have coached. The job has changed.

The modern AD is a fund-raiser first, the day-to-day administrative duties carried out by a lieutenant or many lieutenants. There are likely just as many administrators coming from a business background today, or perhaps from the school's development office, than come from a coaching background. The challenges facing today's athletic directors are largely financial.

The sportsworld has changed quite a bit since my years in Arlington. Some changes have been for the better and some are certainly open to debate. I know that I couldn't have dreamed of a better introduction to the sports world than what I experienced so many years ago.

Chapter Two —
Harvard University

"So, when you go out into the world, and someone asks you where you went to school, look them in the eyes and say to them, 'I went to school ... two miles south of Tufts!'"

Harvard alumnus Conan O'Brien, in his address
to the Harvard Class of 2020 graduates

There is a familiar dynamic where a Harvard graduate, more commonly a recent graduate, is reluctant to tell people where he or she went to school. It usually goes something like this:

"So, where did you go to college?"
"Ah, Boston."
"No, where exactly did you go to school?"
"Um, ah, Cambridge."

Maybe there isn't one reason that many people act this way. Maybe it is a sense that people have preconceived notions of Harvard and Harvard people, and you don't want to deal with that. Maybe they think you must be smart, and you don't want to have to live up to that. Maybe they think you are a communist. (Former Olympic coach Lou Vairo was fond of calling Ben Smith and me, "Those two Communists from Massachusetts.")

I once had a friend say to me, "You know, you are the least Harvard of any Harvard person I have ever met." I wasn't sure how to respond. I believe he meant it as a compliment. But I took it as, "Hey, you aren't as smart as most Harvard people I know."

I would spend many years at Harvard, not only my four as an undergraduate but also many years drawing a paycheck from the University. I was the director of sports information, I was a goalie coach (unpaid position), I was the co-coach (along with my old roommate Kevin Hampe) of the men's junior varsity, I was the head coach (first one) of the first women's varsity and I was the executive director of the Harvard Varsity Club. I also edited a coffee table-style book, *Crimson in Triumph: A Pictorial History of Harvard Athletics*, which was published in the mid-1980s.

So, it was with some delight that many years later, my son, Joey, was accepted by Harvard and I had another chance to connect with my alma mater. In short, it has been a good relationship and still, when my name appears in a newspaper article, I am often referred to as "former Harvard goaltender Joe Bertagna." And this is nearly 50 years after graduation.

I was recently asked to speak on Harvard to a couple of high school seniors, who were in the process of looking at schools. I had to stop to consider what would be of interest and importance to them as they looked at myriad colleges and universities in the East. It reminded me of a visit I made

In 1998, I presented a plaque to Senator Ted Kennedy when his late brother, President John Kennedy, was inducted into the Harvard Varsity Club Hall of Fame as a member of Harvard's 1938 sailing team. I served briefly as the executive director of the Varsity Club. (Tim Morse Photo courtesy of the Harvard Varsity Club))

to the Harvard Club of Boston when I was in their situation, looking at and applying to schools. The process for me was different in that I had hockey guiding me.

During that visit to the Harvard Club, I was led into a large room and told to sit and wait for my contact, who would be with me shortly. The wait was a little longer than I had been led to believe and, looking back, I think that was deliberate. As the time went on, I got up from my chair and started to look around the room. Scores of wooden panels were engraved with the names of Harvard alumni who had become Governor, Senator, President or a Supreme Court Justice. The message, inherent on these walls and, as I would learn, in so many other places at Harvard, was pretty clear. People who come here go on to do something special.

That message can be embraced or can intimidate or, perhaps, both. Certainly, there is a great sense of expectation. You are about to enter this world of great resources and opportunity, and you will have the chance to make your own special mark on the world. That thought would return to me often over the years, particularly when I would receive my Class Reports every five years.

I could read about Benazir Bhutto, Prime Minister of Pakistan. Or perhaps watch the Sunday morning news shows where classmates William Kristol or E.J. Dionne might be talking about Benazir, or "Pinkie," as we knew her. Or maybe it was Evan Thomas, talking about his latest book. Or maybe it was Senator Al Franken, before his fall.

Me? I was putting on sweats and packing my hockey equipment as I shut off the television and went off to play hockey or maybe coach some goalies. The gravitas with which my classmates covered — or made — headlines was not my burden.

Case in point: The day after Grady Little left Pedro Martinez in that Red Sox playoff game against the Yankees in 2003, I attended a panel discussion on the state of the Middle East that was held during the celebration of our 30th reunion. Benazir was on the panel. As was E.J. Dionne and, I think, Bill Kristol. As my classmates spoke with insight and intelligence on a complicated subject, I couldn't stop thinking about the Red Sox game the night before. I am serious. As the complexities of the Middle East were being hashed out, I was still dumbfounded as to how Mike Mussina could pitch so well in relief against the Sox.

Some 14 years earlier, my former roommate, Joe Walker, was invited to a black-tie event in Washington where Benazir was going to speak, the event being hosted by Vice President and Mrs. Dan Quayle. Joe brought me as his date. I rented a tux and we flew to D.C.

It was a big-time event. Chief Justice William Rehnquist was there. As was *Washington Post* publisher Katherine Graham. And D.C. mayor Marion

Barry. Joe and I were seated at separate tables, and I recall the anxiety I felt as people identified themselves at my table and, eventually, asking me what I did for a living. At the time, I was the Boston Bruins goalie coach, which didn't seem to impress this crowd.

During the dinner, I decided that I couldn't come all that way and not try to talk to "Pinkie." I got up from my table and started to approach her and the Vice-President. Suddenly, I was struck with fear. What if she doesn't recognize me? Is there a protocol for approaching a head of state? What if I get tackled by a Secret Service agent?

As I neared her table, she gave me a quick look of recognition. She stood and gracefully extended her hand, giving me a warm welcome. She then turned to Dan Quayle and said, "Mr. Vice-President, this is my friend Joe Bertagna. He was the goalie in *Love Story*."

Really? That's it? I was less than 40 years old and perhaps my accomplishments weren't worthy of anything else. At least that is how she chose to identify me to the Vice President of the United States.*

Before she became a world leader, Pinkie was simply a bright and fun undergraduate who lived in the room beneath mine in Eliot House. While comping for the *Harvard Crimson*, she wrote a feature on me that I still have but, unfortunately, there is no byline. Apparently you don't get one when you are, in effect, trying out for the paper.

In describing her as "fun," I am reminded of the time she asked me to bring a puck home from practice so she could pull a prank on Jay Riley. She had signed up the Eliot House kitchen to bake a birthday cake for Jay. She was planning to cut out a space inside the cake and place the puck there, anticipating Jay's difficulty in cutting the cake.

I delivered the puck as promised, only to receive a frantic call from her. "Joey, I can't get the cover off the puck," she said over the phone. "Cover? There isn't any cover. I'll be right there," I responded.

When I got to the kitchen, it looked like a crime scene. Flour everywhere. The puck showing signs of being stabbed. The weapon in plain view. Apparently, she mistook the textured side of the puck as a covering and tried to cut it off.

As for *Love Story*, the film crew set up in Watson Rink for three days, Bill Cleary serving double duty as coordinator of the hockey scenes and actor Ryan O'Neal's stunt double. O'Neal was from Southern California and couldn't skate. Before subbing for O'Neal, Billy donned the #7 jersey and

---

*In the fall of 2019 and again in the fall of 2020, I was interviewed by National Public Radio and "The Athletic," respectively, on "Love Story." The first was on the 50th anniversary of its filming, the second on the 50th anniversary of its release. It is a story that just won't go away.

the helmet fitted with a wig. On more than one occasion, O'Neal would step off the rubber mats and on to concrete while wearing a pair of borrowed skates. After warning him once, Billy really ripped into him on the set for not showing any respect for the Harvard player whose skates had been borrowed.

Decades later, O'Neal and his *Love Story* co-star, Ali MacGraw, were in Boston to perform in the play *Love Letters*. Billy attended the play and after some hesitation, agreed to go backstage to see if he could meet O'Neal. When the two met, O'Neal embraced Billy warmly and then said, "I still remember how you chewed me out for walking on the cement with skates on."

One last note on Love Story. The Harvard freshman team was allowed to take part on the third and final day of shooting. My role was simple: A puck would be shot on me, I would give it to Bill Cleary and he would take it behind the net. I performed my bit over a few takes and it made the film. After that shot, Ryan O'Neal would be placed behind the net and shot from the waist up, his knees locked tight and ankles turned over.

It's not false modesty when I express a sense of underachieving in my professional life. The career decisions that I made were as much to avoid gravitas as they were to pursue an exemplary career in athletics. To make up

Bill Cleary and I were interviewed by National Public Radio in 2019 on the 50th anniversary of the filming of *Love Story*. He brought along his helmet and wig from the filming of the movie. (Gary Waleik Photo courtesy of WBUR and Boston University)

for the lack of seriousness in my pursuits, I went for volume. At any given moment, I would be a college hockey commissioner, an administrator of a national coaches' association, a small business owner who coached and wrote about goaltending, a broadcaster and a private school goalie coach.

And so, I spent much of my professional career purposely juggling as many things as I could, rushing from one responsibility to another. At times, it was impressive. But it was also selfish, as I often ended up giving each of the jobs, at any given time, less than 100%. Fortunately, I was rarely called on it. But I knew.

To some extent, I felt that I had underachieved while at Harvard. Up to the point of entering Harvard, I had tried hard to do all that I could to get into the place. Once there, I cut myself a deal: play hockey and get Bs. And in retrospect, I regret not taking advantage of so much of what Harvard offered. I could have tried to write for the *Crimson* or work in the sports information office or somehow do something that I could use later on in life. Or, at least in the professional life I eventually chose.

Don't get me wrong. My four-year stint with Harvard Hockey was a life-changing experience. And not just because I was able to forge a professional career in the sport.

I got to be coached by three Hall of Famers: Ralph "Cooney" Weiland, Bill Cleary and Tim Taylor. I made lifelong friends, in and out of the rink. And I learned about myself through success and failure.

It is actually the "failure" that stays with me the most. If I had been hit by a truck in January 1973 and never played another game, I would have an entirely different memory of my Harvard Hockey experience. We were 20-1 as freshmen. I was a back-up goalie as a sophomore, played well in my mop-up minutes and was on the bench when we won the 1971 ECAC Tournament and advanced to the NCAA semifinals.

As a junior, a season in which I started every game for first-year head coach Bill Cleary, we had the lowest goals against average in the Ivy League. During the Christmas holidays in our senior year, we defeated Michigan and Michigan Tech to win the Great Lakes Tournament, earning a No. 1 national ranking. Life was good.

Then it all went south. The team's final record was a respectable 17-4-1. But each of the losses cost us something: a loss to BU gave them the Beanpot; two losses to Cornell gave them the Ivy title and the top seed in the ECAC Tournament. And a home quarterfinal loss to Clarkson, which was win number 17 for a young Jerry York, knocked us out of the ECAC Tournament. In those four losses, I played poorly.

I am fortunate that neither my teammates nor my coaches ever said anything to me about my failures and how it cost the team. In fact, the first time it was even acknowledged came in 2018, when a group of my classmates took me out to dinner on the occasion of my getting an award from USA Hockey. At the time, one of them joked, "We're going to take Joey out for dinner to celebrate the five saves he made senior year."

One other memory from this time: my mother was a terrific hockey fan, a great sports fan in general. I was much more likely to talk sports with her than I

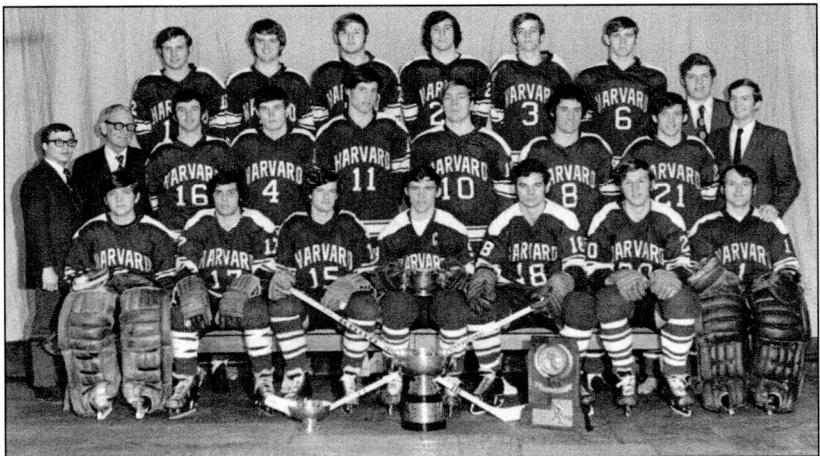

Top: My parents were incredibly, and appropriately, supportive. My mother, Mary, was my biggest fan. An athlete of sorts herself, she spent five years with the Radio City Music Hall Rockettes. That's her, second from the right. We both did a lot of kicking. This picture of my father, Bob, watching a game at BC, appeared in a Boston newspaper. Bottom: The 1970-71 Harvard Varsity Hockey Team. We were ECAC champions in coach Ralph "Cooney" Weiland's final season. This team had 11 players from Massachusetts on its roster. And that didn't count our two Bay State managers, Dan Crane (Cambridge) and Max Bleakie (Wellesley.) (Team Photo by Mel Hookailo courtesy of Harvard University)

was with my father. She would get very nervous at my games and often brought her knitting to Watson Rink, leaving her bleacher seat in particularly tight contests, and taking the knitting into the ladies room. She said that she didn't want to see me give up a bad goal. I often joked that there were some nights that I wished I could have joined her. Four decades later, when my daughter became a goalie, I knew exactly what she was feeling.

Part of the reason that it has been difficult to let all of the failures go is that by staying so involved with college hockey all these years, I have watched so many goalies step up in big games and come through for their teammates. And almost every time that happened, I both marveled at their performances and conjured up painful memories of my failures.

I'm not sure why the failures overtake the successes. Given that I started playing goal in my sophomore year of high school, I should take pride in the fact that I played Division I hockey at all. When I look at the games I started — all 69 games played my freshman, junior and senior seasons — we enjoyed a phenomenal winning percentage of .797. And yet ....

Results aside, I got to play alongside some great teammates who became lifelong friends. As a sophomore, I got to practice with the great Joe Cavanagh every day. A three-time All American on the ice, he was even more impressive as a person off the ice. He centered a line with his fellow Cranston, RI, native Dan DeMichele on left wing and the talented Steve "Cooch" Owen on right wing. Each brought unique skills to the line, making them greater than the sum of the parts.

But Cavanagh was the key. Before practice one day, I read aloud this observation from *The Hockey News*. "With apologies to DeMichele and Owen, Joe Cavanagh could make high-scoring wings out of Rosenkranz and Guildenstern." Not a good idea. I saw more than the usual number of head-high shots at practice from DeMichele (who could really shoot) and Owen.

That season would be the last for legendary coach Ralph "Cooney" Weiland. He actual took in most of the practices from high in the Watson Rink bleachers, donning skates only a handful of times that year. Practice would start with Cooney coming down to the glass, offering a few words, and then Bill Cleary, assistant coach and head coach-in-waiting, would run the practice.

On one of those days that Cooney was on the ice, I was having a miserable time. Pucks were going in with great frequency, and the ones that didn't seemed to find every gap in my equipment. Finally, in disgust, I threw my stick into the balcony behind the locker room-end of Watson Rink. As soon as the stick left my hand, I remembered that Cooney was on the ice, and as I looked up, he was heading right for me.

As I braced for a tongue-lashing, he skated by and, without stopping, said simply, "Can't play goal without a stick." When I went to the bench

This photo came from the day after the first Beanpot in 1952. Harvard won, so Ralph "Cooney" Weiland is seated while fellow Beanpot head coaches "Snooks" Kelley, Harry Cleverly and Herb Gallagher stand behind him. (Photo courtesy of Harvard University)

to get my other stick, Cooney had already delivered a message to manager Dan Crane not to give me my stick. So when I asked, Danny shook his head. "Coach says no."

The image of Cooney that lingers is that of a real character. He was the guy who forgot his own players' names. He could recall Dave Hynes and Bob McManama but forget Billy Corkery's name, sending the line out with, "Hynes, McManama, and, ah, you, you go out there." Billy, of course, became "Hugo" to teammates. He was the guy, concerned about Boston University's Dick Rodenheiser, telling his players to "watch that Eisenhower." He was the coach who eschewed pep talks and simply opened the gate and let his boys play.

But it is an image that, while not altogether inaccurate, undercuts the genius of the man. This was a National Hockey League Hall of Famer, a Stanley Cup winner as both player and coach, who entered a strange new world and continued his winning ways. At Harvard, Cooney won 315 games over 21 seasons. And he did so by being more than just a character.

"He was hard to get to know, and he didn't say very much," remembers Bill Cleary. "But he taught us a lot about life and a lot about hockey. He really appreciated the skill and beauty of the game, and he taught me the way it should be played. Fifteen years after I followed him, I still used his drills at practice."

Tim Taylor, captain of Cooney's 1963 ECAC champs and later head coach at Yale, recalled Cooney's way of preparing a team.

"Whenever I think of Cooney, I think of our teams in the early '60s. I remember practicing, how frustrating it was. It was impossible just to score a goal. We practiced the Cooney Weiland way, with a lot of back-checking. You'd get in a game, and it was an entirely different world. Then you'd realize how right Cooney was."

He was a conservative coach who stressed individual skills and fundamental team play. He did not like the changes that affected the game after his retirement. Speaking in 1977, six years after leaving Harvard, Cooney said, "I'm not knocking it, but they've taken the skill out. Anybody can shoot the puck into the corner, race for it, and scoop it in front of the net. I like to see one-on-one. Today, there's so much confusion in front of the net that by the time the goaltender untangles himself, someone has poked the puck in. I've never seen so many goaltenders on their backs. You don't know half the time who has scored."

As the 1970-71 season progressed, our sophomore class developed a special line of its own. Bill Corkery, Bob McManama and Dave Hynes were all clever forwards. Arriving on campus as centers, they were eventually put together as a line — and what a line they became. Coming from the abutting towns of Arlington, Belmont and Cambridge, respectively, they were nicknamed "The ABC Line" and, later, "The Local Line" and were a force in college hockey for three seasons. Boston University presented the trio its "Most Honored Opponent" award one year. All three went on to play professionally.

By the time the 1970-71 Harvard team reached the ECAC semifinals at Boston Garden, the two lines were clicking on all cylinders, the result being Garden wins over Boston University and Clarkson to give Cooney Weiland a championship in his final season as Harvard head coach. The keys to the wins: taking no penalties in the semis against eventual NCAA champion BU, and Dave Hynes' hat trick against Clarkson's All-American goalie Bruce Bullock in the final.

Speaking of goalies, that 1971 team was anchored by Bruce Durno. I couldn't have had a better experience as a first-year varsity goalie who clearly wasn't ready for prime time. Backing up Durno was a master class for me. And he was so generous with his time and knowledge. How skilled was he? He was only about 5'8" but played so precisely and skillfully.

One of my proudest moments as a goalie came after we had beaten Cornell the first time I started against them. The great Cavanagh-Durno teams had not been able to do that, though we clearly got robbed at Lynah

In my three full seasons of starting (freshman, junior and senior years), we lost a total of 13 games, eight of which were to teams wearing red and white: four to BU, three to Cornell and one to Wisconsin. Above, I follow a loose puck in one of those losses to BU. Also pictured are BU forward Ron Anderson and my teammate Kevin Hampe. (Dick Raphael Photo courtesy of Harvard University)

Rink in 1971 when an overtime goal was denied in a game eventually won by the hosts. Leading into my first year as a starter, the media commonly referred to me as the "heir apparent" to Durno. Following our 6-4 home win over Cornell early in that 1971-72 season, I received a note from Bruce with a newspaper clipping from our win. He wrote on it, "Heir confirmed."

It didn't start off so well. Our first game was at the University of Pennsylvania's new Class of '23 Rink. At some point prior to getting on the ice, I must have recalled my sophomore year roommates telling me that when I got to start, we'd probably have to win "a lot of 9-8 games." Funny guys.

So we open up at Penn, quickly take a 3-0 lead, and then the Quakers' first three shots go in. I scrape up some snow and act like nothing has happened but start thinking, "Hmm, this might be harder than I thought." Two hours later, we are on the bus, 11-3 victors.

During the early part of that junior year, Bill Cleary's first as a head coach, we ran afoul of some disciplinary rules. When a number of players stayed out after curfew during a road trip to West Point, Billy suspended all

The 1969-70 Harvard Freshman Hockey Team. We went 20-1 for Bill Cleary. Our only loss was to Boston University, 6-5, when Stoneham's Billy Flynn scored four goals on me. I believe I got a piece of each one. The following year, Bill Cleary was assistant coach to Cooney Weiland and 10 of us made the varsity. And then the following year, 1971-72, Bill became head coach. By my count, 15 of us were either from New England or attended school in New England prior to Harvard. (Mel Hookailo Photo courtesy of Harvard University)

This was from a 4-1 ECAC consolation game loss in March 1972. The Wildcats are Gordie Clark (9) and John Gray (14), who had 27 and 29 goals, respectively, that year. Both went on to the National Hockey League. Gordie followed a playing stint with a long coaching and scouting career. Charlie Holt's team also beat us, 4-3 in OT, at UNH in December. It was our first loss of the season. (Photo courtesy of Harvard University)

In January 1973, we tied Dukla Jihlava, the top team in Czechoslovakia, 4-4, in the Boston Arena. I actually stopped this shot from Josef Augusta, with Dave Hynes coming in to help. Not sure what it means that my most memorable game was a tie ... in an exhibition game. Part of the memory is that the game story in the *Boston Globe* was written by future baseball legend Peter Gammons. (Photo courtesy of Harvard University)

who were out late. He actually told us at the first practice after the weekend that he wanted everyone who was out after curfew to come into his office after the skate. Many of us were sure he had no idea that as many as seven players would come and own up to the violation. He decided to suspend all of them for the next game, which was against Billy's arch-rival, Boston College.

It was a bold move for Cleary, and it paid off when we beat BC on the road, 6-4, many JV call-ups playing their first and last varsity game. I once had an old Harvard alum from the Class of 1939 tell me that the three things that saved Harvard Hockey were: a) building Watson Rink before BC built its rink; b) giving Cardinal Cushing an Honorary Degree, thus making Catholic families comfortable sending their sons to Harvard; and, c) getting Billy Cleary to choose Harvard over BC.

When we returned home for the next home game, the students had a banner that read, "Free The Harvard Seven!" This was the same group that had fun with opponents on a regular basis. When Cornell came to town, a school whose roster was 99% Canadian and many of whom were (purportedly) enrolled in the School of Agriculture, the students hung a large sheet emblazoned with, "Welcome Future Farmers of Canada!"

Our hockey Class of 1973 was unique in that so many of us grew up within Route 128. In addition to myself and the Local Line, there was our esteemed captain Kevin Hampe of Dedham (also captain of baseball), there was Wenham's Harry Reynolds, and Bobby Muse from Newton. Jay Riley was from West Point, where his father Jack was head coach. But he attended Philips Andover with Corkery and seemed like a local to us. (His father grew up in Medford.)

Our final team in 1972-73 also had a talented and fun group of undergraduates who grew up in Massachusetts. They included junior defensemen Mark Noonan of Arlington and Levy Byrd of Chestnut Hill, along with my back-up goalie, junior Steve Perry of Concord. The locals in the sophomore class were exceptional: forwards Steve Dagdigian (Needham), Leigh Hogan (Belmont), Jimmy McMahon (Brookline) and Ted Thorndike (Chestnut Hill). There were also sophomore defensemen Larry Piatelli of Brookline and Eddie Rossi of Winthrop. That's 16 players from Massachusetts on one Harvard roster. Today, you might have to look at three or four years of Harvard rosters to find 16 Massachusetts players.

Our power play that final year was something to behold. As goalie, I was both participant and spectator, and I loved watching our PP at work. With David Hynes and Bob Goodenow at the points and McManama, Corkery and Randy Roth up front, we were successful more than 30 percent of the time.

As I mentioned earlier, that 1972-73 team had a lot of potential and, in the end, it did not win a championship. At least that's what I thought when I graduated. Some 40 years later, I was sitting in the Bright-Landry Center, on the site of the old Watson Rink, and I looked at a banner hanging across the ice listing ECAC regular-season titles. And I saw "1973" listed there.

There were no regular-season trophies back then and the whole idea of a regular-season champion was never discussed, to my knowledge. Schools made their own schedules and did so without everyone playing everyone else. "Standings," as they were, were kept by percentage.

I do recall that we ended up tied for the best record in the East with Cornell, but since they had beaten us twice, we were seeded #2 in the ECAC Tournament and the Big Red was #1. Looks like someone in the sports information office realized we tied for top regular-season record and determined, in today's world, that would make us 1973 co-champs. I'll take it.

It was a different game back then. In 1985, researching a book on Harvard athletics, I learned that hockey was a seven-man game in the early part of the 20th century. Defense partners once played in front of one another, and it was a major innovation when Harvard coach Alfred Winsor played them adjacent to each other.

Wrote Winsor, "In the first years, the two defence partners stayed fairly close to the goal, one behind the other ... This method was found very faulty as the clever dodger had a chance to dodge each man consecutively and the defence had no chance to stop a clever passing game. Gradually, the defence was widened out until the 'point' and 'coverpoint' were playing side by side or parallel."

As late as 1930, players could only pass the puck laterally or behind them. To move the puck forward, one had to stickhandle. Reading this recently, I was reminded of the changes in the game since we played in the 1970s. The obvious ones? We didn't wear facemasks. We didn't have video replay. Freshmen were not eligible for varsity play.

But there were more obscure differences. We could not check in the offensive zone. We had a penalty called "Leaving your feet to play the puck." One skate blade had to be in contact at all times when blocking a shot, for example.

Two on-ice officials were sufficient to do our games. And, as mentioned in the previous chapter, without realistic professional opportunities for the best players, some of the best college players became refs. There was never any question about respect when your officials were former All-Americans or Olympic stars.

Bobby Barry may not have had Cleary-like skills, but he was a Northeastern Hall of Famer and a great referee. In the Beanpot my senior year, we lost to BU, 8-3. When Buddy Powers scored the final goal, Barry reached into the net behind me to retrieve the puck and said, "Don't worry, Joey, it's almost over." If a ref did that today, he'd get a stick across his helmeted head.

It was common for us to go right from our secondary school to college. In my case, I wore two jerseys from the eighth grade through college: I wore an Arlington jersey for five years and a Harvard jersey for four. Yes, it took me nine years to go from eighth grade to college graduation and I was 21 when I graduated.

Today, it might take a hockey player 10, 11 or even 12 years to cover that period. They might transfer from a public school to a private school and repeat a year. They might play one or two years of junior hockey between high school and college. With college players staying on campus in the summer, working out with teammates and taking courses, many will have enough credits to graduate after three years. This allows them to transfer to another school and take graduate courses while they play for a new program.

Some coaches have pointed out that all of this moving from program to program, or school to school, might provide new experiences. But it also leaves the player as "the new kid," one who might not be given the same responsibilities and leadership roles as someone who puts down roots in one place.

Add all of this up. My nine-year journey, wearing those two jerseys, now becomes that double-digit stint, the practitioner wearing five or six jerseys and graduating from college at 24 or 25. And that is if they stay in school and don't leave for the NHL. One year, Boston College had so many players leave early for pro hockey that they had no seniors on the roster. As Jerry York noted that year, "The only parents who got flowers on Senior Night were the manager's parents."

There was a time that when six new players entered school as freshmen, you could expect to get 24 cumulative seasons from the group. With pro opportunities now more plentiful and the NCAA making transferring easier, a coach is lucky to get 18 years from six incoming freshmen.

One other observation about time. A few years ago, I was at Harvard's Bright-Landry Center for some afternoon meeting when I saw that the men's varsity was taking the ice for practice. For a moment, I thought I would go down and introduce myself to the goalies. For many years after graduation, I got to know the goalies, helping them on the ice sometimes. But it had been a while.

On this day in 2018, I did some math and decided not to go down to ice level. My talking to a goalie in the Class of 2018, as cool a guy as I'm sure I was, would have been akin to the 1973 me talking to a former Harvard goalie from the Class of 1928. I remembered what I thought of them back then. So I kept to myself that day.

Beyond my playing for Harvard, I had an opportunity to coach for Harvard. And to make history in the process. In the fall of 1977, I was starting my first full year as Harvard's sports information director and coming off a year in which I served as "co-coach" of the Harvard men's junior varsity with my old teammate Kevin Hampe.

It was understood that with my new duties as SID, I would give up my JV role and Kevin would run it himself. But then a telephone call came from men's coach Billy Cleary with a simple request.

"Joey, a couple of the girls came by to see me about starting up a girls' hockey team. They need a coach. What do you say?"

Without thinking for more than a second or two, I agreed to become the first coach of Harvard's women's ice hockey team.

Once word got out about my new responsibilities, the reaction was interesting. One particular conversation clued me in on what women's athletics were up against in those days. The first was with a rather crusty alumnus who was finishing a workout at Harvard's Dillon Field House.

"Say, Joe, I understand you'll be coaching a girls' hockey team here. Is that right?" he asked, mopping his brow and kicking his Adidas into the bottom of his locker.

"It's a women's team, not a girls' team," I said.

"Now, tell me why a girl would want to play hockey," he asked.

"Why not? It's a beautiful game and —"

"Joe, they can't be serious," he interrupted. "They're just going to get hurt, and they'll be taking ice time and funds from the men, I imagine. Next thing you know, they'll want to play football."

Thursday, October 27, 1977: Organization Day. First came an afternoon meeting with the powers that be in Harvard's athletic department. Then came an evening meeting with candidates for the first Harvard women's ice hockey team.

Before the meeting with the department officials, I had a visit from Nelia Worsley, a Harvard junior who was the prime mover in getting this team started. She had a list of 40 names of would-be female players. It was encouraging. It was also the only visible evidence that interest in women's hockey existed.

The first meeting went well. The department was willing to grant club status to a women's ice hockey team. It would provide a coach and two hours of practice time per week, 6:15-7:15 p.m., Tuesday and Thursday. A limited number of games could be scheduled at a later date.

Because the team would have club status only, the department wasn't obligated to fully finance it, which meant that the women would have to pay for equipment, transportation to away games and the like. I addressed the equipment shortage by donating my $500 "salary" for the purchase of 10 sets of elbow pads, shin pads, hockey pants and gloves.

A great deal of concern was immediately expressed for the women's safety. Though the department couldn't provide the equipment, it was still responsible for seeing that anyone representing the university was properly equipped. And for the women, even though they would play no-check hockey, that meant adequate protection, including face shields, something not yet mandated in men's college hockey. Though I agreed that this was a good idea, I anticipated that someone would quite rightly wonder why the men didn't have to wear shields and the women did.

The two hours of weekly practice time wasn't much, but the 6:15 p.m. time slot was a blessing. Even more established women's teams were dealing with 6:15 a.m. ice times.

As I awaited the meeting with the women, I wondered if anybody outside of the organizers would show up. Would there be three women or 33? Were those 40 names on the list really future forwards and defensemen and goalies? Would there be *any* goalies?*

A member of the Radcliffe crew, Nancy Kerrebrock, volunteered to play goal in the first season but she was not always available. We actually used three non-students, high schoolers, when no other options were available. They were Sue Mead, Jesse Hill (whose sister Alice was on the team) and Lisa Whitcomb, who went on to lead Boston University to its first Beanpot championship. In 1978-79, the first varsity season, Nelia Worsley became our first legitimate goalie.

About 15 students arrived for the meeting, which accomplished little more than to introduce their coach to them and explain what the department would and would not provide.

I had them all fill out questionnaires so I could get a rough idea of their backgrounds and their commitments to hockey. Their answers identified three distinct groups of candidates.

There was a nucleus of five students who had played ice hockey before. This group included Lucy Wood, the senior captain of the field hockey team, who had gained some notoriety the year before by becoming the first woman to play in Harvard's intramural ice hockey league.

The next group was comprised of five or six women with figure skating experience who had had enough of compulsory figures and double axels and wanted to give hockey a try.

Then there was the largest block of students, who simply had athletic interests and thought it might be fun to take up a new sport. These were the ones — along with most of the figure skaters — who, when asked what position they played, would put down a question mark. Half didn't know what they wanted to play. The other half didn't know the names of the different positions.

History was made at Watson Rink on November 8 when the first practice for Harvard women's hockey became a reality. Figure skates — some with fur trim — outnumbered hockey skates. Brightly colored mittens and hats took the place of hockey gloves and helmets, as hockey gear was at a minimum.

I was in no hurry to blow the whistle and ruin the moment. It was quite enough to watch the 18 skaters who would soon become a hockey team and observe the varying degrees of skill.

My eyes immediately focused on two players, Tania Huber and Lauren Norton, who were passing a puck back and forth as they skated the length of the ice. They had played three years at Concord Academy, and as I watched them skate around and through the others, I knew I was watching my offense at work. Their obvious ability was the first of many encouraging signs on Day One.

Now it was time to play coach. I had spent the better part of the day scribbling down X's and O's, planning what I would do in this first hour of practice — aware that for all but five skaters, it would be their first hour of hockey ever. Both Bill Cleary and Yale coach Tim Taylor had advised me to keep it simple for the first night. My initial observations of the team made it clear that I had no other choice.

I blew the whistle and called the group to center ice. Sixteen skaters negotiated their way to where I stood, some with more ease than others. Norton and Huber found time to rifle a few fluttering slappers after the whistle and arrived at center ice just late enough to irritate the rookie coach.

But in a way it was encouraging. I have never played on a hockey team that didn't have a couple of bona fide rink rats who couldn't resist the temptation to take a few extra shots after the coach's whistle.

I instructed the group to stretch and skate slowly before picking up the pace on my command. As the skaters dispersed and began the counterclockwise flow around the rink, I soon discovered that the difference between half speed and full speed was negligible for most.

Two days later, Harvard's men's varsity team, which practiced from 4-6 p.m. daily, was just finishing up when the women — in larger numbers than the first day — arrived for their second practice. A few of the men stayed out when the women took the ice. One of the guys took a group of women into the corner and explained the proper way to take a wrist shot. Another player was slowly skating up the ice, passing a puck back and forth with one of the women. In other spots, men were offering various hockey tips to interested women.

As the regular practice began, the women were encouraged to ask questions if something wasn't clear. The encouragement wasn't necessary. The questions came freely, for the women were sincerely interested in learning the game.

I was fascinated by two phenomena. First, the questions were quite basic, and I found myself poorly prepared to answer them. What do you say when someone asks simply, "How do you stop when you're skating backward?" or, "How do you lift a puck?" It had been years since I had to deal with this stuff, and it wasn't enough to say, "Well, you just do it, you know? I mean you, ah, skate backward and then you just, ah, stop."

This is the first women's ice hockey team to represent Harvard. It was a club team for the 1977-78 season, taken in the final year of Watson Rink. (Photo courtesy of Harvard University)

I found myself struggling with the mechanics of a sweep shot. How *do* you lift a puck, anyway? For the first time in years, I had to think about placement of the hands, shifting of body weight and so on.

The other phenomenon was a treat. I have worked with boys, mostly goalies, from youth programs through high school age. Too often they have the attention span of a shoehorn. They have all the answers, so why listen? But the women caught every word and followed every detail closely. Sometimes too closely. One time I demonstrated a simple drill where I stickhandled through cones on the ice. By mistake, I missed one of the cones, and every one of the women followed me exactly, missing that same cone.

The season opener was just one week away. So we held a team meeting to tie up some loose ends and to view some hockey films.

After looking at demonstrations of skating, passing and shooting, my assistant, John Christensen, and I fumbled our way through a chalk talk. Christensen was a member of the Harvard JVs who had learned his hockey in Waterloo, IA.

We tried to introduce simple breakout and forechecking concepts that seemed to elude the grasp of most of the squad, and then decided that a simple review of the rules was in order. After covering offsides, icing, and the various infractions, John and I felt reasonably confident that we had given a thorough presentation.

"Are there any questions?" I asked. "I have a question," said Elaine Galler, a rapidly improving right wing. "Can you grab their facemasks?"

It was apparent that we still had some work to do.

History was made again on Saturday, December 10, 1977. In our first game, Boston University came from behind on its home ice to ruin our debut and Tania Huber's hat trick, taking a 4-3 overtime decision from us. A disappointing loss, yes. But in overtime? I had expected worse.

Since the game was a last-minute addition to our schedule because of a cancellation, only eight players showed up, and John Christensen ran the bench in place of an absentee head coach. Christensen rotated the eight players on and off the ice skillfully and found his only tricky situation was entering the locker room to hand out jerseys before the contest.

Loss or no loss, there were three encouraging signs. After the game, the women couldn't stop talking about how much fun it had been. Also, the game was close. Finally, just like any established team at any level, this squad found reason to complain about the officiating after the game. For a group that didn't know the rules a little while back, that was a sign of progress.

The second game was the next day. Watson Rink, a cinderblock and bleachers facility, gave new meaning to the word "cold." And when the game is at nine o'clock on a Sunday morning with 15 people in the stands, the experience could be numbing.

Harvard's first women's varsity ice hockey team had its team photo taken at Dartmouth's Thompson Arena. Without money in the budget for a photographer, I convinced the Dartmouth photographer to take our picture. (Photo courtesy of Harvard University by way of Dartmouth College)

Such were the conditions for our home opener against the Nashua (New Hampshire) Elks, an amateur women's team made up of high schoolers, collegians and ex-collegians, and a 32-year-old mother of two. Not exactly the Montreal Canadiens, but our squad needed to experience victory.

The eight skaters from the previous night's loss were joined by three fresh bodies to give us two full units and a goaltender. Again we had our act together early and found ourselves with another 3-2 lead as the game wound down. There would be no letdown this time as Tania Huber's rink-length dash made it 4-2 and preserved the Harvard women's team's first triumph.

That all seven goals on the weekend were scored by freshmen was an encouraging sign for the future. So was the very evident enjoyment that the women were deriving from the experience. And with each game, new lessons were being learned.

Take Alison Bell, for example. When the referee caught her breaking the rules, he routinely intoned, "Number 15 — two minutes for tripping!"

Alison wasn't fazed by the referee. In fact, nothing registered.

"Alison, that penalty is on you," I said. She pulled her arm around so that she could see the number 15 sewn on the sleeve. "Oh, you're right," she replied, as she laughed and skated to the penalty box.

Small lessons, perhaps. But definitely a learning experience.

In our first Ivy League game, we lost to Dartmouth, 9-2 score. Still, the little things were starting to come around. Players were starting to look up and spot open teammates. Sometimes the passes were there, sometimes they weren't. But the players were looking for people. The skating was improved. The shots were finding their way on goal more often. Individual and team skills were now identifiable. And most important, the enthusiasm was still there.

One afternoon, it occurred to me that a number of players had taken to removing their helmets when they got hot. After speaking to a couple of the more frequent culprits, I felt compelled to announce that we had a new helmet rule. Any time they stepped on the ice, helmets had to be worn.

The next day, a number of the players were smiling, seemingly out of context, and I soon figured that something was up with this group. Apparently a few of them had taken markers to helmets and written, "The helmet rule sucks." We enjoyed a group laugh, and I asked them to remove it by the next day. Practice resumed.

A little while later, I heard from Bill Cleary. He thought the players were being disrespectful and suggested that discipline was in order. I didn't agree. It was a joke and, given our primary mission of keeping things loose and fun and having everyone stay with the program, I took a more liberal approach. The helmets were cleaned up in short order by the players.

By mid-February of this first season, the team had not won a game since that December 11 win against the Elks. But on February 14, we celebrated a different kind of victory. We got the word that the Harvard athletic department had given us the green light for next year. The first-year club team would be a "Level II varsity," eligible for department support, and that was the sweetest victory the group of hockey pioneers could imagine.

For the record, the team did win two more games on the ice, finishing the season with 3-0 and 7-2 wins over Boston University and Ithaca College, respectively. The first season as a club team ended with a 3-5 record.

I'd like to offer a couple of anecdotes about the first varsity season. I was living in Oak Square in Brighton with two friends from Harvard and one from high school. Leigh Hogan was a hockey teammate I had known since I was nine. His father was my first youth coach and Leigh was attending law school when we roomed together.

Don Driscoll was a Harvard baseball teammate of Leigh's, a highly competitive pitcher who was in medical school when we were roomies. How competitive? I was told he once stormed off the mound after striking out a batter to end an inning. He was livid because the pitch wasn't where he intended it to be.

The third roommate was Rick Rigazio, a friend since seventh grade. His father had been a shortstop in the Chicago Cubs organization when the Cubs had Ernie Banks at that position. Rick's uncle Don was a goalie on the 1956 Olympic Team that won silver in Cortina d'Ampezzo. I assigned Rick to referee our home games, and as the team got to know him, I had to remind them not to say, "Ricky, how is that a trip?" Instead to say, "Ref, how is that a trip?"

The other story is about the rink. Harvard Athletics was in a major facility renovation around this time, one that was long overdue. In short order, Blodgett Pool, Gordon Track and Bright Hockey Center were constructed.

The latter rose up on the site of Watson Rink and meant that the first women's varsity team would not have a home rink.

We practiced (at 6:30 a.m.) and played our home games at the Buckingham Browne and Nichols School, a mile or so away from Harvard's athletic facilities. That meant two vans had to leave Dillon Field House shortly after 6:00 each morning, with captain Alison Bell and myself usually behind the respective steering wheels.

It was in this context that I attended a planning meeting with architects and members of the Department of Athletics to review blueprints and the like.

At one point, it dawned on me that the plans for the new rink called for a men's varsity locker room, a men's JV locker room and two visiting team rooms. But no women's varsity room.

On further study, I saw that a women's varsity room existed within the adjoining track building, a short walk from the actual rink. Given that I was invited to the meeting as the representative of women's hockey, I thought I should pose a question: "Call me crazy, but shouldn't the women's ice hockey team have a room that's actually inside the hockey rink?"

I suggested that there should be both a men's and women's varsity room of equal size and location, a men's JV room and one visiting team room. If they were to host a tournament, that room in the track could be for a second visiting team. That was what ended up in the Bright Hockey Center when it opened on November 10, 1979. (The men's varsity was shutout by Jim Craig and the future miracle workers of Team USA, 4-0.)

For the record, we went 6-11-1 in our first varsity season, which included Ivy wins against Dartmouth and Yale, and an impressive 4-4 tie at Brown, that program having been around since the mid-1960s.

We also launched the Women's Beanpot Tournament that year, the original porcelain Beanpot being one that I purchased for $6 in an Essex, MA, antique shop.

I stepped down at the end of the season and was allowed to interview candidates for my successor. Thinking that a female role model was in order, I hired former Brown player Rita Harder. I recommended the runner-up for the job to Northeastern, which was also hiring. NU hired him, and Don MacLeod would go on to win 210 games for the Huskies over an 11-year career.

Harder would coach two seasons before Harvard Women's Hockey was stabilized by the two lengthy and successful tenures of John Dooley (162 wins in 13 seasons) and Katey Stone (494 wins in 26 seasons). Stone, the U.S. Olympic head coach in 2014, ranks fourth overall in NCAA wins and has been a strong voice off the ice in promoting the interests of women's ice hockey. It was during her time that the true potential of Harvard women's hockey was realized. In 1999, Harvard won the national championship, at the time hosted by USA Hockey. (The NCAA first hosted a championship in 2002).

Harvard coach Katey Stone has 494 wins through 26 seasons. Stone brought the program to new heights, winning a national championship and producing many Patty Kazmaier Award winners. In June of 2021, she became the first female recipient of USA Hockey's Distinguished Service Award. I was fortunate to receive this award in 2017, following my fellow Harvard alumni Bill Cleary (1992), Ben Smith (1998) and Tim Taylor (2006). (Photo courtesy of Harvard University)

Another indication of Harvard's success can be seen in the past winners of the Patty Kazmaier Award, given to the best women's ice hockey player in the NCAA. Harvard has had six recipients since the award was established in 1998, Jennifer Botterill being a two-time winner.

Chapter Three —
Coaching Goalies

"If Ken Dryden is so smart, how come he's a goalie?"
　　　　　　— Title of a cover story in a 1970s hockey magazine

In the beginning, there was street hockey. We would most often use a tattered tennis ball and play on the street or in the large driveway at the house next door. As previously noted, the neighbors had a three-car garage and a wide driveway so we could start on the street, Brantwood Road, and move into their driveway, which was walled in on two sides. And I was the goalie. Always.

Without pads to take up any space, I learned early that the best way to play was to wear small knee pads, stand wide and drop, centering the wide upper body on the ball, covering low with the legs and then using the hands laterally for any number of shots. It was a technique that would eventually translate to the ice very well.

Other than family, food and the Red Sox, few things have inspired me as goaltending has. I have spent a half century playing it, studying it and writing about it. It has been a passion. And on occasions like this, when I put things down on paper, I am forced to consider why this has been a life-long pursuit.

While playing defense for the North Cambridge bantams, I got my first opportunity to move from the streets to the ice when our goalie, Dave Egan, got sick on the way to a game at the Loring Arena in Framingham, MA. The Egans continued on to the rink and when Mr. Egan dropped the pads at my feet in the locker room and suggested I put them on, my goalie career was born. (I believe he made a remark along the lines of, "You seem to have

I am kneeling, first on the left. This North Cambridge bantam team had six guys who would play hockey in college and one who played football in the NFL. The coach was Dick Rigazio, a former professional baseball player. (Paul Chalue Photo)

something to say about goaltending so why don't you try it." But my memory could be faulty.)

I do remember three things about that first game as a goalie. I put the pads on the wrong legs before being corrected, the first shot I faced hit the post and died in the crease but was called a goal, and we lost the game. It wasn't until a year or so later that I made the permanent switch to goaltender.

For the record, I became a goalie in November 1966, after two years as a defenseman on the Arlington High School freshman team. (Eighth graders could play.) As previously noted, our MVP goalie, Ed Walsh, left the Arlington public schools to attend Browne and Nichols, eventually making it to the NHL. Ed's departure opened up competition for the goalie slot in my class, and so the week before Thanksgiving of 1966, I scrambled to obtain goalie equipment and make a change that would affect me for the rest of my life.

This is at the heart of my lifelong study of the position. Starting late, and at a time when there were no goalie schools or dedicated goalie gurus, all goalies of our time had to be their own coaches. There wasn't much to see on television, there was no internet and there were no books dedicated to goaltending. There were general hockey books — by Lloyd Percival and Eddie Jeremiah and Jim Fullerton — and the sole chapter on goaltending, looking at them today, was pretty basic.

I demonstrate at an early camp alongside my friend and former BU All-American Ed Walsh. I never would have become a goalie had Eddie not left Arlington schools to attend private school.

I did attend one summer hockey camp, a week in the summer of 1967 at the first Hockeytown rink in Melrose, MA. It was co-directed, for many years, by the rival high school coaches Eddie Burns of Arlington and Henry Hughes of Melrose. The former had played at Boston College and the latter at Dartmouth. The camp's resident goalie coach was Ralph "Ike" Bevins, a physical education teacher and football coach at AHS. He was also a First Team All-American goaltender for Boston University in 1950.

Bevins was an old-school guy who, according to legend, played center in football, goalie in hockey and catcher in baseball. There were plenty of the "tools of ignorance" in his locker. A tough taskmaster, he once told our gym class that we had lowered the age of "middle age" to 16. Taking it as a compliment, a few in the class attempted to leap into feeble "high fives," most unable to gain much elevation with their jumps.

At the Championship Hockey School in the summer of 1967, Bevins taught angles and basics, perhaps too basic for a 15-year-old goalie today, but exactly what I needed in my ninth month as a goaltender. It must have helped as, seven months later, I was in goal when AHS won the Eastern Massachusetts championship and I began to be recruited by Division I schools.

I have to believe that my lifelong study of goaltending stemmed from these beginnings. It was hard to play a new position alongside friends who were in their usual roles, they only having to face the routine challenges of improving at the normal pace experienced by all. I had to learn in a hurry, the failures of a goalie being more readily evident and costly to the group pursuit.

And I did learn. I put in the time, leaving my name and phone number with the people at Hockeytown. If a team needed a goalie in the summer league, I would get a call. Some nights, I would play the 7:00 game, watch the 8:15 game and then play the 9:30 game. I remember specific nights. Like when I was told I would be playing against Paul "The Shot" Hurley, a Melrose legend who went on to play for Boston College, the U.S. Olympic Team and the fledgling New England (later Hartford) Whalers.

It's funny, but I can remember the first piece of sound goalie advice I ever received. I believe I was playing at the Boston Skating Club, so it must have been in the Mayflower League, a Monday night schedule of games in the spring that brought together a mix of high school, college and adult players.

Bill Langone, my brother's goalie at Arlington High School and later an All-East goalie at Merrimack College, saw me play and came up to me afterwards to offer some advice. Bill noticed when I extended my leg pad to make a save, on a deke or perhaps a deflection, I would drop straight down and extend my pad laterally. He pointed out that this method wasn't as fully effective because the opponent only had to chip the puck over my pad.

Instead, I should push off from the skate away from the puck and "launch" my entire body toward the puck so that the enemy attacker had to deal with my entire upper body and not just my pad. This tip was a significant help.

The on-the-job learning continued through high school and college as team goalie coaches did not yet exist. It wasn't until I started working for Tim Taylor at his West Suburban Arena Hockey Camp in Natick, MA, that I learned a structure with which to teach goalies. And that was after I had graduated from college.

Former Dartmouth goalie Warren Cook, a contemporary of Tim's, was the resident goalie guy at the WSA. It is from Warren that I first learned about a teaching structure. By my second year with Tim, I took control of the goalies and this grew into my own summer camps, which are approaching 50 years. I wrote my first book on goaltending in 1975 while doing double duty in Milwaukee as a semi-pro goalie and a student at Marquette University's School of Journalism. This helped establish myself as a goalie coach.

Jump ahead 45 years and I self-published a second, smaller book on goaltending in the summer of 2020, co-written by Darren Hersh, a goalie coach of considerable talent and a former student of mine.

The staff at the West Suburban Arena Hockey School in Natick, MA, early 1970s. From left, Warren Cook, Jake Heartl, Dick "Lefty" Marr, Jim Cross, Teddy Morse, Dick Rodenheiser, Gene Kinasewich, Tim Taylor and Paul Schilling.

In between books, I enjoyed some unique goalie coaching assignments. In 1986, I received a phone call from Mike Milbury, asking me if I had interest in being the goaltending consultant for the Boston Bruins. Mike had recently moved into the front office after a 12-year playing career with the Bruins. He was attempting to upgrade many areas of the organization and, toward that end, brought in Dr. Fred Neff as a team psychologist, introduced new scouts in the U.S. and Europe, and sought out a goalie coach.

I passed the interview process and began a six-year stint as the B's goalie guy, at a time when the only other such coach was Warren Strelow with the Washington Capitals. Strelow made a name for himself in Minnesota and as Herb Brooks' goalie coach on the 1980 U.S. Olympic Team. I was actually there six full seasons, left, and came back for the lock-out-shortened 1994-95 season.

While with the Bruins, I worked for five head coaches: Butch Goring, Terry O'Reilly, Mike Milbury, Rick Bowness and Brian Sutter. Overall, the experience was positive, particularly under Messrs. O'Reilly, Milbury and Bowness. Coaches Goring and Sutter did not engage me very much.

I was particularly fond of Mike Milbury. He combined equal amounts of intelligence and passion, using the combination to succeed both on and off the ice. He probably engaged me more than the other coaches.

A part-timer with the Bruins, I was a regular at games but less so with practice. On those occasions when I did attend a practice, Mike would say to me the night before, "Bring a drill."

During games, I would often watch from the old Boston Garden coaches room so I could see all the replays and be able, at first, to defend my goalies if I felt the need. Mike made me be more objective and not just take the goalie's side.

There was that time he stormed into the room between periods and bellowed, "Your goalie was horseshit that period, Joe. Tell me why I shouldn't pull him."

"You're right," I said. "Pull him." I don't think I had ever done that before.

My friendship with Mike, which remains solid today, was cemented when I was no longer with the Bruins and struggling through a divorce. He called me out of the blue and said, "I hear you are going through some hard times. We have a charter leaving for Quebec City tomorrow. Do you want to join us? Spending a day or two with a bunch of hockey players might be good for you."

I wasn't able to take him up on his offer, but I never forgot the gesture.

The goalies played well during my time with the team. Not having played at that level, I was somewhat self-conscious at first but became more comfortable with time. Part of this had to do with the confidence that came with each new annual agreement from Harry Sinden. In short, if the head coach wanted me back, Harry was supportive.

I had great respect for Harry. He was much maligned by some of the younger members of the media, but his record spoke for itself, both as a coach and a GM. What Mike was trying to do in bringing the organization into the (late) 20th century only happened because he had Harry's blessing.

I have framed on my wall a letter from Harry and a returned check. In one of my seasons, I thought I wasn't giving the Bruins the time I should have because of my college hockey responsibilities. So I wrote the Bruins a check for $500. Harry returned it with a note saying, "Consider this payment for past services."

Mike's hiring of Fred Neff paid dividends as well. The Bruins had not beaten Montreal in a playoff series in 45 years when, during the 1987-88 season, Fred took a video crew on an in-season trip to Montreal. Every part of the trip was taped. Arriving at the airport, getting on and off buses, entering the Forum, before and after the game, etc.

Returning to Boston, Fred held a session with the team where they were shown various parts of the trip and asked what they were thinking at those times. After the obligatory smartass comments, one by one, the players started revealing themselves. "I never play well here." "The refs always screw us here." "We never get the bounces up here." And so it went.

Fred was able to point out that the team was halfway toward defeat before the puck even dropped. While every game might have a first period penalty called against us, in Montreal it triggered a "here we go again" reaction. Maybe it was coincidence but that year, the Bruins beat the Canadiens in the Adams Division final, four games to one, the final game coming at The Forum.

The Bruins went to the Stanley Cup Finals in 1988 and 1990, losing to Edmonton both times. Among the Bruins goalies in this period: Reggie Lemelin, Andy Moog, Bill Ranford, Pat Riggin, Doug Keans and Cleon Daskalakis.

With my reputation peaking while with the Bruins, my summer camps grew to 10 weeks and over 500 goalies annually. It has been funny to run into people who attended my camp. Often, they are fathers of young goalies and I end up coaching multiple generations in one family.

A number of years ago, I stopped into a sporting goods store in Kingston, MA, and as I was looking around, I noticed an old Ernie Higgins fibreglass mask hanging above the skate-sharpening machine. When I asked about it, a shaggy-looking fellow with a beard and braided hair came out and told me it was his. He was clearly burned-out from some ordeal, perhaps involving pharmaceuticals, and appeared to be many years older than me. As I left the store, I heard him call out to me, "Hey man, I went to your camp. It was awesome."

In 1991, Bob Johnson invited me to be the goalie coach for Team USA in the Canada Cup series, and three years later, Tim Taylor asked me to serve that same role, among other duties, with the 1994 U.S. Olympic Team in Lillehammer, Norway.

The goalies on that 1991 U.S. team were Mike Richter, John Vanbiesbrouck and Pat Jablonski. It was a particular pleasure to work with Mike as he had attended my summer camp for two summers when he was 15 and 16. I later got to work with John when he was in charge of international teams with USA Hockey and I was a USAH "Director."

One of the sadder memories of my hockey life came in September 1991. We were finishing up our pre-tournament schedule with a game at Sask Place in Saskatoon, Saskatchewan. Before the final game with Canada, the staff was meeting in an area under the stands when we became inundated with a swarm of flies in our meeting area. Bob Johnson looked at me and said, "Goalie coach, get rid of these flies and waved his hand toward me."

On the flight home, I had the pleasure of sitting next to Bob and had a memorable multi-hour flight, listening to him go over his memory of previous international tournaments, turning pages in old reporter-style notebooks.

I first met Bob when I was playing for Harvard and we lost to his Badgers, 2-1, in a Christmas Tournament in St. Louis. Later, while at Marquette University's School of Journalism, I interviewed him after his experience as our 1976 Olympic coach. (I had tried out for that team.)

The flight from Saskatoon ended in Toronto, with a connecting flight to Pittsburgh where we were training and where we would open up our Canada Cup schedule against Sweden the next day. I was going through that divorce and opted to go home to Boston for a few hours and then connect to Pittsburgh the next morning. That night, while dining with members of the staff, Bob suffered a major stroke, one from which he would never fully recover.

Upon arriving in Pittsburgh on Saturday morning, I went to the hospital with the rest of the staff. Bob was unable to speak but could communicate by writing on a yellow legal pad. He told Tim Taylor to "look out for the trap," Sweden's preferred defensive tactic. He apologized to the coach with whom he had been dining at the time of his stroke. And then he turned to me and waved his hand at me.

For a second, I thought he wanted me to leave the room. But then he wrote something on his legal pad and turned it toward me. He had written one word. "Flies."

At left: Lou Vairo, Bob Johnson and Tim Taylor. All three coached Olympic teams. I became good friends with Lou over the years. Bob Johnson hired me to be his goalie coach for the 1991 Canada Cup. Tim, one of my hockey mentors, brought me along as his assistant for the 1994 Olympic Games in Lillehammer, Norway. At right, our Olympic goalies, from left, Mike Dunham and Garth Snow. (Photos courtesy of USA Hockey)

The Olympic experience was tremendous for many reasons. First, I got to spend time with old friends Tim Taylor and John Cunniff. Second, it was the last U.S. men's team to get together for a 60-game pre-Olympic schedule, using amateurs and what were once called "semi-professionals," subsequent teams being populated by NHL players. Third, I got to perform multiple duties.

We assembled in Cromwell, CT, in August 1993, lived out of the local Holiday Inn and skated at a nearby Olympic-sized rink. Tim worked out a schedule that balanced games against international, professional and college teams that provided, in most cases, appropriate competition along with fund-raising opportunities. Whenever possible, we found other Olympic sheets on which to practice and play games.

My job, or jobs, involved serving as Tim's assistant general manager, public relations liaison and, when those duties had been met, goalie coach. In the assistant GM role, I helped arrange flights (working with the incomparable USA Hockey travel contact Carol Rauch), procure ice, facilitate hotel arrivals, provide per diems to the players, keep stats on the road and keep everyone in good humor.

One of the things I enjoyed doing during the college hockey season was to keep all the former college players updated on how their alma maters were doing. Every Saturday and Sunday morning, I would type out a list of scores from the night before and make sure I included all the appropriate schools. When it came to the alma mater of captain Peter Laviolette, I would be sure to list, "Westfield State: Did Not Play." The school, at that time, had dropped hockey, only to pick it up years later.

The goalies on our roster were Mike Dunham, Garth Snow and John Hillebrand. Dunham and Snow had enjoyed outstanding careers at the University of Maine, and Hillebrand had played at Colorado College. Hillebrand had basically been told that he was going to be slotted as the third goalie, regardless of what happened on the ice.

I recall a game against Binghamton of the American Hockey League. Hillebrand had left the team and was now playing for that AHL club and, on that day, we played Dunham, Binghamton being his home town. We ended up winning the game by a score of 10-9.

At some point in the third period, Lewis Gross, a player agent who was sitting next to me in the press box, turned to me and said, "Excuse me, do I understand that you have coached both of these goalies this season?" As he asked the question, he glanced up at the scoreboard.

Dunham and Snow could not have been more different. Both were nice guys and both were talented. And both went on to the National Hockey League.

But Dunham was clearly a more complete goalie and Snow was clearly a more personable, fun-to-be-with teammate. Dunham was slated to be the heir apparent to a long line of great U.S. Olympic goalies. Jack McCartan, Lefty Curran, Jim Craig, Ray LeBlanc. He could do it all and showed it in our higher-level games against NHL teams.

On the other hand, Snow was a talent in his own right. In the 1993 NCAA Championship Game against Lake Superior State, Maine coach Shawn Walsh faced a 4-2 deficit heading into the third period and knew that the Lakers would likely do a lot of dumping the puck into the zone, nursing their lead. And so he took out Dunham and installed the better puck-handler in Snow. While other factors surfaced, Maine scored three times and shut out LSSU in the third period to win the national title.

I experienced a funny thing prior to starting with the Olympic team. In almost every conversation I had with Hockey East coaches who knew Dunham and Snow from their Maine days, I would hear a variation of the same theme: "In the end, you will go with Snow."

I didn't understand this. Dunham was clearly the more naturally talented goalie. But Snow kept coming. He didn't lose a start from mid-November up until the Olympic Games began. (Granted, Dunham drew more of the tougher games.)

Snow had a larger personality. He had a great sense of humor. He was more likely to stay out when practice time was optional.

When the games began. Dunham struggled a little in the early games. A 4-4 tie with lowly France set the stage. There was a soft goal or two here and there. And when we got to Canada, a team we had played a dozen times on the tour, the staff went with Snow. (Another tie.) When we finally reached the medal round, a tough decision had to be made.

It was always assumed that for us to succeed, we needed a goalie to stand on his head like other U.S. medal-winners. Dunham clearly had the high side in talent. And yet when this moment came, as those Hockey East coaches had predicted, we went with Snow. In the end, it wasn't enough and we finished without a medal, having tied three games and won only the game against Italy. It wasn't the goaltending. It was our depth.

After the Bruins, I served two seasons as goalie coach for the Milwaukee Admirals when they were in the International Hockey League. That was my last "big" coaching job, as my college hockey work intensified with my move from part-time ECAC Hockey administrator to full-time Hockey East commissioner.

In my nine Hockey East contracts, covering 23 years, I insisted on keeping my goalie coaching business, short of another pro stint. In addition to the summer camps, I spent nearly a decade of my Hockey East years coaching at the prep level, first with St. Sebastian's and later at The Governor's Academy.

There are moments from this long coaching trek that stand out and bring a smile. And that doesn't even cover the countless smiles from young goalies when they finally get the hang of something they have been working on.

I remember the long list of coaches who have graced my summer camps, including Brett Abel, John Aiken, Bob Bartholomew, John Binkoski, Michelle Collett, Bob Conceison, Bob Deraney, Kelly Dyer, Mike Geragosian, Darren Hersh, Bob Houston, Andrew Huntoon, Todd Lampert, Dan Lombard, Paul MacAuley, Brad Michals, Rick Mills, Kevin Morrison, Mike Morrison, Conor O'Brien, Cap Raeder, Mo Randall, Garry Scott, Alex Westlund and so many more.

I remember legendary NHL administrator Brian Burke, when he was a player agent in Boston, asking to work a week to better understand goalies. He has reminded me many times that my camp was the only one he ever worked that cost him money. He forgot his skates on the first day and bought a pair in the pro shop at the Pilgrim Arena in Hingham, MA. The skates cost more than I paid him for the week.

Then there was BU All-American, and Boston Bruin, Cleon Daskalakis who, working in that same Hingham facility, was found to have written, "Cleon D" inside his staff jacket. While picking up the locker room after one day's session, I came upon the jacket and stared at Cleon's name. I thought to myself, "What possessed him to write the 'D' after Cleon? Was

This has been a familiar scene at camps and clinics for nearly a half century.

he concerned that there might be another Cleon, maybe 'Cleon F' joining the staff that week?"

Through the years, whatever connection I had would result in a guest coach making an appearance. While with the Bruins, Doug Keans and Reggie Lemelin visited the camp. After the Olympics, Todd Marchant and Garth Snow appeared on the ice. My favorite guest coach might have been Mike Richter, primarily because he had attended the camp for two summers while a teen. A Stanley Cup champion and Hall of Fame inductee, Richter made the camp Hall of Fame when he refused to accept a paycheck for the week he worked.

Equally memorable are the goalies who have attended the camp. Alongside Richter, there was Jim Carey, who won a Vezina Trophy with Washington. There was a very young Cory Schneider, who went on to great success in college and the NHL. So, too, did Rick DiPietro, a No. 1 overall pick who played at BU and with the New York Islanders.

Dan Lombard was another of my favorites, shining at Belmont Hill and then Yale University. There was Mike Ayers, who played at UNH and coached at BC. There was 10-year-old Erin Whitten, who would go on to UNH and Team USA as one of the best female American goalies ever produced. And I have a special spot for Chuckie Hughes, who attended for 10 summers, including the summer of 1988, right before enrolling at Harvard and helping lead the Crimson to the 1989 NCAA Championship.

There were also some notables who did not go on to such hockey glory. One of legendary singer-songwriter James Taylor's sons attended our camp in Burlington. So, too, did the son of the actor Robert Vaughn, who was

Two of my favorite students: Hall of Famer Mike Richter and Erin Whitten, now Erin Hamlen, head coach at Merrimack College. (Richter Photo by Jennifer Ziegelmaier)

Here are 12 of the 13 goalies who attended my wedding reception in September 1995. Kneeling in front: my nephew, Timmy Sheehan, in front of me, and Bobby Quinn to the right. Five people across the middle: Ron DeGregorio, John Binkoski, Michelle DiStefano, Paul MacAuley and Mike Gough. Standing in the back: Eddie Walsh, Bob Conceison, Garry Scott and Rick Mills. The 13th goalie was Jimmy Logue, but the Ryder Cup was on television and we couldn't pry him away.

one of *The Magnificent Seven* on the big screen and was Napoleon Solo, the *Man from U.N.C.L.E.*, on television. There was Gray Weicker, son of Connecticut governor Lowell Weicker, the father being part of the Watergate hearings, the son a St. Lawrence and AHL goalie. And I once coached a Dartmouth goaltender, Anne Albright, whose mother, Madeleine, became Secretary of State under President Bill Clinton.

After decades in the goalie coaching world, I had made a name for myself, not only locally but across North America. Maybe beyond. While my "day job" for nearly four decades was as a college hockey administrator, nothing gave me more pleasure and pride than the work I did with goaltenders.

The visibility sometimes led to unique opportunities, and one in particular I feel compelled to share. A meaningful part of my late summer calendar is the day after the final on-ice session. I review attendance by week, I list the coaches who worked (and who will be invited back), what drills were effective, what changes to the curriculum might be in order, what rinks should I repeat and so on. Then there is the putting away of things. Take stock of jerseys by size and color, wash and store coaches' jackets, and secure things that won't be needed until the following summer.

In this last category falls my Boni puck-shooting machine. I first met Orlando Boni in the early 1970s when one of his first models (maybe the actual first one) was delivered to Tim Taylor's West Suburban Hockey School in Natick, MA. This one, named "Shaibu," held more than 200 pucks, evenly distributed through eight columns. When one sleeve of pucks was done, you stepped on a release, pivoted this huge cylinder, and then locked in another column, ready to go. I've seen many of his machines but none like Shaibu which, I was told, meant "puck" in Russian.

I always stored my puck machine in a plywood mini-shed that my late father built for me many years ago. If a tornado came down my street and ripped my house off its foundation and reduced the neighborhood to rubble, I am pretty sure that shed and my machine would be the only things still intact. (In March 2021, I returned the machine to 89-year-old Orlando Boni.)

I am haunted by a memory of an unexpected turn of events involving the machine that took place in 2008. I call it "The Bird Incident."

Early that year, I received a phone call from Eric Handler, a television producer at WGBH in Boston. Eric worked on a show called *Fetch*, a children's program that taught science through an animated dog and a cast of precocious children. A future script called for the kids to make a set of goalie pads out of various materials, eventually showing how rolling newspapers and weaving them at an angle would create more strength than one might imagine.

A key component of the script was pelting the animated "Ruff Ruffman" with pucks through a puck-shooting machine. Someone in Eric's circle of contacts knew that I had just the type of machine that he needed, thus the call.

I arranged to meet Eric at my house and give him a demonstration of what the machine could do. A few days later, he arrived with a female assistant, whose name escapes me at the moment, and the demonstration followed. With one unfortunate twist.

While waiting for my public broadcasting guests, I lugged the machine out of its winter home, connected it to an extension cord and dragged it down the gravel driveway. That's no small feat given its weight and proclivity to sink into the stones. I dropped in the black plastic tube that holds the pucks, having sprayed it with silicon, and then filled it about halfway with pucks.

At the other end of the driveway, I emptied a couple of puck-filled milk crates and stacked them on top of each other. Looking around, I spotted a small bucket that I placed atop the crates and thought to myself, "That will make a good target so I can show them how accurate the machine can be."

Right on schedule, my guests arrived and we exchanged pleasantries. I'm sure we all tried to stifle the urge to stereotype. My trying not to see them as PBS elitists who, as Bill Cleary might say, "wouldn't know if a puck was blown up or stuffed." Their trying not to see me as some crude jock who owned a puck-shooting machine.

After some mindless chitchat, I led them over to the machine and explained how it worked; how the power cord was unique to the machine, how you could adjust the speed and how you could raise and lower it and so on. I started the machine and turned the dial so I could get significant speed for the steel wheels that would propel the pucks.

As fate would have it, at that very moment, a small bird landed on top of the bucket that I had set up as a target. Without giving it any thought, and I mean ANY thought, I turned to my guests and said, "Hey, watch this."

I grabbed the handle used to put the pucks into firing position and cranked it hard. The puck flew in a straight line and made a direct hit on the defenseless bird. A few feathers went up and one tiny bird went down. And stayed down.

I turned toward my guests. I turned back to look at the bird. I turned back to my guests. They had that exaggerated jaw-dropped look that actors in bad sitcoms use. I started my defense.

"Oh my God," I began. "I did NOT do that on purpose. This is not that precise a machine. It was an accident. Really."

If I had tried to do that intentionally — I have been using this particular machine for more than three decades — there is very little chance that I would have succeeded. And I am not saying that because I have tried. It was an accident.

My PBS friends, who were really nice people, seemed to accept my story and seemed genuinely torn between feeling sorry for the bird and feeling sorry for me. Now perhaps they were really thinking, "What kind of sadist kills birds with a puck machine? Are these hockey people even worse than we thought?" I can't recall how hasty their departure was that day, but Eric did call back and arranged to use the machine in his program as planned.

Further proof that they had accepted my defense came through an offer to actually appear in the episode (which first aired on October 29, 2008).

When the producer of the PBS show *Fetch* called, I was ready to lend my puck-shooting machine. Little did I know it would result in tragedy.

The original plan called for Christina Kessler, a goalie on the Harvard University women's team, to appear as the goalie in the episode. But Christina, a Canadian citizen, was stopped at the border when she revealed she was coming down to work on a television show. Customs officials would not let her through without the proper papers and the people at *Fetch* were suddenly in need of a goalie.

Having steadfastly turned down offers to appear on film as a goalie ever since *Love Story*, for fear of being typecast, I relented and took the job. Some friends have told me that they have watched the episode with their children. It's actually kind of a fun show, and I was happy to be asked. Actually, I was happy to receive any correspondence from WGBH, given "The Bird Incident."

When I watched the finished product, I was reminded of those disclaimers that you often see at the end of a television show or movie or commercial. You know, the ones that say, "No animals were harmed in the making of this program." I always thought, in the interest of full disclosure, that Series 59, Episode 19 of the PBS program *Fetch* should have ended with a narrator intoning, "Only one animal was harmed in the making of this program. It was an accident. Really."

All this aside, the lifeblood of a half a century of coaching remains all the goalies who, perhaps, did not gain notable fame but maybe won a pee wee championship or a state high school title. By conservative estimate, I have been on the ice with more than 12,000 goalies. I have used that number for some time, so it probably needs adjusting upwards. Going back to the start of this chapter, when I wondered what led to the passion for studying goaltending, I believe it is my desire to make learning the position easier, to make playing goal more fun.

I have a memory of leaving a college hockey game decades ago where the Boston College goaltender, Paul Skidmore, put on a show, making close to 50 saves, many of them acrobatic and spectacular. Walking out of the arena, I overhead a conversation between two pro scouts. One of them was raving about Skidmore's performance and the other said, "Yeah, he's pretty good. He'll be even better when he learns how to play the position."

That remark stayed with me. I spent time thinking about what it meant. Skidmore was, as I said, spectacular. Was the scout suggesting that "spectacular" wasn't a good thing? Over the years, I have come to understand that it is good to have the ability to be spectacular, but it's hard to sustain your game counting on the ability to make one flashy save after another. The goal is to play such a smart, position-solid game that you never have to be spectacular.

And so I set out to explore and explain what it means to "know how to play goal." What can you do to take the burden off your reflexes and ath-leticism? When I played Division I college hockey and in Europe, I wasn't a great physical athlete and yet I succeeded at a high level. How was I able to do that? What was it about my thought process that allowed me to get in position and succeed despite the lack of exceptional physical strengths? If I could study that and articulate it, could I help others with average skills play better?

I recently sent a copy of my new goaltending book to Bill Fitzsimmons, the longtime Dean of Admissions at Harvard University. Bill and I have enjoyed a running gag over the years, stemming from some research I did on Harvard goaltenders. He had 1,085 career saves before he graduated in 1968. When I finished my Harvard career five years later, I came in at 1,084. When I discovered this, I sent the stats to Bill with a note reading, "One save better. Obviously, an icing that found its way on net." He responded, with an inscription on the same piece of paper, "Obviously a breakaway save in overtime."

Upon receiving my latest work, Fitz wrote back, "Imagine if we had something like this to help when we were learning how to play goal." And that, I believe, has been the point of my efforts all along.

Over the years, in addition to my writings, I have been able to produce a number of instructional DVDs. The first, in the early 1980s, was part of the ESPN Instructional Series. Later, working with Dave Peterson and Al Godfrey, I did one for USA Hockey. One of the highlights of that period was working the first USA Hockey goaltending camps in Colorado Springs.

One area of the position that I have started to emphasize is what I call "managing the game." This covers all those things that influence the outcome of a game that are NOT about making saves. Communicating with teammates, handling pucks, tying up pucks, etc. I preach this to high school and older goalies.

Recently, I watched a 14-year-old goalie make about 30 saves in a game and tie up the puck for a whistle 15 times. It was a terrific perfor-mance, those whistles preventing any second shots and also allowing his coach to send fresh players over the boards. That was a game well managed.

When I was a senior in high school, my back-up goalie was John Aiken. John left Arlington High School to go to Belmont Hill and then on to Harvard. He was one of seven goalies in his freshman class, and, by the time he was a senior, he was the only one on the varsity. Today he is a pedi-atric surgeon in a Milwaukee suburb and one of my closest friends.

John and his wife, Mary, raised three hockey-playing sons who went on to Notre Dame, Harvard and Colgate. But what really shows their intelli-gence is that none of them became goalies.

John and his brother, Jimmy, were featured in the photographs of my first book on goaltending. And Johnny put in many hours as a member of my summer school staff in the early years.

This is a long way of introducing the other John Aiken, my friend's father, who lived a unique goaltending life and from whom both John and I have learned plenty about goaltending. In the fall of 2020, I was thrilled to receive a long hand-written letter from the 88-year-old Aiken shortly after I sent him a copy of my newest goaltending book.

John Aiken Sr. was the Boston Bruins' reserve goaltender from 1953-64, a period that overlapped his actual college playing experience. And that's part of his story.

It was the receipt of my book that triggered the elder Aiken to pen the 16-page letter to me. Some background to the younger readers: It wasn't until the mid-1960s that the NHL completely abandoned the one-goalie-per-lineup policy. Prior to requiring two netminders, each team had a practice goalie who was expected to attend all home games and suit up if either team needed a goalie.

That opportunity for John Aiken came on March 13, 1958, when the Montreal Canadiens visited the Boston Bruins. In that game, the legendary Habs goalie, Jacques Plante, was injured in the second period when Montreal defenseman Doug Harvey drove the Bruins Vic Stasiuk into Plante, who hit his head on the crossbar.

Down 1-0 already, Montreal summoned Aiken from the stands. Except the young goalie, about to make his NHL debut, had left his equipment in his dad's car. The father ran to get it, delivered it to the son and the nervous 26-year-old suited up. The game ended in the home team's favor, 7-3, but

The two John Aikens from Arlington: one briefly in the NHL, the other a member of our camp staff after a career at Harvard.

John Aiken had made it to the NHL. His 35-minute career started off a little bumpy, but he stopped eight of nine shots in the third period after he settled down.

How he got there was somewhat improbable. His college career began at West Point, playing for Jack Riley. But while there, his twin boys, John and Jim, were born. Aware that this might force him to leave the Academy, he shared his situation with BU coach Harry Cleverly after a 60-save performance against the Terriers.

"Harry told me he would have a spot waiting for me at BU, and he did," recalled Aiken. And so he transferred to BU and was forced to sit out a year. It was during this time that he received a call from Lynn Patrick, coach of the Bruins, offering him a chance to be the team's practice goalie for $25 a game. (Later $100 a week.)

"It took a while to be accepted by the players," said Aiken. "Ferny Flaman hits me with a wicked slapshot, left ear badly cut. Coach Lynn Patrick asks if I can finish practice, and I do. Six hours and 35 stitches later, I was accepted by everyone from that point on."

He would also practice with Montreal or Toronto on Sunday mornings after Saturday night games. He watches today's hockey and marvels at the goalies. ("We were Model T's and today they're a Lexus.") He watches the goalies intently, still. I remember him grabbing line charts before his son's games, looking for guys with a lot more goals than assists. ("See the guy with 17 goals and four assists? Those guys like to shoot the puck. I would tell Johnny to watch them.")

I feel an urge to include some technical writing on goaltending, some sample or two that captures what I have been trying to say for close to 50 years. I have written a couple of books on the subject and considered reprinting full chapters here. But if I over-do this, I can see readers quickly flipping the pages to Chapter Four. So let me share a couple of stories that might accomplish what I have in mind without losing any of you.

I have written quite a bit about how a goalie thinks during competition. Beyond reacting to shots, a goalie has to anticipate where the action is going to come from and how he can get in the best position to, simply, "get hit" with the puck. That is, let's take the burden off of our reflexes and fill the net so a shot *must* hit us.

In the next chapter, I describe how I ended up sitting in the living room of Hall of Fame goaltender Ken Dryden, going through the manuscript of my first goaltending book. I first connected with Dryden to get permission to use a speech he gave on goaltending. I remember he allowed me to do so but asked that I clean it up, as transcripts of speeches can be choppy.

I wanted to write about some of the mental skills that a goalie needs to possess and I came across a speech where Dryden addresses the psychological

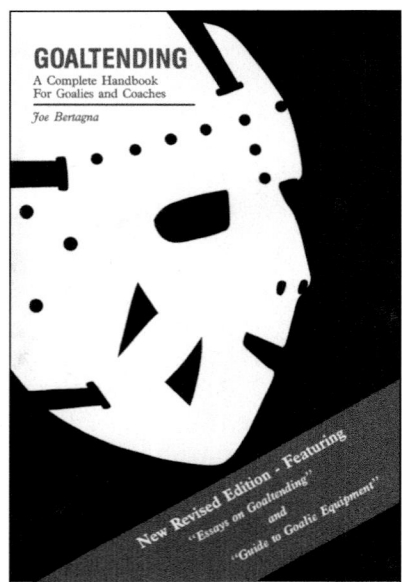 

Much of my work on the study of goaltending can be found in these two books, the first written in 1975, the other in 2020. Both were self-published.

warfare that goes on between the goalie and the shooter. Here is his view of the psychological battle.

"You [the goalie] have the direct confrontation all the time. You are intimately involved with the team; but ultimately there is that one man and you. You can either love that sort of thing or it can get to you after a while. It is he and you, you see what happens, it works out well, and you get a tremendous sense of satisfaction. In order to keep your sanity as a goalie, you have to think of yourself, not as a target, not as somebody out there to be hit by pucks. You act on the puck yourself. It is not that somebody is acting on the puck and it is bouncing off you. But you are actually sort of aggressively or almost offensively playing goal. You are in a sense acting on the forward; not always sitting back there receiving everything, but actually psychologically moving ahead. Maybe physically and position-wise you stay where you are but you are always being aggressive. I think if you look at it any other way, in a passive way, just sort of being back there, you are going to run into a lot of problems, mostly psychological. You know what it is: you just sit back all the time and get hit, get hit and get hit. Well, what you'd like to do is give the hit back. You know you can't do it physically but you do it through a save or whatever.

"You always want to put the pressure on the opponent and again, you can't do it physically. But you can do it many, many ways psychologically.

I became a Goalie Dad in 2017 when Grace, my daughter, took up the position. She remains my all-time favorite goalie, just ahead of my niece, Michelle, and Glenn Hall. **(Larry Bella Photo)**

You sort of move out a bit to cut down the angle; you take an inch or two away here and you are acting on the forward's mind like, 'I had six inches a second ago and now I only have four.' And his confidence disappears and you know you have defeated him at that point. This is something you have to do subtly in many ways. And you can do it."

The other story involves my daughter, Grace, who took up goaltending at the age of 15, when a high school teammate had to give up the position due to concussions. This story explains how experience helps goalies antici-pate what might happen in a given situation.

The more one watches (and plays) hockey, the easier it is to see the options a puck carrier has at a given time. This is the first step in reading plays. And, of course, the more you play, the more you file little "movies" in the back of your brain. After a while, almost every situation you encounter reminds you of something you have seen before and you know "how that movie ends." Or, perhaps, how it CAN end.

As Grace was about to assume the starting job in her junior year in high school, she entered a summer league to begin the learning process. To start creating those movies in her head.

One game, a soft shot came from the wing to her right. A VERY soft shot. She tried to steer it to her left but ended up placing it deliciously out front where an opposing forward played it and scored. After the game, I asked her about the play. She said I had taught her to steer on-ice shots away from the net and that's what she was trying to do. I told her that is difficult to do on such a soft shot as the speed of the shot helps you steer it away. And I added, "On such a shot, you'd be better off killing it and tying it up."

She responded, with poorly disguised irritation, "How would I know that?" And she was right. It was the first time she had faced that particular situation and had no reason to know the distinction between a soft shot and a hard shot. Movie created. As you expand your "film library," you are able to identify plays, "read" them sooner, and prepare for your eventual response. Much of this based on knowledge of the game and personal experiences.

When I was coaching elite goalies, I had a technique that I found helpful. I would ask them, "What will I see in your game when you aren't playing well?" Most goalies answered the question with candor, a few hesitant to acknowledge that there might be something they didn't do well. My favorite answer came from Andy Moog. He answered, "I want to arrive WITH the puck, not AHEAD OF the puck. Sometimes I over-anticipate."

A goalie who arrives ahead of the puck gives the puck carrier a chance to adjust. Consider this situation: There is a pass being made to a goalie's left where there is quite a bit of open net for the player receiving that pass. If the goalie is late getting to that open space, he can be 100% sure that the opposing player will shoot for that space.

On the other hand, if you are "early" and the opposing player sees that the open net is about to be covered, he can keep the puck a little longer and move past the goalie. And, in the process, the play ends in a different place, and a different time, than it might have. The goalie "over-anticipating" and arriving early has actually created a more difficult play. A goalie has to know where and when the play is likely to end and adjust accordingly.

Chapter Four —
Adult Hockey

"It's a wonderful thing, like never-never land, where we never grow up and we never grow old ... as long as we do it together."
E.M. Swift, on adult hockey, in "Our Boston"

I can't recall the year, but I was asked to play goal with some of my wife's friends at a mini-rink just north of Boston. I was putting on my gear in a public part of the rink when I became aware of a young boy, maybe 9 or 10 years of age, holding an oversized soda and watching me put on my goalie pads.

"Aren't you a little old for this?" he asked, about three minutes into his examining the scene. I was probably in my late 50s, maybe early 60s, at the time.

"Yes," I said. "I probably am a little old for this."

I moved to the other leg, wishing we still had toe straps and buckles and not this winding skate lace thing of today. The boy had paused but then resumed his interrogation. "Do you enjoy it?" he asked.

I actually had to stop to think about the question. "Sometimes," I said. He waited a few more seconds, and as he walked away, I believe he was shaking his head.

It is an interesting concept, this "adult hockey." We are, technically, adults. But there is something adolescent about the experience. (Listen to the locker room banter.) There is a clinging-to-our-past element to it and once in the blood, it is hard to give it up.

Like many of my hockey peers, I have had trouble walking away from the game. To be more exact, from playing the game. There are probably many reasons for this, but one that I have hit on is that when you *don't* do something anymore, it is a short walk from acknowledging that you *can't* do that thing anymore. And we don't want to go there.

In the half century since I last played college hockey, I have been fortunate to experience a variety of post-graduate playing experiences, some for pay but most solely for pleasure. As I write, I am two months into my 70th year and have a skate tonight with "The Former Legends," a group of mostly senior citizens, many with Ivy degrees, who have been skating at a local prep school for a couple of decades. It was the Legends whom E.M. Swift was referencing in his wonderful essay in *Our Boston*, a collection of contributions by local writers to support the One Fund, which was established following the Boston Marathon bombing in 2013.

I technically qualified as a professional hockey player during my first three years out of Harvard. The pay varied. In my first year, while teaching American history at my old high school, I made $20 a game playing for the Framingham Pics. In my second year, I abruptly ended my teaching career and moved to the Italian Alps, earning about $10,000, which was approximately $2,000 more than my teaching salary. And in a truncated third year, I had the most intriguing compensation package while playing in the old United States Hockey League for the Milwaukee Admirals: $18 a day, a room in a hotel, and $10 for every road win.

When I decided to leave the Admirals in midseason, my professional career was over. Little did I know that I would have another 40+ seasons as an adult hockey player. Let's take a look at a number of these experiences.

1973-74: The Framingham Pics

When the fall of 1973 arrived, I was a little burned out from tending goal and was not inclined to pursue any significant professional options that might have been there. I returned to Arlington High School as a social studies teacher and earned the $20 a game playing for the Framingham Pics in what was left of the old New England League. Thus began nearly a half century of one form or another of "adult hockey."

For many years, the New England League was a great post-college option for scores of players. Teams moved around a bit, with traditional sites being the likes of Braintree, Fitchburg, Lowell and Framingham in Massachusetts, and Concord, Manchester and Nashua in New Hampshire.

By the fall of 1973, my first year out of college, when I had a chance to play in the league, the only teams remaining were Framingham, Concord and Manchester. There were also some Canadian teams that were occasionally scheduled, billing the combined slate as "The Can-Am League."

The best college players were now signing NHL contracts, and the Big Bad Bruins were must-see viewing on TV-38. Suddenly, the lure of paying to watch ex-collegians was not as attractive.

The three New England teams created a schedule where each team had a home night. Manchester played at home on Friday, Concord on Saturday and we played our home games on Sunday night at the Loring Arena. This was a notable place for two reasons: It was managed by 1960 Olympian Dick Rodenheiser and it was where I first played goal as a bantam.

I was Mr. Bertagna, history teacher, by day, and alternating in goal with former Clarkson goalie Kevin Woods and former Norwich netminder Tom Smelstor by night. We practiced on Thursday nights and then played our two weekend games to earn our $40.

I remember Jack Norwell, a diminutive forward from Walpole and Brown, telling me that the envelope we were handed at Thursday's practice contained "flying twenties." I didn't know what he meant until I left the Happy Swallow bar after practice with little of my pay left in the envelope.

We had a roster of mostly Division I alumni. I had played against Kevin Woods in college and first knew him as the Walpole High School goalie who shut out my brother's Arlington team, 1-0, in the 1965 State Tournament. Kevin was also the nephew of the great Clarkson and BC coach Len Ceglarski.

My Harvard teammate, Leif Rosenberger, was briefly with the Pics. I say "briefly" because he broke his wrist when he collided at mid-ice with a menacing-looking defenseman named Baine Donovan. I recall that before leaving the ice, Rosie told Donovan, "Nice hit," his wrist dangling at his side.

My one-time Harvard roommate, Kevin Hampe, was another of the "Pics." When we had the New Hampshire road trips, Kevin, who was living in Brockton and attending law school at the time, would drive north to pick me up in Arlington, and Kevin, his wife, Diana, and I would head to Concord or Manchester. I guess I can admit now to our having a cooler of Budweisers next to me on the back seat for the ride home. I'm hoping we kept the beers from Diana and let her do the driving. But I can't be sure.

Another defenseman on our team was 16-year-old Richie Dunn, whose skills were far too great to play for Canton High School. He ended up play-ing 483 games in the NHL, mostly with Buffalo.

Our coach was Ralph Toran, a public school administrator who had played at Boston College. I liked Ralph, but I do remember him getting worked up between periods. He once told the team that if any of the Manchester Monarchs continued to play dirty, that we should "take our sticks and stick them in the Monarch," the logo on the jersey's front.

Manchester had some memorable French-Canadian players. There was the hulking Ron Dubreuil, the tiny but clever Norm "The Kangaroo" Hebert and the tough and talented Andre Prefontaine. All were transplants from Quebec and made the games at Manchester's JFK Coliseum tough to play. And if there was a fight one week, you knew you had them on the schedule the following week for a likely rematch.

I might have this wrong, but I recall that the three teams in New England were tightly matched, the standings being 19-17, 18-18 and 17-19. We finished on top but lost the playoffs to Concord.

1974-75: S.G. Cortina Doria (Italy)

In the summer of 1974, I had the pleasure of playing summer hockey in a pick-up league in Quincy, MA, just south of Boston. I say "pleasure" because those were the days before entrepreneurs discovered you could get rich selling the concept of "exposure" to parents who were scared to death of missing an opportunity to promote their child's hockey talent.

Before "Hockey Night in Boston" or the "Chowder Cup" or any of the other showcase events that now dot the hockey landscape, friends got together and put teams into leagues. You enjoyed the hockey and the post-game beers, and you went home without worrying about who was watching you and how well you played.

One night, as I was entering the rink and others were leaving, I crossed paths with Paul Giandomenico, a friend I had known through college competition. Paul had grown up in the hockey town of Walpole, and I was from Arlington. The two public high schools had won numerous titles in the 1960s and twice in my brother's three-year high school career, Walpole had ousted Arlington from the State Tournament.

But our connection stemmed from the Boston University-Harvard rivalry. Paul and I had faced each other three times during the 1971-72 season, my junior year at Harvard and his senior year with the Terriers. We played in a terrific 4-4 tie in December, followed by BU wins in the Bean-pot Tournament (4-1) and the ECAC Semifinals (3-1). We then spent the 1973-74 winter playing together on the Framingham Pics.

As we crossed paths on this August Wednesday, Paul told me that he had accepted an offer to play professionally in Italy and was leaving in a couple of weeks for Cortina d'Ampezzo. Half jokingly, I said to him, "Well, if they need an Italian goalie, give me a call."

When I returned to my teaching job in September 1974, it was soon apparent that I no longer wanted to be Mr. Bertagna of Room 4A. The desire to play hockey, which was not there upon graduation from college, had returned. In early October, I saw an ad in *The Hockey News* for a senior team in Milwaukee that was looking for players. And so on Columbus Day weekend, I arranged to try out for the Milwaukee Admirals, precursor to today's AHL franchise.

I impressed enough at the tryout to be offered a spot on the team. On the flight back to Boston, I decided I would quit my teaching job and become a member of the Admirals.

Before I could tell the high school administrators, I received a call from Paul Giandomenico in Italy. The Cortina goalie, a Vancouver native, had blown out his knee skiing in the Dolomites. The team needed a goalie and Paul had convinced them that I could play. I remember having two questions: What does it pay and do you trust them?

Paul told me the deal was $7,000, an apartment, $500 a month for expenses, and $2,000 if we won the league title. And this was for just October through February. Everything he had been promised up to that point had been delivered. He trusted them. I went through with my conversation at the high school, but it wasn't to inform them that I was going to Milwaukee.

The reaction at my alma mater was interesting. The administrators threatened to hold me to my contract, which required three weeks notice. And they worked hard to make me feel guilty about breaking the contract. The teachers, on the other hand, urged me to leave as fast as I could. I remember one conversation with a 15-year veteran of the math department, who had been my math teacher when I was a student. He explained that he had been given chances to leave and pursue dreams when he was younger. But then he got married. Then he bought a house. Then he had kids. All of a sudden, the choices he once had were gone. I never forgot that conversation.

A week later, I was unpacking my goalie equipment in beautiful Cortina d'Ampezzo. On my second day in town, the team embarked on a week-long trip to France, Germany and Switzerland. This is not going to be a day-by-day account of the season. But I would like to offer a few observations.

The 1975 S.G. Cortina Doria squad won the "scudetto" as Italy's national champions on the final day of the season. The other American on the team, former Boston University winger Paul Giandomenico, is back row, first from the right.

• Upon arriving in town, I learned that my salary had been reduced from $7,000 to $5,000. It seems that the departing goalie's wife was an attorney, and she was playing hardball with team ownership over her husband's damaged knee. To remove her from the scene, they agreed to give them an additional $2,000, which they took from me. As I was told, and not just once, "You are not in America anymore."

• After a rough start, I played up to expectations before the initial road trip ended. It was only then that I learned that the team had made plans to trade me to nearby Auronzo had I not lived up to Paul's recommendation. The difference between Auronzo and Cortina, from both aesthetic and hockey viewpoints, would have been considerable. However, had I been traded, one of my teammates would have been former Colgate University star Dave Conte, later a longtime NHL player personnel executive, most notably with New Jersey.

• It took me a while to learn the language. Teammates implored me to learn a little more quickly when in-game action put my teammates in peril, I couldn't even muster the Italian equivalent of "Look out!" The learning process was not without humor. Before one road game, I was introduced this way: "Numero uno, Bertagna Giuseppe," which was followed by a chorus of, "Figlio di putana!" When I asked the teammate standing next to me what they were saying, he answered, "They just called you the son of a whore."

• At that time, Cortina's hockey team had won the Italian championship in 12 of the previous 16 seasons. Its roster was dotted with veteran national team members. Its venerable arena was built for the 1956 Olympic Games, where Russia won its first gold medal, and the United States, with Willard Ikola in goal, John Mayasich and Bill Cleary up front, and John Mariucci behind the bench, won silver.

• For most of the season, the two imports performed well for S.G. Cortina Doria: Giandomenico led the team in scoring in what would be a 40-goal season, and I led the league in goals against average. Yet, entering the final game of the season, we were in second place, a point behind league-leading Bolzano. And here is where I pick up the narrative once again.

To my friends and family, I was off to the Alps to play hockey and eat pasta and have yet another memorable hockey experience. To me, it was a little more than that. Teams for which I was the starting goalie had always finished in second place. Two years in high school and two years in college, second place. And what made this sting was that these were teams fully capable of finishing first. At Arlington High School, the Spy Ponders finished in first place in the five years before me and again in the five years after me. Get the picture?

At Harvard, we finished second to Cornell in my two seasons. On a team dotted with stars and future professionals, we should have accomplished more.

And so when I reached the final game of my last competitive season in February 1975, and faced the possibility of finishing second again, it was a personal challenge that I took very seriously. I had to break this streak, both for my team and for my sense of self worth. Well, for my hockey self worth, at least.

We had played Bolzano three times that season, tying them twice at home and losing the one game at Bolzano. And now, we were returning to Bolzano needing a win to give Cortina its 13th "scudetto" in 17 years. The "scudetto" was referenced like we would say "the pennant" in baseball. It was a shield featuring red, white and green vertical sections, and the reigning Italian champion would wear it on their jerseys for the following season. Every time you took the ice, you had the visible reminder that you were the defending champs.

The expectation was that Bolzano would prevail and the "scudetto" would transfer to them. On the day of the deciding game, the local newspaper, *Alto Adige*, featured a photo of a Bolzano player taping his stick, with the headline, "Tonight the Dinosaur Falls." That would be us.

I recall that around that time, I was trying to make a little adjustment to my game. I was too wide in my stance a little early in the play. That is, before I could ascertain whether a shot was coming or if the puck carrier was going to move laterally or pass it, I was getting a little wide, which would have been fine if the guy shot. But if he did almost anything else, I was making movement difficult.

Shortly before that final game, while flipping through the limited television channels we had, I came across a replay of a Philadelphia Flyers game. I noticed on a defensive zone face-off that Flyers goalie Bernie Parent's skates weren't completely parallel. He was standing in a somewhat erect stance, face-off to his right, and his right skate seemed to be a little behind his left skate. I guessed that this position helped him push off that right skate since he was most likely going to move to his left off the face-off.

Then it occurred to me that if, in facing an offensive rush, I kept my feet a little closer, with my right skate a little behind my left, only as a mental device, I might not get spread out as early as I had been. If nothing else, I gave myself something to focus on, a distraction from worrying, perhaps. I am sure that others could challenge this theory in a number of ways, but for me, at that moment, it worked.

We won the game, 5-1, and I had the pleasure of feeling that I contributed in a very direct way to a team championship, a feeling I had not known for quite some time. And, I immediately realized, Paul and I also won that extra $2,000 apiece as provided for in our contracts. (My share eventually arrived in a large stack of 10s and 20s that I stuffed in my pockets for the plane trip home.)

Oddly, Cortina's 13 championships in 17 years would become 13 championships in 48 years. Through the 2005-06 season, Cortina was still looking for its 14th title. On the positive side, every time I returned to visit, it was a reason to celebrate. I was the goalie on the last championship season. Let's have a drink! And on a number of visits, we did.

Then one night, in February 2007, I received an e-mail. A journalist had tracked me down and sent a two-line message: "They are dancing in the streets of Cortina tonight. Cortina has won the scudetto."

On that championship roster were a couple of former U.S. collegians. One was Mike Souza, who had played at the University of New Hampshire and who is currently the UNH head coach. And one of his teammates was Jeff Dwyer, formerly of Yale University.

I had an opportunity to go back for a second playing season in Cortina in the fall of 1975. I had no other job lined up at home. I was just 24 years old and was playing well. Why not consider a second year in the Dolomites?

In a rare moment of maturity, for me anyway, I decided not to play a second year. The 1974-75 season was perfect. Winning the championship on the final day of the season, being the toast of the town, how could a second year ever live up to that standard? Unbeknownst to anyone else, I was just starting to get a little "puck shy," the goalie equipment of those days not being what it is today. This is not a good thing for a goaltender.

But more to the point, I thought it highly unlikely that I could ever match the experience of that first season playing for Cortina. In fact, I convinced myself that going back for a second year would almost certainly detract from the memory and experience of Year One. What if I played poorly? What if they traded me or I quit in midseason? And so I never pursued a second contract, content to retain the memories of that championship season intact.

1975-76: The Milwaukee Admirals

I spent the 1975-76 season in Milwaukee, WI. In addition to playing for the Milwaukee Admirals, I attended the Journalism School at Marquette University. Two of the year's best memories: 1) watching Carlton Fisk's home run in Game Six of the World Series while wearing a rented tuxedo; and 2) writing my first book on goaltending.

Both the Admirals and the Journalism School were struggling a bit. The Admirals were not the AHL team they would become. Or even the IHL team. They were part of the United States Hockey League, with stops in Sioux City and Waterloo, IA, Stevens Point, WI, and Traverse City and Calumet, MI.

And Marquette's Journalism School was trying to regain proper accreditation. Toward that end, it brought in as its Dean the esteemed George Reedy, former press secretary to President Lyndon Johnson. He would walk the corridors of Johnston Hall in bedroom slippers and regale us with stories from his White House years.

The one story I remember most, for some reason, was about antimacassars. They are the small pieces of cloth that would hang on the back of your grandmother's arm chair to protect the chair's fabric from oil that, in olden days, was used on hair. The oil was macassar oil and, thus, the small piece of protective cloth came to be known as an antimacassar. Don't say you didn't learn anything from this book.

The graduate experience would have resulted in a master's degree had I stayed to complete the two-year program. But all my friends who were writers advised me to focus on actually writing and getting by-lines, downplaying the value of academic degrees. And so I hustled to get my name out there.

Using my hockey connections, I interviewed Bob Johnson, the 1976 U.S. Olympic coach, who had taken a sabbatical from the University of Wisconsin. I also wrote a story for a new magazine, *Hockey*, out of Norwalk, CT. Upon receiving a subscription offer, I wrote back asking if they would publish a diary of an American playing in Italy. When they answered "yes," I had to create a diary of my various exploits in Cortina. The stories were true, but I had never kept a diary.

And after leaving the Admirals in mid-season, I wrote a story on how they won the league championship and declared bankruptcy in the same season. In fact, Milwaukee County officials seized the gate receipts on the night the championship was won, portions of the money used, I was told, to pay the hotel that housed the team. These stories — on Bob Johnson and the Admirals — appeared in *The Milwaukee Journal* and *The Milwaukee Sentinel*, respectively.

I recall that we had to go out and rent tuxedos for our *Face-Off with the Admirals* preseason dinner for the team and our fans. It was to be held at the Marc Plaza hotel and took place on the night of the fabled Game Six of the 1975 World Series between the Cincinnati Reds and my Boston Red Sox.

The guest speaker for the evening was former Marquette basketball coach Al Maguire, who, at the time, was the Director of Athletics at MU. Al started his remarks by noting that it was the first team dinner he ever addressed where there were no "Black guys" on the team. He then regaled us with stories about riding his motorcycle and walking barefoot in Kenya and all sorts of other adventures. By the time it was over, we were pretty sure that the guests left the hotel talking about Al and not us.

I was able to get to the bar at the top of the Marc Plaza to watch that World Series game, arriving in time to see not only Bernie Carbo's home run that tied the game but Carlton Fisk's game-winning home run off Fenway Park's left field foul pole.

One more Al Maguire story. When his son Allie was the starting point guard, the back-up guard worked up the courage to visit Maguire to plead his case. "I believe I should be playing. I'm just as good as Allie," he said.

Maguire looked at the young man, smiled and said, "You're right. You are 'as good as' my son. But I love my son. To play, you have to be better than him."

Playing for the Admirals was a trip. We were put up in the once-posh Knickerbocker Hotel, which at the time the team occupied it, was otherwise filled with senior citizens. As previously noted, we were paid $18 a day, plus $10 for every road win. That led to frequent pep talks prior to the third period on the road, ending with, "You need that money. I need that money. Let's go!"

The speaker was our coach, Andre Caron. Doing his best with a heavy French accent, the coach might order breakfast with, "I'll have two eggs, side by each, and a pair of toast." Or perhaps he would urge us to "Make some skate" or "Have some proud." But my favorite was, "If you give these guys a hinch, they take a feet."

Andre wasn't the only one who struggled with language. We had a talented defenseman on the team by the name of Rene Daze, which was properly pronounced *reh-NAY dah-ZAY*. One night, on the road, the PA announcer introduced him, phonetically, as, "And on defense, number twenty, *RAINY DAYS!*"

While in Milwaukee, I wrote my first book, *Goaltending: A Complete Handbook for Goalies and Coaches*. Self-published, the book was printed at the Cosmos Press in Cambridge, MA. The company was owned by the family of Bill Lamarche, a former Harvard teammate of Tim Taylor's and my summer roommate at Tim's house on Miller Road in Newton.

I banged out the manuscript on a manual typewriter in my post-Admirals apartment on West Wells Street, the original copy now residing at the Charles Holt Archives at the University of New Hampshire. I had left the Admirals around holiday time, having played much more poorly than I had planned.

My roommate, Mike Halloran, was a fellow Marquette student who was in need of someone to pay the rent, and it was only after a month or so together that we discovered we shared a birthdate: Halloween of 1951. This led to decades of correspondence where one or the other would sign off with, "10/31/51." On our 50th birthday, I awoke in Gloucester, MA, to discover 50 pumpkins on my front lawn, displayed to form a giant "50."

It was Mike who, upon seeing a draft of this chapter, reminded me that our apartment was "above Katsune's Grocery Store and Schlonsky's Pharmacy. I could never figure our how Mr. and Mrs. Katsune made any money, as there was never much stock on their shelves. The place always had the look of an East Berlin grocery store at about the time of our birth."

Where was I? Oh, my goaltending book. The illustrations in the book were either hand drawn by myself or were photographs of my fellow Arlington and Harvard goalie John Aiken, with his twin brother, Jimmy, as a shooter. Between writing and printing, I had a promotional idea. I would ask former Cornell University and then-Montreal Canadiens goalie Ken Dryden to write an introduction to the book.

I checked the NHL schedule and found a date when Montreal would visit Chicago. I made a copy of my manuscript, tucked it inside a manila envelope and, on February 4, 1976, made the 90-minute drive to Chicago Stadium.

After the game, I waited with autograph seekers outside the door that led the visiting team to its bus. When Dryden came out, I engaged him in conversation while he was signing for the fans.

I tried to make our Ivy League connection work by telling him I had beaten Cornell once. Without putting his head up, he asked me the names of the Cornell goalies against whom I had competed. I mentioned Brian Cropper and Dave Elenbaas. I told him why I was there and handed him the envelope containing the manuscript. He took it and walked to the team bus.

It was several months later, while I was painting a house that my father owned as a rental property, when my mother drove up. Through an open window, she told me that she had just taken a call from Ken Dryden and that he had left his phone number. My first thought was that there was an equal chance that the caller was my old Harvard coach, Bill Cleary, claiming to be Dryden. (My old coach had a habit of using celebrity names when leaving messages with third parties.) But when I saw a Quebec area code on the paper my mother handed to me, I thought it could actually be Dryden. And it was.

When I got home that day, I called him. He explained that he would not write the introduction I sought, partly because he was not inclined to put his name to someone else's work and partly because he planned to write a book of his own some day. He certainly followed that notion up spectacularly.

He did, however, offer to read the manuscript and, when the Stanley Cup playoffs were over, he would be happy to sit down with me and go over what I had written. For the record, Montreal won the Cup that year. In fact, Dryden won an incredible six Cups in eight seasons. And, as promised, Ken Dryden sat down with me and reviewed my work.

It was like winning some sports fantasy contest. I drove to his house in Ste. Anne de Bellevue, sat on his couch and reviewed the manuscript with him, page by page, had a cheeseburger cooked by his wife and drove home the same day. He had substantive suggestions. He had grammatical corrections. And he talked me out of including a section on the burdens of playing goal: nerves, little injuries, responsibility.

It wasn't until after college that I got to wear my Higgins mask fulltime, in Cortina (at left) and with the Milwaukee Admirals.

He asked, "Why include something so negative in an otherwise positive book?" And so I took the section out. But let the record show that in his terrific book, *The Game*, published in 1983, there is this passage on page 117. "Playing goal is not fun. Behind the mask, there are no smiling faces, no timely sweaty grins of satisfaction. It is a grim, humorless position, largely uncreative, requiring little physical movement, giving little physical pleasure in return. A goalie is simply there, tied to a net and to a game; the game acts, a goalie reacts." Really?

My book was a modest success, even without Dryden's endorsement. I sold about 10,000 copies, re-printing the book twice. It remains somewhat relevant, even with all the changes in the position. And it helped propel my reputation as a goalie coach. Just as an artist has to be skilled in both art and self-promotion, so does a freelance goalie coach. It is important to know how to teach, but it is equally important to attract goalies and be a viable business. The book helped both.

While my playing time with the Admirals did not last very long, I later added a goalie coaching gig with the team. Former teammate Phil Wittliff, who had become coach and then GM of the Admirals, brought me in for a couple of seasons in the mid-1990s. This stop also introduced me to Don MacAdam, an Admirals coach with whom I became good friends. The Admirals had moved from a sleepy semi-pro league to the International

Hockey League, a step just below the American Hockey League (where they play today). It was a great job where I made one trip a month to Milwaukee, stayed in a Holiday Inn, went to two practices and two games, flew home and got $500 each month. And that doesn't even include the benefit of the warm chocolate chip cookies they served on Midwest Airlines.

One of our goalies was Mark LaForest, a veteran who had played more than 100 NHL games before nearing the end of his career with the Admirals. LaForest had one of my favorite nicknames, "Trees." For goalies, the only other nickname in this class was given to Norm Foster, a former Michigan State goalie I coached when he played for the Maine Mariners. When the 5´8´´ Foster chirped at practice, teammates would say, "Shut-up, Speed Bump!"

The time playing with the Admirals ended my "pro" days. From there, it would be "beer league" hockey, as some call it. "No-check" hockey. Adult hockey. While no longer being paid to play, the levels that followed allowed us to play for free, goalies being harder to secure with each decade.

While I will try, I'm not sure that I can match Chip McGrath and Ed Swift, professional writers whose work on this subject set a fairly high standard. McGrath, with *The New York Times* and *The New Yorker* on his resume, did a piece on the Depot Cafe Bombers for the now defunct *New England* magazine.

Swiftie, my rival goalie when he played at Princeton the same years I was at Harvard, wrote for *Sports Illustrated* and published a number of books, notably *Eleven Seconds*, with Travis Roy. In 2013, after the Marathon bombing, Eddie contributed that chapter in *Our Boston*, the fund-raiser for Marathon victims. His chapter on The Legends is a classic.

Their efforts in mind, I will not attempt to equal or better what they have already produced. But I will try my best to give my first-person accounts of the various non-paying stops I have made along this journey.

The City Point Clovers

I spent countless hours enjoying summer hockey in places like Melrose, Lynn and Quincy, free of all the nerves that rattled me in those high school and college winters. I probably played my best hockey in the summer, particularly in my early 20s.

The most memorable of these experiences was with the City Point Clovers, a team put together by Bob O'Connell that played Wednesday nights in Quincy in the mid-1970s. The roster consisted primarily of players with roots in South Boston. While I was actually born in Southie, I don't think that had anything to do with being asked to play. Fresh out of Harvard, I was a Division I goalie and that was my main calling card.

The competition was very good. The teams had plenty of D-I players, either still in college or recently graduated. And there were a few guys who had professional experience or maybe were future NHLers. The Clovers, for example, featured veteran John Cunniff, with whom I would work as a coach on U.S. Canada Cup and Olympic teams 20 years later. And they had a teenage Bill O'Dwyer, who would be on the Boston Bruins teams for which I served as goalie coach.

Cunniff was a great student of the game. As a member of the New England Whalers, he would pick the brain of goalie Al Smith and share nuggets of information with me. We also had P.J. Flaherty, a star goalie at UMass, who played up front for the Clovers. He helped me with my game as well.

John Cunniff was a quiet man, physically powerful, who had a lighter side that I found I could tap into. I had gotten to know him through Tim Taylor, as John and I would occasionally work Tim's camps. I remember the 1993-94 Olympic experience, when John and I served with Tim, the head coach of our Lillehammer team. On long bus trips, John might be reading military histories. Tim would have worn out copies of books by great coaches, perhaps by John Wooden or maybe Anatoli Tarasov.

I also recall that John had a tattoo on his arm, "Johnny," in cursive. During our Olympic year, I asked him how that came about. He told me that when he was 12, a bunch of friends stole some tattoo equipment and gave each other tattoos.

John had once worked a summer painting job and one of the other workers was the notorious gangster Whitey Bulger. At John's wake in 2002,

Before summer hockey was about "showcasing talent," we played for fun. The City Point Clovers were based in South Boston in the mid-1970s and housed a lot of talent. Among my favorite teammates: former BC star John Cunniff, back row, first from right. We would coach together two decades later.

I had an awkward Bulger-related experience when Bob O'Connell came over to me and said, "Joe, I'd like you to meet a friend of mine, John Connolly. He's a big college hockey fan."

I had just finished reading the book *Black Mass*, which was about Whitey. John Connolly was the FBI agent who, at the time of my introduction, was awaiting trial for his actions in that Bulger saga. O'Connell told me that Connolly was a big Boston College fan. Wanting desperately to end the conversation, I said to Connolly, "Well, maybe I'll see you at a BC game this winter."

He laughed. "Oh, I don't think you'll see me at any games this winter." He was right. By that point, he had been incarcerated.

I also remember that when I left the funeral home, I made the short walk to where I had been born. The old Carney Hospital was now Marion Manor, a nursing home. As I entered the facility, I chatted up the reception staff and told them why I was there. When they reminded me of their current services, I said, "Well, maybe I'll end up a resident here. You know, go full circle."

My hockey memories of the Clovers are of good competition and single moments. I remember Paul Stewart, just out of the University of Pennsylvania, showing me the hockey bag from his first pro team. He was not yet the fighter he would become or the Hall of Fame referee.

As previously stated, I remember former BU forward Paul Giandomenico, my teammate with the Framingham Pics, telling me he was going to be playing in Italy and how that led to my joining him.

And for some reason, I remember that we played two 15-minute periods and one 20-minute period. If you had the last game of the night, which began at 10:30, that damn 20-minute third period never seemed to end.

The Bud Kings

Few things go together better than beer and adult hockey. So it is not surprising that one of my adult teams was sponsored by Budweiser. The Bud Kings, formerly the Carling Black Labels, gave me a place to play in the late 1970s and early 1980s.

The team had a heavy Boston College flavor to it by the time I joined them (Tim and Joey Flynn, John Monahan, Kerry Young, Chuckie Lambert). Other stalwarts included Tommy Colby (UVM), Bob Hayes (Dartmouth), Rico Graham (Saint Anselm) and my Harvard buddies Bill Lamarche and Leif Rosenberger.

The Kings played a schedule that mixed other senior teams with college JV teams. Our schedule, in fact, wasn't as long as the one that Jack Norwell put on his refrigerator, one that had a number of fake dates and opponents and got him out of the house more often than the rest of us.

I remember a couple of funny moments from this experience. We played a game out in western Massachusetts, maybe in Chicopee. My driving partner that night was Chuck Lambert, a small but skilled defenseman from Needham and BC. Midway through the drive home, we pulled off to get a bite to eat. We found a diner whose interior was in the shape of an "H." There was the dining area on one side, with a small passageway mid-diner into the bar. The sign in the window advertised "Live Entertainment."

While we sat in the diner, attacking a couple of burgers, we could hear the sound of that live entertainment coming through that passageway. While I couldn't put my finger on it, something wasn't right.

We finished our meal, paid up and wandered into the bar. Once seated, I figured out what didn't sound right. The live entertainment was provided by a drummer and a jukebox. The drummer would wait for someone to drop a coin or two in the jukebox, and when the song began to play, he would keep the beat on his drumset.

The other anecdote comes from the team break-up dinner the year I decided to "retire" from the Kings. I remember my closing line was to thank Johnny Monahan for providing the impetus for my retirement by showing us all "what it looks like when you play one year too long."

The Depot Cafe Bombers

I have been blessed with great and unique hockey experiences. Arlington High School, Harvard University, Cortina d'Ampezzo. And right up there is my experience with the Depot Cafe Bombers of Gloucester, MA. Our motto: "Hockey the way it was meant to be played. Only a little bit slower."

We played in the Sunday night Industrial League at Gloucester's O'Maley School Rink. It was a pretty local league with teams named Cranston Electric, Boulevard Grocers and J & P Trucking. The average age of the league was probably late 20s/early 30s while the Bombers were mid-40s and above.

We had a local core of players but weren't above bringing in outside talent, almost always *younger* outside talent. Offsetting our age was the fact that most of the players had been D-1 calibre at one time or another and many were still on the ice as coaches at elite levels.

The team was founded by Russ Smith, older brother of Ben Smith, a talented player at Gloucester High School and Harvard, who went on to a Hall of Fame career as a coach. He had been a longtime assistant coach to Jack Parker at BU and Tim Taylor at Yale. But his HOF credentials were secured when he led the first U.S. Women's Olympic Team to the gold medal in Nagano in 1998.

Once I started with the Bombers, the job was pretty much mine but my work schedule provided plenty of openings for Bob Deraney, Peter Fish, Tad Doherty, my niece Michelle DiStefano Collett and Bob Higgins, who actually preceded me with the Bombers. "Higgy" had been my resident advisor freshman year at Harvard and was a huge success in the venture capital world.

Peter Fish went on to a successful career as a player agent, having played his hockey at Boston University. While most of our games were played on Sunday nights, we had one opponent that only played Mondays. When apprised of this, BU coach Jack Parker quipped, "Don't play Fishie on Mondays," a reference to Fishie's Beanpot history. (Mine wasn't much better.)

While I like to think my goaltending helped the Bombers, I have to admit that our defensemen may have had something to do with our success. Let's see, we had a Hobey Baker Award winner in Mark Fusco. We had the future head coach of the New York Rangers in David Quinn. We had Kevin Burke, a former UConn player who served as Secretary of Public Safety in Governor Deval Patrick's cabinet. We had Ben's Harvard roommate and longtime Harvard JV coach Bob Carr. We had former St. Lawrence University defenseman John Gummere, whose college roommate was the legendary college coach Ron Mason.

Oh, did I forget former Harvard-Yale rivals Mark Noonan (H) and Kirk Bransfield (Y)? Or 1972 Olympian Stu Irving, a small forward who, like

The key to being a successful "adult" goalie is making sure you have good defensemen. My Bombers teammate about to hook an opponent above is David Quinn, who, between playing at Boston University and coaching the New York Rangers, found time to be a Bomber. Oh, and that puck did not go in. I believe the attacking forward is former Holy Cross All-American Matt Muniz. (Photo courtesy of the *Gloucester Daily Times*)

Ben, might drop back on "D" when needed?

Up front, goals came from the likes of Gene Kinasewich, Jim Turner, Donald "Toot" Cahoon, Kenny Irving, Jay Somers, Frank Haskell, Ian Wood, Peter Noonan, Jay Valade, Georgie Mechem, Tom (as seen on "Cheers") Babson, Dwight "White Dog" Ware, Tommy Mutch, Tom Livingston and others. Two of the others provided a lot more than goals.

As much as we had talent, we had humor. The spiritual leader of the team was Ben's first cousin, Tom "Red" Mechem, another former Crimson skater. And we had a former Northeastern University alum, who died way too young, who kept us all laughing. That was Dave Murphy.

Red's pre-game pep talks invariably referred to our opponent as "a pesky bunch." Some of his best work was saved for the annual break-up dinner at the Annisquam Yacht Club, where the latest in Bombers swag might be unveiled. Bombers lore has it that Red, also known as the "GM," once lifted $10 out of the wallet of a player who was being transported to the hospital after breaking his leg. After all, the cost of icetime still needed to be covered.

But no one provided more laughs than Dave Murphy. Whether in the locker room or postgame at the Depot Cafe, Murph was the best at cracking us up. One of the Industrial League referees worked in a flower shop by day. He wasn't a large man, leading Murph to make this comment after being penalized more than once in a particular game: "If he keeps that up, I'll knock the diminutive florist all the way into his perennials."

Or Murph might skate up to the two senior members of the league officiating crew, Skip Gove and Warren Silva, and say during a showdown with the Truckers, "Skip, this game has gotten too big for you. Too much glitter, Skip." Or he might tell a stranger, "Hey, you can sell me a fifty-four portly, but I'm really a forty-eight long."

When Murph worked for me as a Hockey East observer, I saw a different side of him. He took the job very seriously and was not afraid to challenge me when we disagreed on a referee or an on-ice situation.

But even within that job, Murph's humor would surface. He was fond of assigning nicknames to people. One of our officials, who worked as an undertaker by day, would be referred to by Murph as, "Sorry For Your Loss." And another, a small Irishman, came to be known as "Lucky Charms."

The Rest

Scattered through the years are a number of other "Adult Hockey" experiences that kept me going. When the paying gigs were over, I started the adult no-check experience in my hometown, where there was a Sunday night league populated mostly by former Arlington High School players. Our team was called the "Green Machine," and it gave me a chance to play with my brother Bob as well as some of my Harvard teammates.

From time to time, we would put together teams to play in tournaments, often in Fitchburg, MA, or in Montreal. One of these travel teams was the "Boston Merchants." Again, I got to play with my brother and other older guys of his vintage.

One year, I had the pleasure of playing with former Boston Bruins defenseman Gary Doak, a great guy. That year, the final game in each bracket was played in the old Montreal Forum. When we came up short, someone said, "Doakie, you still haven't won a big game in this building."

I tried the "Hockeytown Over-50 League" for a while but the more that 50 was in my rearview mirror and "younger" 50-somethings joined the league, I struggled. But I made some new hockey friends there, most notably Steve Artick, Bruce Hutchinson, Tom Moulton, Kevin Pierce, Paul Bastarache and Norm Bent.

I am now with the "Former Legends," the subject of the Ed Swift piece. In that essay, Swiftie seemed to suggest that adult goalies look like we shouldn't really function but we do. He wrote, "They are the black-and-white TVs of the hockey world." To bolster that observation, I can report that when I took the ice in the fall of 2020, I was wearing a chest protector that was older than the other goalie on the ice that night.

As I said earlier on these pages, the adult hockey experience needs to match the moment. And The Legends came along for me at just the right time. We are, for the most part, guys in our 60s or 70s and so we have contemporaries who "get it." They want a nice skate with no one acting up, and while the pace is slow, it is the right level of competition for who and where we are.

When it was just "us," the senior citizens, I could still make plenty of saves. When, because of the small numbers showing up (especially in the year of the virus), and some Legends brought their sons and daughters, things changed. One night, the only goals I allowed came off the stick of a young woman who was, at the time, on the Colby College varsity.

Actually, the standards have changed as well. A successful outing is no longer determined by how many goals I allow. It is now whether or not I make it through the hour without getting hurt.

But I still get to see my hockey friends, some I have known for half a century, and I still get to put on the pads and stop pucks. It's not pretty but it's a continuation of something that has been part of who we are for so long. It will have to do.

In March 2003, I wrote an essay for *U.S. College Hockey Online* titled, *"Time to hang 'em up?"* It was the 52-year-old me pondering the annual question that comes at the end of an adult hockey season. Looking back at this, 18 years later, it is clear that "time" has not yet come.

The Green Machine played Sunday nights in Arlington. I'm pretty sure we were the only team in that adult league with former members of the Boston Bruins (Dave Hynes - front row, first on left) and Montreal Canadiens (Eddie Walsh - back row, first on right).

The Boston Merchants were put together to play in tournaments, often in Montreal. In this event, I got to play with former Boston Bruins defenseman Gary Doak (front row, third from right). (Photo courtesy of JAS International Sports Photography)

In the article, I identified some of the things I'll never experience again if I decide to hang 'em up.

• I'll never experience lugging the oversized bag of equipment up the cellar stairs, through the kitchen, through the breezeway and out to the car. Nor will I ever experience going back and picking up the nine things I knocked over in the process, including my two-year old daughter, Grace. (That only happened once and I still think she could have seen me coming and moved.)

• I'll never again have that uneasy feeling when you are more than halfway to the rink and you are running late and you realize you have absolutely no recollection of putting your cup in your equipment bag.

• I won't get dressed for the first time in October and discover that my hockey pants have somehow shrunk since the last time I wore them. Or maybe ...

• I'll miss locker room talk. Subtle put-downs. Not so subtle put-downs. Being 20 years older than the youngest guy in the room and not feeling out of place.

• I won't be the first one in the locker room and the last one out. Again. So I like to talk. What's wrong with that?

• I'll never again stretch so long that I miss most of warm-ups. My theory on warm-ups is this. I don't play it like a game so more pucks just hit me, as opposed to me going after them. The ones that just hit you hurt more. Second, at this age, I feel I only have so many saves left. Why waste them in warms-ups?

The Legends, after an end-of-season brunch at The Country Club in Brookline, MA. The group afforded me the opportunity to play again with former youth, high school and college hockey teammates.

• I'll miss that mental sequence that unfolds each year.

Week One: "I have no expectations of playing well. I just don't want to get hurt."

Week Three: "Hey, I'm playing better than I thought."

Week Five: "Can't any of these guys cover anyone? Where the hell are the back checkers!"

Week Twelve: "I hope this is almost over. I just don't want to get hurt."

• I'll certainly miss the characters. There's that one guy who is better than the rest but doesn't acknowledge it. He makes everyone around him play better and is unselfish, never showing everything he could do. There is that little guy who buzzes around and makes you wonder why he didn't make it at some higher level. There is that guy who wasn't ever a star when he was younger but is now playing better than he ever has at any other time in his life. And, of course, there is The Mouth. That guy who has something to say about everyone, knows exactly which buttons to push to get someone's goat, and usually has one poor foil who takes the brunt of his verbal assaults.

In looking back on my adult hockey years, I was reminded that it's not just the ice time that kept us going. If the 60 minutes became 30 minutes, many of us would still show up, for the locker room, the reduced ice and the postgame beers. It is all a part of who we are. And when each winter begins, we want to make sure there is a hockey schedule on the refrigerator door that is our very own.

Chapter Five —
The ECAC Years

"The ECAC (Eastern College Athletic Conference) is an eighty-year-old organization ... that exists to enhance the experience of student-athletes participating in intercollegiate athletics, and provide great value for universities and colleges, by sponsoring championships, leagues, bowl games, tournaments and other competitions throughout the Northeast."

— ECAC Web Site, 2020

Having decided that my days as a professional hockey player were over, and passing on a second year of journalism school, I found myself needing something to do in the fall of 1976. Enter Bill Cleary. Again.

My old coach continued to be a major influence on my life. First, he arranged for me to serve as co-coach of the 1976-77 Harvard junior varsity team, along with my old roommate Kevin Hampe. That assignment would start in late fall.

Then, he told me about a relatively new internship being offered at the office of the Eastern College Athletic Conference in Centerville, MA, not far from his summer home on Cape Cod. I applied for the position and was accepted. The internship would run from September through Christmas, and Bill even offered me the chance to rent his summer home.

It was through the ECAC, and Commissioner Robert "Scotty" Whitelaw and Associate Commissioner Clayton Chapman, that I was officially introduced to the world of sports administration. That four-month immersion into college athletics exposed me to the staples of so many of my lifelong work experiences: media relations, (preparing and running) meetings, budgeting, scheduling, officiating, tournament administration and more.

This position began my two decades involved with ECAC Hockey. The internship led to a job at Harvard (1977-82), which led to a 15-year stretch as an ECAC Hockey administrator (1982-97). For the record, the ECAC came to me when Hockey East was born. As the story goes, some Ivy League presidents were concerned that their hockey rosters increasingly had a number of players who were struggling academically. They connected this to keeping up with other programs whose academics might not have been at their level.

So the Ivies began talking to other ECAC schools that might want to join them in a new hockey structure. This process left out a number of schools, the schools that eventually became Hockey East. There has been some debate over the years as to who left whom. As one observer characterized it to me, "The Ivies were planning a party, and they weren't going to invite a group of schools. So those schools went out and had their own party."

It was in this context that Scotty Whitelaw turned to me, as the ECAC now had to contend with the launch of Hockey East. It started with modest assignments. Edit the media guide. Direct the Division I men's tournament. Direct the other men's tournaments. Launch women's hockey. The title then became Executive Director of Ice Hockey and then, finally, ECAC Hockey Commissioner.

But first there was the Asa Bushnell Internship, named after the former ECAC Commissioner. This internship launched some significant careers in amateur athletics. The first Bushnell Intern was John Humenik, who served as the Sports Information Director at Michigan and Florida before becoming the Executive Director of CoSIDA, the national SIDs association. I followed him, and in short order came (and titles they achieved): Tom Odjakjian, Senior Associate Commissioner of the American Athletic Conference; Dave Ogrean, for many years Executive Director of USA Hockey; Connie Hurlbut, Senior Associate Commissioner of the West Coast Conference (also Patriot League Commissioner); Jen Heppel, Commissioner of the Patriot League; Julie Ruppert, Commissioner of the Northeast-10; Paul Schlickmann, AD at Fairfield University; Jeff Schulman, University of Vermont Director of Athletics; and Patrick Summers, Commissioner of the NEWMAC. And I'm leaving out so many others.

Looking back, in addition to specific skills gained, I also learned how to treat employees and co-workers. Scotty and Clayt were such terrific role models. It was a privilege to learn from them at a time when an agreement might just as easily been concluded with a handshake as with a signed contract. Decades later, when I had moved on from the ECAC to other pursuits, Scotty Whitelaw would call me annually to catch up and tell me how much he admired and followed my career. It meant a lot to me.

The Bushnell Internship at the ECAC launched a number of long careers in the field of sports administration. Following my internship in 1976, these four interns had hugely successful careers. Clockwise from top left: Jen Heppel, Connie Hurlbut, Jeff Schulman and Tom Odjakjian. (Photos courtesy of Patriot League, West Coast Conference, the University of Vermont and the American Athletic Conference)

The ECAC launched in 1938, working out of New York's Hotel Roosevelt. Asa Bushnell and a small staff administered to the needs of fewer than 50 institutions at the time. As schools and leagues realized they were duplicating services, the idea of a central office providing such things as scheduling, officiating and media services became attractive.

By the time Scotty Whitelaw became commissioner in 1972, the ECAC was on the verge of major changes. At the suggestion of Boston College AD Bill Flynn, Scotty engineered the move of the offices out of New York to a former private estate in Centerville, MA, in 1974. The membership swelled to just shy of 300 schools and the ECAC was administering some 90 championship events.

Of particular note was the leading role that the ECAC played in advancing the interests of women's athletics and Division III athletics. I don't think it is a coincidence that I received my education in administration from the ECAC and that throughout my professional career, I, too, sought to advance the interests of women and Division III athletics.

My theory was that Division I men had too many stakeholders to be allowed to fail and most of what I contributed in my 38 years as a conference administrator to Division I men would likely have happened on anyone else's watch.

As the presence of individual conferences made a rebound, the ECAC billed itself as "the conference of conferences" and continued to provide a number of services, most notably media relations, officiating and postseason championships.

Looking back on the ECAC Internship, I recall an enjoyable work experience. Having spent all my summers on Cape Ann, I didn't have much appreciation for Cape Cod. And experiencing it in the fall, when most of the tourists had retreated, maximized the pleasure factor.

I did much of my work, as an intern and later, with John Garner, an associate commissioner at the ECAC. Many years later, when both of us were no longer with the ECAC, John covered the Women's Hockey East Championships for the *Cape Cod Times* when that tournament enjoyed a four-year run at a rink in Hyannis.

The internship flew by. Starting in September, I experienced the fall season, highlighted by the Sunday morning "Service Bureau," when ECAC staff and local sportswriters would assemble to prepare a weekly release, featuring results from the weekend and the "Players of the Week" we would choose.

As I write in early 2021, I am still receiving nominations for individual honors, only now it is the college hockey "Players of the Month," sponsored by the Hockey Commissioners Association. Back then, we received forms via telecopier; now they are emailed to me. But the protocol is the same: identify the best performances and if there are multiple candidates, spread the wealth to schools that may not have had many opportunities for such honors.

These programs have dual purposes. First, they honor the athlete by providing some special recognition, a chance to shine a light on unique performances, log it for history and promote the school.

But at its core, such a program exists to promote the given sport. Where my internship was from September to December, we were honoring football players. Over the rest of my career, it was in ice hockey, a sport that needed more exposure than football or basketball. Over the years, schools had to be reminded that what we were doing was for the conference and the sport, not just for their program. And it could get contentious.

I learned multiple lessons during this internship that lasted a lifetime. On one Sunday, one of the local sportswriters, who volunteered each week, thought he would have some fun by burying a double entendre remark in a release. A Williams College running back had a great afternoon and in the one-sentence blurb noting this guy's Honorable Mention performance, the writer said that the halfback "ran for 184 yards as the Ephmen mastered Bates by ... " It did not take long for someone at Bates to contact the ECAC and call attention to the sophomoric take.

We were reminded that people actually read these things. They don't just exist in our office. I can recall two examples, one when I returned to the ECAC and another at Hockey East, when verbiage in a press release was appropriately challenged.

It was in the late 1980s when the Brown men had won only three of 44 games played over a two-year period. After one of those wins, we referred to Brown "upsetting" its opponent. It seemed like an appropriate way to describe the result, given that Brown was struggling for wins and its foe that day was well above .500.

After the release, we heard from Brown coach Bob Gaudet. He did not care for the characterization of the victory being an "upset." He explained that he was trying to change the program's culture and didn't want his players to think that their winning a game was some sort of aberration. He wanted his players to start expecting to win. If nothing else, I was reminded that writing for a conference press release is not the same as being an objective sportswriter. We serve the schools and should be sensitive to their needs.

The other situation occurred when I was with Hockey East. Two schools that were picked to finish at the bottom in the preseason coaches' poll were scheduled to open the season against each other. My assistant wrote in that week's release that this game could determine who avoids finishing last in the conference. This time, the schools weren't given the chance to complain because I caught it before it went out. I had to tell the assistant that just because a poll suggests a long season for these teams, we can't be validating that with such a comment or projection.

My philosophy on the weekly selections has always been this: When there is an obvious winner, the four-goal game or the 50-save effort, take the obvious. But more often than not, there isn't that clearcut choice. So you entertain other factors.

You try to give an also-ran some love when they are having a tough year. You check who the opponents were that week. What is better: two 40-save efforts in 2-1 losses or two 17-save shutouts against weak teams, 8-0 and 4-0?

Late in the year, you might favor candidates for postseason national honors. Remember, it is a PR program for the conference. Favoring a leading candidate for the Hobey Baker Award or Patty Kazmaier Award, given to the nation's top men's and women's collegiate hockey players, respectively, might be helpful for that candidacy down the line.

Another example of being reminded that people read our releases: parents. Twice, once at the ECAC and once at Hockey East, I had goalie parents call the office and ask why we cut off the statistical "leaders" after five people. Yes, their goalie sons were ranked sixth that week in one goalie stat or another. (Bill Cleary used to joke that if he ever came back to coaching, he would coach at an orphanage to avoid dealing with parents.)

The selection of honors also extended to the postseason. And that led to some noteworthy exchanges with coaches. One year, RPI head coach Mike Addesa left blank one of the first team defense slots. When I called to get his missing vote, he explained it this way. "You are asking me to be dishonest. I know my defenseman is one of the top two defensemen in the league, but you won't let me vote for him and that forces me to be dishonest."

I explained to him that all coaches, in all leagues, were not allowed to vote for their own players. That was how it was done, and it had nothing to do with "honesty." By leaving that slot blank, he was denying another defenseman in the league a vote and, actually, that could be construed as dishonest.

Another time, Princeton coach Jim Higgins voted for Harvard defenseman Mark Fusco as Player of the Year but then pegged him as Second Team Defense. Jim did not have any defensemen on the ballot, so he wasn't doing this to protect one of his Tigers. So I called him.

"I thought about this for a long time," he said. "Mark was clearly the most dominant player in the league, the guy that could take over a game. He had 20 goals as a defenseman. But when I think of a defenseman, I have different qualities in mind, and I just though these other two guys were better 'defensemen' than Mark."

It was an honest answer and not one that I had any reason to question. We did, however, have a more serious issue with the All-American votes one year, the balloting conducted by the American Hockey Coaches Association. The coach counting the ballots called me to report some irregularities. The All-American ballots are made up of each league's first and second all-league teams. On this occasion, the coach in question appeared to vote for the six weakest forwards on the ballot. Why did we think of them as the "weakest?" In just about each case, every one of those six only received one vote: the vote from this coach.

So we confronted the coach, and with very little coercion, he admitted he did it on purpose to protect his forwards on the ballot. He felt that his players had been slighted in the past and he wasn't going to let that happen again. So he

When I started at the ECAC as an intern, I worked closely with two of the people in this photo: Rich Hussey, at far left, and John Garner, at far right. Between them are Rich Sturcio of Cramer Productions and legendary broadcaster Marv Albert. (Photo courtesy of John Garner)

withheld votes from anyone he thought might be a challenger to his guys. The coach was subsequently reprimanded by the AHCA Ethics Committee.

Also falling under media relations was the production of the annual media guide. This staple of media coverage included rosters, schedules, photos and statistical leaders from the year before. Those were the days before digital publishing when endless visits to a small print shop, in this case Patriot Press, had you laying out copy and photos, cropping the latter and proofreading large galleys provided by the typesetter.

One of my bosses at the ECAC was Rich Hussey, a great guy who went on to a stellar career at NBC. After hours, we would often retire to a small bar called Jack's Lounge, galleys in hand, to have a glass of wine and proof copy. Rich, who called the joint, "La Lounge de Jacques," would attribute typos that made it into the finished product as the result of "wine reads."

I still maintain a collection of ECAC media guides. It's kind of fun to re-visit the 40-year-old rosters and find names of people with whom you have done some hockey business over the years. When Hockey East was born in 1984, one of the many innovations was a more robust branding effort that caught the ECAC trapped in the past. Our media guide, for example, treated all divisions equally, existing primarily as a helpful tool for all media covering ECAC teams.

By contrast, the Hockey East media guide was not only that but was

I learned the sports information business from two of the best: Dave Matthews (left), who was my boss at Harvard; and Jack Grinold, a mentor to so many in Boston. (Grinold Photo courtesy of Northeastern University)

a recruiting vehicle for its coaches. It was slick and dedicated solely to the seven schools (later as many as 12) and their needs. I can still remember Clarkson AD Bill O'Flaherty lobbying for the ECAC to follow suit and separate the Division I schools from the Division II-III programs. I held on as long as I could because I knew that once Division I got its own guide, there would be no Division II-III version at all.

It wasn't the last time I was criticized for supporting the underdogs. When I was Harvard SID, the policy was separate guides for football, basketball and hockey, with all other teams included in what was called the "All-Sports Guide." Women's athletics were just being taken on by the Harvard Department of Athletics, and I decided to give them some attention on the cover of that publication. I commissioned Larry Johnson, the talented cartoonist at *The Boston Globe*, to create an image of a female Harvard athlete in a sweat suit, standing next to a young girl who was literally, and figuratively, looking up at her. My statement on the changing times.

No sooner had the guide been distributed than the men's swim coach, Joe Bernal, walked into my office, dropped the guide on my desk and said, "What's this crap?" I was young and didn't have a lot of power, but I knew that the people for whom I worked would back me on this one.

The production of publications was one of the great perks of these jobs. And at Harvard, we were fortunate to be able to tap into some great talent to help us along. Even though attendance at Ivy League football games was, with the exception of The Game, not significant, advertisers still coveted the

Ivy audience. So our football programs, filled with high-end advertisements, could be special magazines.

Our publisher, Harold Zimman, was a former Tufts University football player who created a terrific company in Lynn, MA. Not only did they do the Ivy League ad inserts, they were also a big player in the world of tennis, producing the U.S. Open program and its daily updates. As I write, my wife, Kathy, works for H.O. Zimman, now under the watchful eyes of Harold's son Josh. Among their publications: programs for the Super Bowl, The Masters and, still, the U.S. Open.

And so we got to produce slick football programs, with ads from the likes of Rolex, investment firms of the day like Paine Webber and E.F. Hutton, cars like Volvo, local banks and other upscale firms.

The Rolex ad, for many years, was placed on the inside front cover and, by edict from the agency, featured an action photo that was reversed. You could see that the numbers and any other such image were backward. Their tag line was, "Rolex. Unmistakable Quality." We would always get calls pointing out the "mistake" and had to explain it was intentional.

Given our audience, we could also tap into some heavyweight contributors. Paul Szep, a Pulitzer Prize-winning cartoonist at *The Boston Globe*, contributed some cutouts of what the "right people" would wear to the Harvard-Yale game. In 1978, on the 10th anniversary of the fabled 29-29 tie between the schools, I was able to convince the great Roger Angell to write a piece for the occasion.

I laugh when I think of receiving Angell's story over the telecopier late one November afternoon, instinctively reaching for my red pen as I set out to proof it. Right. I'm going to edit Roger Angell. I was struck then, as I am now, by this passage.

"I come back to The Game, year after year, not so much for the sport as for a feeling of renewal. It has become a rite, and its capacity to move me does not have much to do with the final score or even the pleasures of meeting old friends there, before the kickoff and after. It has something to do with the turn of the seasons; winter begins here, every year, when the gun goes off and the last cries and songs are exchanged across the field ... the Game picks us up each November and holds us for two hours and then releases us into the early darkness of winter, and all of us, homeward bound, sense that we are different yet still the same. It is magic."

During Yale week in one of my Harvard years, possibly 1978, I was having difficulty getting access to a famous photo. It was the picture of Harvard tight end Pete Varney holding the football aloft, having just caught the two-point conversion that completed the improbable comeback in Harvard's 29-29 "win" against Yale in 1968. The photographer, Dick Raphael, was my regular football photographer but on that day in 1968, he was on assignment for *Sports Illustrated*. The magazine was making me pay an exorbitant amount of money for a one-time use of the photo, again, not a digital image back then but an actual 8´ x 10´´ glossy photograph.

At the same time, I was getting a string of phone calls, increasingly frantic, from someone at *Sports Illustrated* who was looking for good seats for The Game. Considering these two matters, I finally called the person at *SI* who was looking for the tickets and explained the matter of the photograph. I don't recall having to connect all the dots. The photo arrived the next day, at no cost and with unlimited use granted, and in turn, I found some very nice tickets.

Speaking of game tickets, I tried to get the great John Updike to write a story for one of our football programs by offering him a check and a few tickets. He politely declined, typing his response on a white postcard and signing his name. When Updike died in 2009, his obituary made reference to his habit of communicating via white postcards. (I still have mine.)

One other story about publications. Every fall Sunday, during my Harvard SID days, my staff and I put out a newsletter that chronicled that weekend's games, leading with a football game story. One of my student assistants back in 1978 was Jon Ledecky, later an owner of the New York Islanders and proud uncle of Olympic swimmer Katie Ledecky.

On home weekends, the aforementioned Raphael would leave a large white envelope under the door, filled with a stack of photographs. Any possible image I might desire to accompany the game story would be there. I remember one game when the starting quarterback was injured and a combination of a late turnover and the back-up quarterback stepping up combined for a Harvard win. Raphael's photos included the turnover, the winning score and a great sideline shot of the back-up talking with coach Joe Restic, and the injured starter in the background on crutches.

Normally, the home games were covered by Will Cloney, Harvard '33. Will had a long career in journalism but was better known to the Boston sports culture as the director of the fabled BAA Marathon.

Will became a mentor to me and taught me valuable lessons. When I referred to Harvard's "sloppy tackling" in a game against Princeton, I was reminded of my audience. "You can't say that," he told me. "Refer to Princeton's 'elusive ball carriers.'"

When I edited a coffee table book on Harvard athletics in the mid-1980s, I was obliged to send each chapter to Will and a couple of other alumni. Upon receiving one such chapter, Will returned the chapter, marking up the copy with, ",,,,,,,,,,,,,, Commas. USE THEM!"

In recalling my relationship with Will Cloney, I am reminded of another elder statesman at Harvard with whom I was fortunate to create a friendship. When Harvard athletes in and around my time suffered a sports-related

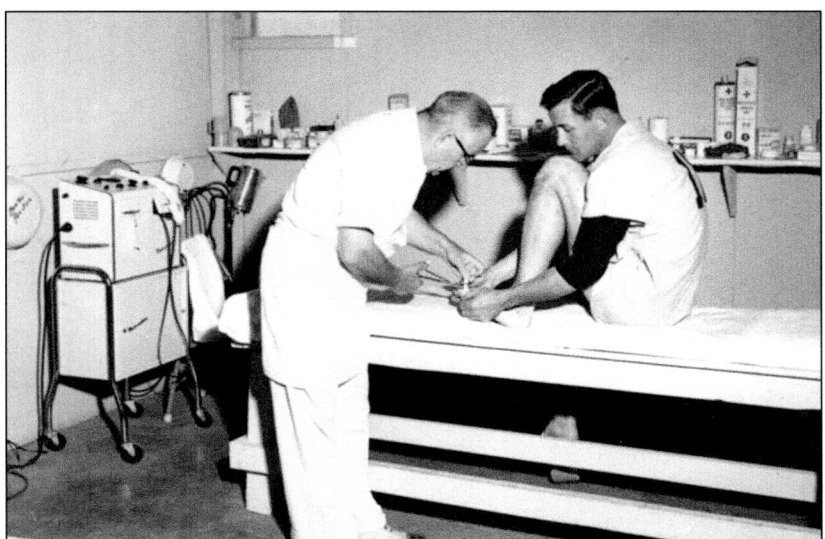

My Harvard education was not limited to my four years as an undergraduate. I also learned life lessons from Harvard trainer Jack Fadden. Jack, as shown above, was also the trainer for the Red Sox. (Photo Courtesy of the Boston Red Sox)

injury, it was a bad news/good news situation. Yes, there might have been some pain and a missed game or practice. But there was also the chance you would receive treatment from legendary trainer Jack Fadden. Former Harvard quarterback Jim Kubacki, upon receiving an award named for Fadden, said, "I feel sorry for all the Harvard athletes who were NOT injured. They never got to form a relationship with Jack."

Fadden served as athletic trainer for both the Boston Red Sox and Harvard Athletics, and long after he was fully employed, he would hold office hours early in the morning at Dillon Field House. They weren't formal office hours. But Jack would be there before the work day began, available to Harvard employees and alumni alike, dispensing first aid and practical wisdom in equal doses.

When I worked as the Harvard SID, I often parked my car behind Dillon and stopped to see Jack and share a cup of tea before walking up to my Harvard Square office. I have a vague recollection of Jack working on a minor knee injury I had as an undergraduate goalie. But it is the memory of these post-graduate mornings, and subsequent mail correspondence, that have remained with me.

Two anecdotes of my mornings with Jack have stayed with me. One involved a Harvard baseball player, Chet Boulris, who had severe vision problems. Said Fadden, "I swear he saw three balls coming at him and swung at the one in the middle."

The other story was about Ted Williams. Fadden and Williams had a close relationship while both were with the Red Sox. During one of Williams' many feuds with the media, perhaps when Ted made a gesture in the direction of the Fenway Park press box, the newspapers were full of criticism directed toward the slugger.

While being worked on by Fadden one day, Williams said, "Everybody has something to say to me, but you haven't said a word. Don't you have an opinion on my behavior?"

Fadden waited for effect and responded by telling Williams, "I know a lot, Ted. But I'm no child psychologist."

Somewhere in my basement, buried with family photos and sentimental letters and documents, I have a few letters written to me by Jack Fadden when he used to travel around the world during his later years. I have to find and preserve those.

I recently came upon a collection of ECAC Championship programs while doing research for this book. It is clear that the frustrated writer in me took advantage of those annual programs to insert all sorts of stories, many historical, to provide an outlet for my urges to write.

I chuckled while perusing the 1984 program, which contained an article titled, *Opinion: Where are the great forwards?* In it, I tried to make the argument that great forwards, the ones that everyone knows and talks about, are not coming along like they used to. I cited changes in amateurism rules that kept some Canadian talent up north, the fact that the most dominant players the year before were defensemen Randy Velischek of Providence and Mark Fusco of Harvard, the depth of third and fourth lines taking ice time away from star players and even the advent of facemasks making it more difficult to see the personality of star players.

I tried to cover myself with this final offering: "Of course, now that this theory is in print, watch some left wing come into the Garden this weekend and go absolutely wild." Well, he wasn't a left wing. He was a center. And in that 1984 tournament, RPI's Adam Oates continued a performance that left him with 13 points in the two weekends of tournament games, second all time, leading RPI to the ECAC crown. RPI became the eighth different school to win the championship in eight years, and Oates went on to a 19-year NHL career, being inducted into the Hockey Hall of Fame in 2012.

It was during the ECAC internship that I was introduced to one of the necessary staples of athletic administration: meetings. The fall is a time of numerous meetings. The administrators meet. The coaches meet. The on-ice officials meet. Everyone meets the media. Long before conference calls and Zoom meetings, people got together, in person, and held meetings to conduct business.

All these years later, I take for granted that at some point I had to learn about selecting a meeting date, gathering agenda items, preparing handouts, and prepping all participants — including the meeting chair. September (October back then) is "Meeting Month" for ice hockey as everyone needs to focus on the season that is about to begin.

The ECAC always hosted a fall convention on Cape Cod, and my memory is of: a) running from meeting to meeting, delivering handouts and eventually keeping minutes of each of them; and b) chalky clam chowder. I found the actual meetings themselves to be fascinating in my early years.

Perhaps there were proposed budgets. Maybe someone was suggesting a restructuring of the many hockey divisions. Or it could be an officiating issue, on which system to use or how much to provide in travel expenses to the on-ice crew. Pretty dry stuff, but it was all new to me.

While I'm sure I attended multiple meetings in the fall of 1976 as an intern, the first meeting that remains vivid in my mind came a year or two later when I was working in the sports information office at Harvard. Harvard was hosting a meeting of Ivy League directors at the beautiful Chatham Bars Inn in Chatham, MA.

The only substantive issue I remember is that they were discussing a lot of financial concerns and yet, when it came time for lunch, they all dined on lobster salad in this beautiful New England inn. More than the issues, I remember the personal dynamics of a meeting involving eight schools.

There were people who spoke a lot but didn't seem to be making any points. There were people who said little but when they spoke, they seemed to command everyone's attention. One of these was Dartmouth's Seaver Peters, a former Big Green hockey player who had ascended to the AD role.

There was my boss at the time, Jack Reardon, who was a brilliant administrator and one of the best bosses I ever had. Smart, fair, to the point, Reardon served Harvard at a crucial time when women's athletics were absorbed into the athletic department and just about all of the university's athletic facilities needed an overhaul.

Most of all, I remember Cornell director Dick Schultz, who chaired the meeting. A former head coach of both baseball and basketball at the University of Iowa, Schultz went on to Virginia and then served as the executive director of the NCAA.

Not that I had anything to which I could compare his efforts, I thought Schultz gave a master class in how to run a meeting. I would learn over the years that there is an art to it. You had to know how long to let a discussion go before shutting it off and calling for a vote. There was a sweet spot between letting something go too long and cutting off people who still had new points to make. He seemed to know exactly when everyone had heard enough.

Over the years, I had the opportunity to chair scores of meetings and attend hundreds of others. I learned that where an issue is placed on an agenda can impact what kind of scrutiny it receives. A conference officer can't do a lot to make sure a measure passes but if the issue is placed at the end of the day's agenda, you could increase the chances that the proposal will die or be tabled. I also found that pre-meeting preparation went a long way toward running a successful meeting. One challenge, however, was getting participants to actually read the meeting materials before they walked into the room.

Hockey was a sport that was relatively successful for most of the schools for whom I worked over the years, whether they were the ECAC schools or those in Hockey East. I only mention this to establish that most directors were likely preoccupied with other challenges on their campuses. Maybe they had facility issues or needed to replace a coach or perhaps they had to cut sports due to budget constraints.

For the most part, ice hockey worked and worked well for these schools. And so, I often felt that the first time many an AD addressed a certain hockey issue was when he walked into our meeting. And I say "he" because more often than not, the AD was male. The ECAC was more progressive in this regard. In my 23 years at Hockey East, I calculate that I worked for 44 athletic directors, 42 of whom were male. Often, the only female at a Hockey East AD meeting was my associate, Kathy Wynters. (As of this writing, five of the 12 ECAC Hockey directors are female.)

Another factor at work here was that the associate or assistant AD might have been the actual "hands on" person for hockey, with the Director of Athletics more removed from the minutia of day-to-day operations. Over

Former ECAC coaches at a reunion in 2019. From left, Don "Toot" Cahoon, Mike Gilligan and Joe Marsh. (Rich Gagnon Photo)

This photo must have been from an ECAC media event, possibly at tournament time. It also shows how hockey careers intertwine. At left, Boston Bruins coach Mike Milbury, who played at Colgate. In the middle, then-Colgate coach Terry Slater. I was the Bruins' goalie coach and ECAC Hockey Commissioner at the time. (Rudy Winston Photo courtesy of the ECAC)

the 38 years I was a conference administrator, the job of athletic director had become more of a development officer/fundraiser position than actual day-to-day administrator. The larger the school, the less likely I would see the AD. When Notre Dame was in Hockey East for four years, the only time I was in the same room as the AD was at the press conference announcing its entry into the league.

While with the ECAC, I often chaired meetings. Not all the time but depending who a given committee chair was, he might defer to me to run the meeting. And this included coaches meetings.

Some of my best memories are of ECAC men's coaches meetings when the roster included the likes of Herb Hammond at Brown, Mark Morris at Clarkson, Terry Slater and Don Vaughan at Colgate, Mike Schafer at Cornell, Bob Gaudet at Dartmouth, Bill Cleary and Ronn Tomassoni at Harvard, Don "Toot" Cahoon at Princeton, Mike Addesa and Buddy Powers at RPI, Joe Marsh at St. Lawrence, Bruce Delventhal at Union, Mike Gilligan at Vermont and Tim Taylor at Yale.

The meetings were serious but never over the top. The humor emanating from the likes of Marsh and Gilligan would never let that happen. Perhaps more than any other time, I felt like I was contributing by bridging the needs of the administrators and coaches at the same time. Later, when I moved to Hockey East, coaches ran their own meetings.

I remember one misstep when I reprimanded veteran coach Terry Slater for being late to a meeting. Of course, I never bothered to find out why he was late and it turned out that his wife had been ill.

From that point on, Terry was pretty much the first guy at every meeting and when the clock turned 1:01 for a 1:00 meeting, he had something to say to me. All in good fun but his point made.

Current Colgate head coach Don Vaughan shared a story about Terry. The Red Raiders had been swept in Boston and Coach Slater was not happy with how they played. At the next practice, the players arrived to find Slater sitting on a lounge chair at center ice, wearing a floral shirt and smoking a cigar.

"You guys took a vacation last weekend so I will take one today," said Slater. "Everyone, on the goal line." And he proceeded to skate them hard, to send a message.

One of my saddest memories from my ECAC years came on December 6, 1991. I was going through the early days of a divorce and sleeping on a mattress thrown down on the floor of my home office. In the middle of the night, my telecopier turned on.

I got up off the mattress, turned on the light and waited for the transmission to finish. But I already knew what it was. It was a press release announcing that Terry Slater, who had suffered a stroke four days earlier, had died at the age of 54, one day after his birthday.

The highlight of each season was the end-of-season tournament. And while at the ECAC, that meant *tournaments*. We administered seven championship tournaments by the time I had finished my ECAC tenure. We had Division I men and women, and we had five Division III playing structures: East-West-North-South-Central, all of the latter being men's events.

The first Division I men's championship was held in 1962 at the Boston Arena, and the first women's championship was held in 1984, when there was no regular-season structure for women. The first 10 women's postseason events mixed Division I and Division III programs. It wasn't until the 1993-94 season that a structured ECAC Division I women's regular season was inaugurated. I made the successful presentation to ECAC directors the year before to make this a reality and had the privilege a decade later to do the same to launch Women's Hockey East.

At the time of my 1976 internship, the ECAC had a firm grip on college ice hockey in the East. All of college hockey in the East was played under the ECAC banner. There were three levels of play, commonly referred to as Division I, Division II and Division III, though those designations were not necessarily consistent with NCAA nomenclature.

At the Division I level, there were 17 programs that played at the top level. These were a mix of NCAA Division I or II or III programs, the latter two groups formally "playing up" at the D-1 level. The remaining teams were classified as "ECAC Division II" or "ECAC Division III," though a school's NCAA status might be different.

For example, schools like UConn, UMass, Fairfield and Holy Cross were NCAA Division I schools overall. But their ECAC Hockey programs played in lower divisions. Likewise, schools like Bowdoin and Middlebury were NCAA Division III schools but their hockey programs competed for ECAC Division II titles.

It was confusing for anyone other than hockey fans who knew that they were seeing three different levels of competition when, on a given Saturday in the 1970s, you watched Clarkson play RPI, Bowdoin play Norwich and Fitchburg State host Framingham State. All six schools were NCAA Division III schools, but all sponsored hockey programs with distinctly different levels of play.

Eventually, led by complaints from non-hockey ADs, the ECAC changed its nomenclature so that the playing divisions of the schools below ECAC Division I Hockey took on geographic names: the old ECAC Division II became ECAC East and ECAC West, while the old ECAC Division III became ECAC North-Central-South, and tournaments adjusted accordingly.

For decades, most schools in the East were responsible for their own schedules. One exception was the Ivy League, which scheduled all teams to play the others home and away and that crowned an Ivy champion and announced All-Ivy teams even while their schools competed within the ECAC.

ECAC Commissioner Scotty Whitelaw (far right) presents St. Lawrence coach Joe Marsh (left of Scotty) one of many ECAC trophies won on Joe's watch. (The tournament trophy was eventually named for Scotty.) Scotty was one of the best people for whom I had the opportunity to work. (Tim Morse/ECAC Photo)

The result was that ECAC standings had to be listed by winning percentage, given that there was no common master schedule. While this was the way of the world for decades, it came as a shock to college coaches during the 2020-21 season when listing teams by percentage was necessitated by their pandemic-damaged schedules.

Looking back at my own playing experience, we always had 12 games against the other Ivy schools and then a scattering of the non-Ivy schools — but I never played against the likes of Colgate, Providence or RPI in my career. In some cases, schools had logistic difficulties in scheduling a certain opponent. In others, there might have been an ugly incident between two schools that left them with little desire to keep each other on the schedule.

It wasn't until the 1980-81 season that an attempt was made to create some sort of common Division I scheduling. This was done through the creation of three divisions: New England (BC, BU, Maine, UNH, Northeastern and Providence; Ivy (the six Ivy schools) and Empire (Clarkson, Colgate, RPI, St. Lawrence and Vermont). The teams played a double round-robin schedule within the division and there were some crossover games. The division winner was guaranteed a home ice spot in the ECAC Tournament.

At the lower levels, it was even more complicated to come up with anything resembling a common schedule. And this made for a complicated process when seeding teams for postseason play. This was before computer programs were used to calculate "strength of schedule." We had a primitive version of that, one that kept me up late every March prior to the Division II/Division III playoffs.

The athletic director at Lowell, Jim Ciszek, came up with a formula that attempted to recognize strength of schedule. The Ciszek Formula gave a school points for wins and ties that factored in its opponent's record. If you beat a team that had nine wins, you got two points for each of its wins or, in this case, 18 points. If you tied that team, you got one point for each of its wins. So, if you had a win and a tie against a 9-15 Wesleyan team, you got or 27 points (18 plus 9) for those two games. You added up all the points and divided by games played to get that school's Ciszek number.

What fell to me was to stay home on the last Saturday night of the regular season, armed with a calculator, a grid of all ECAC teams with all their results and plenty of coffee. Because, you see, you couldn't start the calculations until the results of all games were known. And for 14 of my 15 years, it went flawlessly. More on that later.

There was no "app" for this. No software. It was me and my calculator and my organizational skills going to work when each division's games were done. Oh, and there was no internet, so we depended on SIDs calling in all the scores to my house. After completing my calculations, I would go to bed around around 2:00 a.m. and then awake to provide my stats to the respective tournament committees that had to seed teams based on what I told them. (No apps for stats either — me entering each goal, assist and penalty.)

So, back to my reference to "14 of my 15 years." In my final year with the ECAC, I completed the Sunday morning seeding calls and felt pretty good about myself. On Monday, after all the pairings had been announced for the various events, I received a call from Worcester State AD Sue Chapman. "Joe, I hate to have to make this call, but I think you might have made a mistake in your Ciszek calculations."

I can only assume that I responded defensively because I had enjoyed such a long streak of perfection. But, at the same time, I must have felt a sharp pain in my gut, knowing she might be right. And she was. I had transcribed a pair of numbers that put Fairfield in the tournament and kept Worcester State out. Once the numbers were fixed, the fates of the two schools were swapped. And I was the one who had to make the call to Fairfield.

Whatever the level, "Tournament Week" was always exciting. Right through my last tournament, the 2020 Women's Hockey East Championship, I never lost that special feeling and energy the tournaments provided. Part of this was the excitement of tournament play and crowning a champion. But there was also the sense of pride the staff felt in pulling everything together. While circumstances changed over my near four decades of running these events, what didn't change was my amazement at how much work a small number of people could produce in so little time.

All of these events, except the men's D-I championship weekend, were held on campuses. So the ultimate running of those events was left to the schools, with policies and procedures established and enforced by the conference. And as the seasons began to overlap, March was a challenging time for schools that were wrapping up the winter season at the same time spring sports got underway.

I had help from the fulltime ECAC staff, and each tournament had an Executive Committee of administrators who established policies down to the smallest detail. My job was to make sure the policies were followed.

This would start with how teams qualified for the postseason, how ties were broken, how they were seeded within the event, and then myriad financial policies governing what was and wasn't reimbursed, what hotels to use, what rates were negotiated, etc. Finally, all the details of game night were articulated, right down to who would present the trophies on the ice.

It is fun to look back on the different formats that tournaments used. The two-game, total goals series was, thankfully, scrapped. It often led to teams running up the score in that first win to provide a cushion going forward.

The other since-shelved format involved the "mini-game." This was a series that should the teams split the first two games, a 10-minute "mini-game" was tacked on to the end of the second night. It was treated as an entirely new game. Line-ups could be changed. Penalties did not carry over from Game Two. And if Game Two was a blowout of any kind, teams kind of coasted at the end, saving energy for that upcoming "mini-game."

Each game or series played had a "Games Committee" that existed to adjudicate any disputes that might arise in the course of competition. While I liked attending these games, I often stayed home on a busy playoff night so that I could be accessible should an unusual situation occur. These early ECAC events, after all, took place before mobile phones and internet access.

What could go wrong? Well, one night I got a call from Colgate informing me that the Zamboni had broken down between periods of a quarterfinal men's game with Yale. The draining hot water had created a deep crater in the ice and it was impossible to continue.

I recall that referee Marty McDonough actually went up to the press box to get on the phone and confirm that there could be no further play that night. The Games Committee, following the NCAA Rules Book, had to determine whether the game could continue from that point or if a new game needed to be started. Then they had to address whether the next night was Game Two or the continuation of Game One and so forth.

Sometimes the issue involved discipline of players, a sensitive subject

The administration of the ECAC Hockey Championships depended on a crew of "men in large blue coats." From left, I am flanked above by Howie Borkan, Bob Olivari, Bruce Bosley and Joel Weisblatt. (Photo Courtesy of Dave Smallwood)

at any time, but particularly in tournament play. Fortunately, players tend to be on their best behavior when a trophy is within reach.

Speaking of trophies, we did have an unfortunate incident during a trophy presentation when Plattsburgh's captain, upon receiving the ECAC West trophy from ECAC Supervisor of Officials Dick "Lefty" Marr, placed it on the ice and skated away. Plattsburgh had been livid when Elmira, due to geographic proximity to more competing schools, got to host the championships ahead of Plattsburgh, which had a better record than Elmira.

The main event was always the ECAC Men's Championship weekend. Everyone moved into Boston for the Thursday banquet and two nights of fantastic hockey. The Friday night semifinals, for many Eastern hockey fans, was the best night of the year, whether you had a semifinalist you followed or not.

All these years later, I can still remember certain Friday nights at the Garden, going back to 1971 when I was the back-up goalie at Harvard. In Cooney Weiland's last year, we didn't take a single penalty in a 4-2 win over eventual NCAA champion Boston University.

I was just a fan in 1977 when the two semifinal games produced 32 goals: UNH defeated Cornell, 10-9, in two overtimes; and Boston University defeated Clarkson, 7-6, the game ending well after 1:00 a.m.

In 1986, it was the goaltending of Cornell's Doug Dadswell that was on display when Cornell defeated Yale, 3-2 in double overtime on Friday and then needed another overtime to win the title with a 3-2 win over Clarkson the next night.

Finally, there was 1989 when Vermont stunned Harvard, 3-2 in overtime on Friday, temporarily stopping a Crimson club that would go on to win the NCAA's in St. Paul weeks later.

Whether the Garden events or those that eventually took place at Lake Placid, what I remember most of all was tending to all the details with a combination of facility staff, SIDs and their volunteer friends, and a group of buddies who took pride in delivering a memorable weekend for the participants.

One group of those buddies came to be known as "men in large blue coats." Yes, that could have been rearranged to say "large men in blue coats" but why quibble? Howie Borkan, Bruce Bosley, Bob Olivari and Joel Weisblatt volunteered at the old Garden and Lake Placid, and when I moved to Hockey East, I was able to recruit all but Howie to come with me. A Cornell alum with strong ties to the ECAC, Howie's allegiance to the ECAC was understandable and admirable.

This group would take on all sorts of duties — from checking credentials to writing quotes at postgame press conferences to overseeing media dining to copying box scores for distribution to teams and media.

Most of all, they provided me an insurance policy, trusted confidants who, when all the pre-planning in the world might go awry, would be there to bail me out.

Years later, when I was with Hockey East and the championships at the new Garden had grown in scope and expectations, the three remaining men in large blue coats were still my insurance policy but the army of staff involved in putting on such an event had grown exponentially. One of my lasting memories from my final Hockey East men's championship was watching the end of the final in the media room with Bob Olivari, Joel Weisblatt and legendary *Boston Herald* scribe John "Jocko" Connolly, while waiting to go on the ice for the trophy presentation.

During those first few years following the ECAC-Hockey East split, both conferences had to deal with attendance issues at their respective tournaments. As noted, the ECAC had held its championship weekend at the Boston Garden since 1967 while Hockey East launched its first such event at the Providence Civic Center in 1985. (And what a "launch" it was, with Providence College goalie Chris Terreri making 65 saves in a triple overtime championship game win over Boston College.)

It was no secret that Hockey East coaches wanted to get back to the Garden. It was the preferred spot in New England, being the home of the

ECAC Commissioner Clayton Chapman, a Hall of Fame oarsman at Cornell as an undergraduate, presents an award to Vermont's Eric Perrin. (Photo courtesy of the ECAC)

Boston Bruins and all. The Hockey East games were broadcast on NESN, which carried the Bruins. And half the league schools were located within minutes of the facility.

The ECAC, now in a competitive situation with the new conference, was reluctant to give up what it perceived to be a valuable asset. But, at the same time, the ECAC schools were predominantly New York-based and the split clearly had an effect on the ECAC attendance.

In short, both conferences were struggling to fill their buildings, no small part of the problem being that they were holding their events at roughly the same time. While they could count on those fans who specifically followed a school in their league, they now were competing for the same "unaffiliated" fans, the college hockey fans who wanted to see championship play whether they rooted for a specific school or not.

Hockey East was able to play its 1987 and 1988 championship games at the Garden but had to settle for Monday nights. One year, the quarterfinals and semifinals were on campus and the other year saw Sunday-Monday semis and final on Causeway Street. With both leagues now at the Garden, the ECAC's hold on the building was no longer a sure thing.

So it was in this context that the two leagues started to discuss how this matter could be mitigated. What if fans didn't have to make a choice? What if the games were scheduled so that fans could see all the games without conflict and that they could do so in the Mecca of New England hockey, the venerable Boston Garden?

Conversations started in 1988, and by the following year, the new event

Left: This program is from the second year of the "Hockeyfest" concept at Boston Garden. Right: Legendary Cornell coach Ned Harkness (at left) convinced the ECAC to move its Men's Division I Tournament from Boston to Lake Placid in 1993. For that year's tournament banquet, he brought Ken Dryden to be the guest speaker. (Photos courtesy of the ECAC)

had a name and a structure. It would be called "Hockeyfest" and roll out as three nights of championship play at the Boston Garden. The ECAC would keep its traditional Friday night semifinals, followed by Hockey East semifinals on Saturday night. And then the crowning glory: two championship games for the price of one ticket on Sunday night.

There was some discussion about going Thursday-Friday-Saturday, to have the championship games on Saturday night. But that would have left an unattractive night for whoever played its semifinals on Thursday. Given that the ECAC still held the primary rights to the Garden, that would have been Hockey East playing on Thursday.

Beyond getting the ECAC and Hockey East to play nice, another challenge was getting the Garden to clear its schedule for three straight days of college hockey at a time when the Bruins, the Celtics and high schools (tournaments) coveted time in the building. Let the record show that not only did Garden VP Steve Nazro play a huge role in making this possible but so, too, did Bruins president Harry Sinden, whose request to move his team's games led to a domino effect where many other NHL games were affected.

While the major decisions for this event to happen were made by athletic directors in each conference, the details had to be worked out and implemented by two people. At the time, my title at the ECAC was executive director of hockey. My counterpart, Hockey East commissioner Stu Haskell, delegated much of the Hockeyfest work to his associate commissioner, Kathy Walsh. Later, when she was Kathy Wynters, we would become co-workers at Hockey East for two decades.

And so Kathy and I, on behalf of our respective athletic directors, spent over a year planning "Hockeyfest" with Steve Nazro and the Garden staff. Given that the ECAC had the Garden contract, my recollection was that we, the ECAC, had some leverage in the negotiations. Still, I also recall that setting the schedule and working out details went fairly smoothly. And then came measles.

An outbreak of 50 or so cases at the University of Maine put a halt on the planning. The Massachusetts Department of Public Health notified us that should Maine advance to the Garden, everyone entering the building would have to be screened, those over 34 years of age would be allowed in and others would need to show proof of vaccination. Everyone soon realized that this could not be done with crowds, hopefully, in excess of 10,000 people.

And so Hockey East directors convened to see where it could play its 1990 event and opted for Boston College, its highest seed. The ECAC stayed at the Garden, but with a Saturday-Sunday schedule and four New York schools, the prospects for large crowds were not good. Some 5,000 fans showed up to see Colgate defeat RPI, 5-4. Over at BC, a similar crowd saw BC defeat Maine, 4-3.

The two leagues were able to pull off Hockeyfest '91 and delivered two great championship games for the fans, BU nipping Maine, 4-3 in overtime, and Clarkson beating St. Lawrence, 5-4. The crowds were larger but couldn't get over the 10,000 mark. And so the two leagues lobbied to move the event to Thursday-Friday-Saturday dates, in the hopes that hosting the two championships on a Saturday night would allow them to crack the 10,000 mark.

Sure enough, on March 14, 1992, just over 12,000 fans were on hand to see Maine defeat UNH, 4-1, and St. Lawrence defeat Cornell, 4-2. It looked like Hockeyfest was finally catching on.

When ECAC directors met for their annual spring meeting that year, a different assessment surfaced. Two issues appeared to sour many of the directors on the future of Hockeyfest. First, they noted that the Boston papers covered the Hockey East final on page one of the sports section, while the ECAC final, featuring all New York schools from 1990-92, was relegated to page eight or worse.

The other issue was financial. There just wasn't enough gross revenue to go around with three partners dividing up the spoils. And so, the ECAC decided not only to put an end to Hockeyfest but also to leave Boston altogether. Former Cornell coach Ned Harkness was now working for the Olympic Regional Development Authority (ORDA), and he was eager to bring the ECAC Tournament to Lake Placid.

I was pretty well invested in the Hockeyfest concept. I thought it was great for fans and provided a terrific championship atmosphere for the schools. Having worked on the details for four years on behalf of the ECAC, I hated to see it end. But the ECAC directors had made up their minds. They were going to Lake Placid.

In my 15 years with the ECAC, I must have attended more than 700 games. The memories that remain are a mix of individual plays and games, and also of the routine and the scenes that played out over time.

I remember waking up on a Saturday or Sunday morning, taking my coffee into my home office and picking up the rolled up pages from my telecopier, box scores from the night before. Long before live stats, I would enter every goal, assist and penalty into a primitive stat program and create the statistics used by the conference.

I remember calling a (906) number for scores late on a Friday or Saturday, hearing the WMPL recorded voice giving me the college hockey results for that night. And I laugh when I recall how the young man pronounced "Schenectady" as "Shennen-decty."

I remember the ECAC Staff. Beyond Scotty and Clayt, I am thinking of Art Hyland, Steve Hardy, John Garner, Bobby Quinn, John Gallagher, Pat Rotondi, Sally Benson, Anne Glover, Sam Gwynne and others.

I laugh when I think of the late Bill Hutchinson, a supervisor of referees, who would write me an annual letter on a manual typewriter from the Veterans Hospital, requesting tickets to the Beanpot Tournament. In one of his final letters, he wrote, "You must be wondering what I do with the tickets each year. Well, I give them to my doctors, and I swear to God the only reason they keep me alive is so they can get the damn tickets."

I remember road trips. Staying at the Hanover Inn to watch Dartmouth and then heading to UVM the next day. Entering Gutterson Fieldhouse, I would walk up to the concourse on the press box side to make sure "my picture" was still there, one from a game in 1973. (More on this in the next chapter.)

I remember staying at a motel halfway between Clarkson and St. Lawrence. And on one visit, I recall serving as site director when Clarkson hosted Wisconsin in the NCAA Tournament on the final weekend of Walker Arena in 1991. When Badgers coach Jeff Sauer kept stalling to rest his star defenseman, Sean Hill, referee Matt Shegos, having already warned Sauer, gave the coach an ultimatum. "Coach, I can't make you take a timeout. But I can give you a delay of game penalty," said Shegos. "What would you like me to do?"

"You can't make me take a timeout," countered Sauer. "You are right, said Shegos. "But I can call the penalty. What are you going to do?" Sauer, reluctantly, called a time out.

I remember the Ivy rinks, but much of that has to do with playing there years earlier. As a starter, I never lost a varsity game at Brown, Dartmouth, Penn, Princeton or Yale. Cornell was another story. Brown's Meehan Rink was dark, and I always got lost finding the right street on which to turn. Entering Brown's press box well before game time, you could smell the weed wafting up from the student section below.

Princeton's Baker Rink looked like a church. Dartmouth's old Davis Rink turned into the still beautiful Thompson Arena. I recall Harvard opening Penn's "Class of '23" rink in 1971.

I remember Joe Marsh at a press conference. Win or lose, he always said the right things. And, usually, he won.

I remember doing the color commentary for Harvard radio in St. Paul when the Crimson beat Minnesota in overtime to win the 1989 NCAA title. The rink, St. Paul Civic Center, had clear glass boards. After the game, Bill Cleary stood on a table in the lobby of the St. Paul Hotel, holding the trophy and declaring that the win was for anyone who ever wore the Crimson jersey. Years later, Ed Krayer, who scored the OT game-winner, bought my wife's childhood home.

I remember also working color with famed Boston sportscaster Bob Gamere. One night, our phone line had not been installed at Harvard's Bright Center, so Bob somehow hot-wired the pay phone, ran a wire into the stands and we did the first period taking turns talking through the phone.

I remember the Sunday morning I received numerous calls from Harvard friends telling me that Mike Schafer, then a Cornell defenseman, allegedly shot a puck in the direction of Bill Cleary behind the Harvard bench. I called Big Red SID Dave Wohlhuter and said with a chuckle, "Hey Dave, my crazy Harvard friends are claiming Schafer shot a puck at Cleary last night." "Yes, he did," replied Wohlhuter.

I remember the first tournament banquet in Lake Placid, with a proud Ned Harkness welcoming us on behalf of ORDA, the Olympic Regional Development Authority. And I recall the guest speaker was Ned's old netminder, Ken Dryden.

Finally, I remember the routine of so many tournament nights at the Garden and at Lake Placid. On one of those nights in the latter, a 50-50 raffle provided hundreds of dollars for its winner, Billy Zito. A former Yale hockey player, Zito was an agent at the time and is currently the Florida Panthers general manager.

Upon picking up his winnings, he said he would give back half of the cash to the charity for which the drawing had been held, provided that the PA announce that the winner was Reggie Dunlop, Paul Newman's character in the movie *Slap Shot*.

With several hundred dollars in his pocket, Zito left Lake Placid for the ride home, only to be stopped for speeding. The New York state policeman who stopped Zito informed him that he had a number of outstanding speeding tickets and, with great delight, further informed him that he had to pay for them all and that they didn't take checks or credit cards. So, unless he had plenty of cash, he was spending the night in jail. I can only imagine Billy's smile.

By my 15th season with the ECAC, the constraints of being part-time started to chafe. Our first son was born in July 1996 and I needed to make more money and receive benefits. And right around this time, a group of Hockey East coaches came to me and started a recruitment effort. They wanted me to come to Hockey East to be their first full-time commissioner.

I listened to the Hockey East people and received an offer. Up to that time, I had been working out of my house with no dedicated hockey staff and no benefits. I say "no dedicated hockey staff" because the ECAC office on the Cape had a number of people I could tap into but none solely working on the interests of the 90 ice hockey programs I administered.

My heart was with ECAC Hockey, so I went to Clayt Chapman and asked the ECAC to match the offer from Hockey East. Not better it, just match it. They came back with an offer that would only reach the Hockey East numbers if I took on sponsor sales and made significant commissions. I was disappointed but the offer from Hockey East was too good to pass up.

Chapter Six —
Hockey East Calls

"... The second aspect of 'corporate' hockey was an increased willingness to embrace business partners to underwrite costs in return for the opportunity to market their products through an affiliation with a team, a player, an arena, or an event. Today's marketers call this 'sponsorship.' It is an expected and necessary practice at almost all levels."

> *— Stephen Hardy and Andrew Holman,*
> *discussing "Corporate Hockey" in their 2018 book,*
> *"Hockey: A Global History" (University of Illinois Press)*

When I was hired by Hockey East in February 1997 (starting the job on July 1), it was primarily because a group of head coaches went to the directors and convinced them that the conference needed a fulltime commissioner and that person should be "a hockey guy." Up to that time, all the commissioners had done "double duty," as Hockey East boss and something else. They were either athletic directors or perhaps commissioner of another entity.

I was excited to start my new job. Having started a family with the birth of my son Bobby in July 1996, it was a time of change for Kathy and me. We had met when she worked in Harvard's sports information office, a job I had enjoyed a decade earlier. I would miss much of the ECAC job, but Hockey East had so many new things to offer.

On my official first day on the job, July 1, 1997, I made sure that the first thing I did was call Lou Lamoriello, the founder of Hockey East, and let him know that I would do everything I could to live up to the legacy he

I sat for an interview with Hockey East's first commissioner, Lou Lamoriello, in 2018 on Long Island. Interviewed by Dave Starman, I had paid the visit to Lou on the occasion of Hockey East's 35th anniversary season. (Photo courtesy of Hockey East)

had created when the conference was founded nearly 15 years earlier. I had great respect for Lou and wanted to show that. Lou's contributions to hockey were recognized with his Hall of Fame induction in 2012.

I always take care, when describing the differences between ECAC Hockey and Hockey East, not to diminish what the ECAC hockey coaches accomplished. In terms of each league's coaches and their desire to win, nothing was different. But there were differences in the business cultures of those conferences.

Steve Hardy, a good friend and a former Bowdoin College hockey player, teamed up with Andrew Holman to write a phenomenal book, *Hockey: A Global History*. Steve and Andrew had been professors at the University of New Hampshire and Bridgewater State University, respectively.

In *Hockey*, they discuss a major change in the game that they estimate started around 1972, a change that led them to coin the term "Corporate Hockey." I can't do their work justice in a small space here, but I can describe how the differences I discovered in moving from the ECAC to Hockey East reflected this new hockey culture.

Right from the start, Hockey East was the more "corporate" of the two entities. With a public relations firm engaged to assist in its launch, Hockey East made it clear that it was not going to be content with old norms. From its hockey-specific logo, to its interlocking schedule with the Western Collegiate Hockey Association (WCHA) to its television contract with the New England Sports Network (NESN), Hockey East was going to be marketed in a way no other hockey conference ever was.

The ECAC was influenced by the presence of six Ivy League schools, which made up half of the league's membership. The Ivies limited their seasons by playing only 29 games (the NCAA limit was 34) and taking the ice weeks later than their non-Ivy counterparts. To their credit, they did not demand that the six non-Ivy schools in the ECAC follow these practices.

While at the ECAC, I was expected to explore sponsorship opportunities and had a full-time staff member at the Cape Cod office who was charged with sponsor procurement for the entire ECAC. However, as I learned fairly late in my tenure, he did not see his job as selling sport-specific sponsorships but selling the ECAC as a whole.

While times eventually changed, some within the Ivy block had not yet embraced the need to pursue sports sponsorship during my time there. My old Harvard coach, Bill Cleary, once remarked to me, "You'll never see a Chevy parked on the 50-yard line while I am here." In all due respect to my coach, Harvard had resources that other schools did not, and for the others, the prominent placement of a Chevy or other marketing initiatives might have been a necessity.

Moving to Hockey East, I'm pretty sure that the prospect of looking for sponsor dollars was not one of the attractions for me, but I certainly welcomed the marketing and branding potential of having a TV partner like NESN. It was something all of us in ECAC Hockey had envied.

The Hockey East broadcasts on NESN helped launch the career of Sean McDonough, son of legendary *Boston Globe* columnist Will McDonough. The younger McDonough teamed up with Bob Norton, a former UNH coach, to give Hockey East a great tandem. Norton, who had played football at Rutgers before coming to UNH, was an encyclopedia of all sorts of hockey knowledge. If it wasn't about the game action itself, it might have been who some goalie's high school coach was or which player's uncle had a cup of coffee in the NHL.

McDonough went on to be one of the most versatile broadcasters in the country, working a number of prime professional and college assignments and, as of this writing, he was tabbed to be one of the lead play-by-play men for the NHL's return to ESPN in the fall of 2021.

So, imagine my disappointment when in the period between my hiring in February 1997 to my first day on the job on July 1, NESN announced it was dropping Hockey East from its programming. I recall meeting with NESN general manager Bob Whitelaw to understand why this was happening.

Whitelaw (no relation to Scotty) explained that NESN was disappointed in a number of developments. Schools were not cooperating when NESN asked them to move some games, either to different dates or, more often, to different start times. Coaches weren't willing to accommodate interview requests. In short, Whitelaw thought Hockey East had taken NESN for granted.

College hockey not being a great draw for ratings or advertisers, the finances of the Hockey East deal probably had more to do with the decision. But, then again, that had always been the case. So, coupled with the grievances aired by Whitelaw, the decision was made.

All was not lost, however, because when the Hartford Whalers announced in May 1997 that they were departing Hartford to become the Carolina Hurricanes, the move left their television partner, SportsChannel New England, with a major programming hole. Even before my first official day on the job, I started talks with SportsChannel and eventually managed to get the 1998 Hockey East Championships on the network. (Hockey East returned to NESN after a two-year hiatus.)

With both Hockey East and NESN being launched in 1984, the partnership was a natural. And the fact that the Hockey East footprint was exclusively in New England created a dynamic that other conferences did not have. This New England footprint also was an asset in making schedules and, eventually, landing regional sponsorships. The scheduling benefits were huge. Where other conferences were limited to weekend play in order to limit midweek travel and missed class time, most Hockey East schools could schedule midweek games against opponents, both league and non-league foes, that were less than an hour away.

This provided two major benefits. Hockey East schools could open up weekends for non-league series by scheduling a few midweek games, and when weather caused postponements, rescheduling was less of a challenge. Only Maine and eventually Vermont were "long" road trips. And they were only "long" to Hockey East, when compared to other parts of the country.

Early in my tenure, I made the mistake of scheduling BU to play at UNH on a Friday and at Maine the next night. That led to a call from BU coach Jack Parker telling me that it isn't done that way. In my thinking, the Friday night game would end around 9:15 and the team could leave Durham before 10:00 and go halfway to Orono. They could get up early, get to Orono for a brief game-day skate and play at night. I checked with other coaches and they all confirmed Jack's observation.

While schools did their own non-league scheduling, league scheduling fell to me (both men's and women's), and given the many variables, there was no scheduling software, certainly early in my tenure, that could provide much assistance. I used to go on-line for a generic 9-team or 11-team schedule, substitute Team 1 with "BC," Team 2 with "BU," etc. This would give me all the match-ups and then I would place them on the calendar, usually working backwards from the final weekend of the season. Not high tech but highly efficient.

The schedules were done in two-year cycles so that everyone played the same number of home and away games and played each opponent the same number of times. If you had to go to Maine, you would host Vermont that year. The next year, you would go to Vermont and host Maine. Those were often two-game series at the same site. In years you played them three times, one was home and two away or vice versa.

The coaches liked playing the same opponent on a given weekend. They could prepare, Monday through Thursday, for one team and its tendencies. For most of the schools, these were "home and home" series. For example, BU might host Providence on Friday and then PC would host BU on Saturday.

Most years, the schools had three games against each opponent, so I placed the two-game series at the end of the schedule and dropped the single games into the early months, through mid-January. I kept Maine and Vermont from being on the road in consecutive weekends and never made other schools go to Maine and Vermont back-to-back.

Special consideration was made on the two Beanpot Tournament weekends so that the three Boston schools played only once, on Friday, allowing them to be well rested for those two Monday nights. While I'm sure some non-Beanpot coaches didn't like our helping the Boston schools in this way, the ADs didn't question this. They understood that Hockey East's success in the Beanpot, with all the media attention it garnered, reflected well on the league. And if Hockey East could take a couple of wins from Harvard, which more often than not had strong teams, it would be good for the conference's computer ranking come NCAA tournament time.

Conversely, Harvard had difficulty getting the ECAC to adjust its schedule in a similar manner for many years. With the ECAC locked into weekend play with each school having a travel partner, it was logistically more of a challenge.

The women's Beanpot was played on the corresponding Tuesdays to the men's Mondays. These were held at the four campus rinks in a set rotation. Kathy Wynters and I served as independent administrators for the women's Beanpot while Steve Nazro of the Garden was the point person for the men's event. Efforts were made over the years (still are) to get the women's Beanpot final into the Garden, the prime target being to replace the men's consolation game.

There were other variables in putting the schedule together and they changed over the years. For a time, the city of Lowell had a winter festival in early January, causing UMass Lowell to request no home games in that period. Other schools wanted no home games in early January because students were not on campus.

A number of Hockey East schools played basketball games in the same building where hockey was played. Boston College had four teams playing in

Conte Forum: men's and women's hockey, and men's and women's basketball. When BC moved into the ACC, with televised basketball games a factor, scheduling got a little more complicated. Late in my tenure, both UMass and UConn submitted blackout dates when I couldn't schedule hockey games, those dates held for basketball. That situation was mitigated by the fact that UConn's women's hockey team played at a different facility and UMass did not have a women's hockey program.

Regarding that last observation, it always bothered me that UMass did not sponsor women's varsity ice hockey. Four of the New England state universities in Hockey East (Connecticut, Maine, New Hampshire and Vermont) have women's varsities, but Rhode Island and Massachusetts only have clubs. Every time a new AD was hired in Amherst, the first question I would ask on my initial visit was, "When will UMass have women's varsity ice hockey?"

As indicated above, the expectations for me to line up sponsors and market the conference were more clearly articulated in my early Hockey East years than they had been at the ECAC. To assist in this matter, Hockey East contracted Craigville Associates to assist us in procuring sponsorships. Craigville Associates was a small company founded by Dan Gavitt, son of former Providence College basketball coach and AD Dave Gavitt, the moving force behind the formation of the Big East.

The "Craigville" in Craigville Associates was a reference to Craigville Beach in Hyannis, where the elder Gavitt had a summer home. I knew this because Bill Cleary also had a home in the area and was a good friend of Dave Gavitt. Once, while working at the ECAC, I had to drive from the ECAC office, which was up the road from Craigville Beach, to Providence for a game, I asked Gavitt how long it would take me. He said, "It should take you a little over an hour and twenty minutes. Wait, you went to Harvard? Four hours."

I believe it was in that same conversation that Gavitt advised me that in promoting a league, you have to ride your best assets. He suggested I use Harvard in specific situations to promote the whole. When I told him I didn't want to be seen as favoring my alma mater, he chided me about thinking small.

Danny Gavitt, who would go on to become the NCAA senior vice-president for basketball, effectively running "March Madness," wasn't able to produce much for Hockey East. And that was through no fault of his own. His experience would be mirrored by countless other firms with whom we would partner.

In my two decades plus, we contracted with a half dozen firms that took over the responsibility of finding sponsors. All of them made impressive presentations before being hired — and all of them failed. In fairness to them, a single-sport conference, one where you don't have direct access to on-campus exposure, is a tough sell. Your primary asset is your tournament but, during my Hockey East years, many of the obvious targets were already TD Garden sponsors and thus had no need to give us any money.

More than a few times, we heard a prospective sponsor say, "You know, you have priced this well and we are very familiar with you. But we are already in the Garden so ... "

The other dynamic we found that was that most of these firms focused heavily on landing that one six-figure, league-wide or tournament sponsor, as opposed to pursuing many smaller partners. As I would say, they all are trying to hit home runs when a bunch of singles and doubles would be more attainable.

Sure enough, some of the better years we had came when the staff had responsibility for sponsorships and followed the singles and doubles approach. Kathy Wynters and I did this in those years between outside firms being brought in. And the best years of all came when we convinced the directors to bring in someone on staff to pursue accounts for us.

That happened in 2017 when Tim Flynn, a former BC hockey player and son of legendary BC athletic director Bill Flynn, joined the office staff. His efforts in my last year at Hockey East, 2019-20, brought in the most sponsor revenue we ever had and more than any of the other single-sport hockey conferences at that time.

This hire also provided us a staff member to deal with sponsor fulfill-ment, always a hidden drain on staff hours. And by being on staff, Tim gave us an extra body for other non-sponsor duties when the office was extremely busy.

At the time I started with Hockey East, the conference by-laws prohibited any advertising that included alcohol, tobacco products or gambling. There was also a prohibition on the use of professional athletes in any advertisements. This particular provision was challenged when an early sponsor of our women's championships, Pure Hockey, featured Boston Bruins star Ray Bourque. When the ad was allowed to stand, the provisions in the by-laws started to dissolve.

By my final years in the league, one of our major sponsors was North American Breweries and beer and wine were sold at many arenas. UMass Lowell had a beer ad on its dasher boards, and Providence College had a sponsorship with Mohegan Sun.

All of this reflects the growing need for schools and conferences to find new revenue sources. Schools were pouring money into aging facilities and, in some cases, not-so-aging facilities. The former was a real world necessity, the latter a nod toward ever-increasing pressure to keep up with the competition.

Fans can be forgiven if they retain fond memories of experiencing hockey at the likes of Tully Forum (Lowell), Snively Arena (UNH) or even early UMass games played at Amherst College's Orr Rink. (No, not named for Bobby.)

But in the new world, where recruited athletes were savvy consumers, the old barns couldn't do the job. And so along came the Tsongas Center, "The Whit" and the Mullins Center, not to mention major renovations to the likes of Northeastern's Matthews Arena, Merrimack's Volpe Center, PC's Schneider Arena and, as I write, Vermont's Gutterson Fieldhouse.

Rarely did I walk into the latest locker room renovation without thinking of my Harvard experience so many decades earlier. The modern Division I locker room is part work space, part sports museum. Athletes might enter through a changing room that leads into the actual locker room. The weight room is likely in close proximity and perhaps there is a mini-amphitheater where videos can be viewed and discussed.

There is usually some sort of players' lounge, perhaps designed for leisure or even as a study room. And then there is the program history, displayed through the latest computer graphics, showing the accomplishments of those who came before, particularly those who went on to the NHL or the Olympic Games.

In the early 1970s, we had loose benches in front of antique metal lockers inside the history-drenched Dillon Field House. The hockey team had to wait for the football team to vacate the room, and the baseball team had to wait for our season to end. And, whether for daily practice or on game nights, we had to take our bags and walk across a patch of lawn to the cinder block and bleachers of Watson Rink to don our skates in a tiny skate room.

I thought of Watson Rink the first time I watched a game at BU's Agganis Arena. I could get a glass of white wine and snack on some sweet potato fries while sitting in a soft movie theater-style seat. At Watson, you would be sitting on a hard bench, the only concession product being the hot chocolate served up by Danny Crane and his brother Kevin, two undergraduates from Cambridge, whose father had once been the city's mayor. Legend has it that the hot chocolate was made with hot water from the Zamboni bay, the powdered mix stirred with a broken Northland stick.

Those thoughts also cue the memory of how much the game night experience had changed over the years. We would hear the starting line-up through scratchy speakers, the Harvard Band providing the soundtrack for the evening. In fact, how quaint it now seems that we let the visiting school's band into the building most nights.

There was no Jumbotron providing a pump-up video of the home team or deafening music alternating with the home school band. There was no dimming of lights with a mascot carrying a huge school flag. The starting line-up was not introduced with individual players, their exaggerated "game faces" and raised sticks aimed at the camera. There were no videos of great goals just scored. Or video review. If a puck went in the net, it was a goal.

And there wasn't the incessant sponsor reads at every stoppage of play, or corporate logos on the video board or actual boards or imbedded into the ice itself. Corporate Hockey indeed.

I once paid a visit to Maine when Shawn Walsh was the coach. Before a game, he introduced me to the team and said, "Hey, guys, the Commissioner wants to say a few words. He isn't pleased with our talking so much to the officials."

That was true. But then he added, "You know guys, we are in the entertainment business and that's not a good look."

When I got home, I sent Shawn a note, praising the team he had and adding a comment on his remarks to the team. "I thought we were in the education business, not the entertainment business," I said. He responded with a note of his own. "Picky picky."

In one of my last years with Hockey East, I mentioned this to an athletic director. He said, "Don't kid yourself. We are in the entertainment business." I repeated this anecdote in a press briefing at the time it was announced that I was ending my time with Hockey East. When my comment went public, I drew some fire by telling that story. Some felt I was suggesting that our ADs didn't care about education. I never said that. I took the AD's remark to mean we are in both the education business AND the entertainment business. And that appears to be true. I just worry that in acknowledging such, decisions could be made that compromise our primary role.

For a single-sport hockey conference, revenue generation is a challenge. All conferences are heavily dependent on their championship tournaments, along with some sponsorship dollars, to attempt a balanced budget. But until money from streaming contracts appeared, outside revenue was limited and so schools were assessed dues, in one form or another.

During my 23 years at Hockey East, I took great pride in balancing the budget for much of that time, particularly since Hockey East was the last conference to assess member schools a dues charge and that didn't happen until 2018, the league's 34th season.

At the 2018 league meetings in Naples, FL, we had a crisis of sorts. It was getting more difficult to balance the budget and I expressed that it was time for schools to pay some sort of dues or at least pay for the on-ice officials. Hockey East was the only conference that paid officials directly from the conference treasury. The schools did agree to pay for officials in non-league games but balked at adding league game fees.

Around 2017, my specific message to the body was that a review of budgets from the previous decade indicated we were only able to comfortably balance the budget in years that we had a special event: Frozen Fenway in 2010, 2012, 2014 and 2017; the NCAA Frozen Four in 2015.

In most instances, these provided the extra income to balance the budget and prevent Hockey East schools from paying dues. They also provided broad exposure and, in the parlance of the day, promoted our brand.

I'd like to showcase three of these events that took place from 2010 to 2019, two being profitable and one setting a precedent in all of NCAA athletics.

Frozen Fenway

Outdoor hockey has become a big draw of late. Whether in a baseball park, a football stadium or on a frozen pond, players and fans are returning to their roots and enjoying the pleasures of hockey as it was in the beginning.

The NHL hit on something with its January 1 "Winter Classic," coupled with other outdoor events under various titles. However, let the record show that college hockey started this resurgence back in October 2001 when Michigan State hosted Michigan in the "Cold War," a 3-3 tie played before 74,544 spectators in Spartan Stadium.

When the NHL tabbed Fenway Park to host the 2010 Winter Classic, the Boston Bruins were slated to host the Philadelphia Flyers on New Year's Day 2010. The Red Sox were thrilled to play host for this game but thought the rink on that fabled baseball field could host so much more. And with COO Sam Kennedy, a former high school hockey player, taking the lead, the Sox made a pitch to the NHL.

Kennedy and the Red Sox brass convinced the NHL to keep the rink up for another week or so, negotiated the appropriate financial details and then set out to create a slate of events that would bring the extended New England hockey community to Fenway. In the process, Fenway Park, which had hosted college and professional football, political speeches and all sorts of other non-baseball events over the years, added amateur ice hockey to its credits.

Kennedy needed an event that could serve as the financial engine to this increased schedule of events. Those "events" would eventually allow high school hockey, Division III college hockey, USA Hockey, a public skating event for then-mayor Tom Menino and corporate rentals. But something had to generate revenue for the Red Sox to pay for the maintenance of the rink and generate an operating profit.

That is where Hockey East came in. The Red Sox pitched the concept to the directors and conference staff and then let us work out the details. Looking back, and without the benefit of seeing how successful this would be, the directors can be excused for being cautious and, in some cases, skeptical. There was concern about ice conditions, weather for the fans and, if this should turn out to be special, who gets to play in the game or games?

At that point, the Winter Classic had already become a big deal, and

Left: When New Hampshire coach Richie Umile retired, I wore a Melrose High School replica jersey in his honor. Right: I held the original women's Beanpot trophy when the event celebrated 40 years in 2018. With me, from left, Julie Starr and Alison Bell, Harvard's first varsity captain. (Photos courtesy of UNH and Harvard)

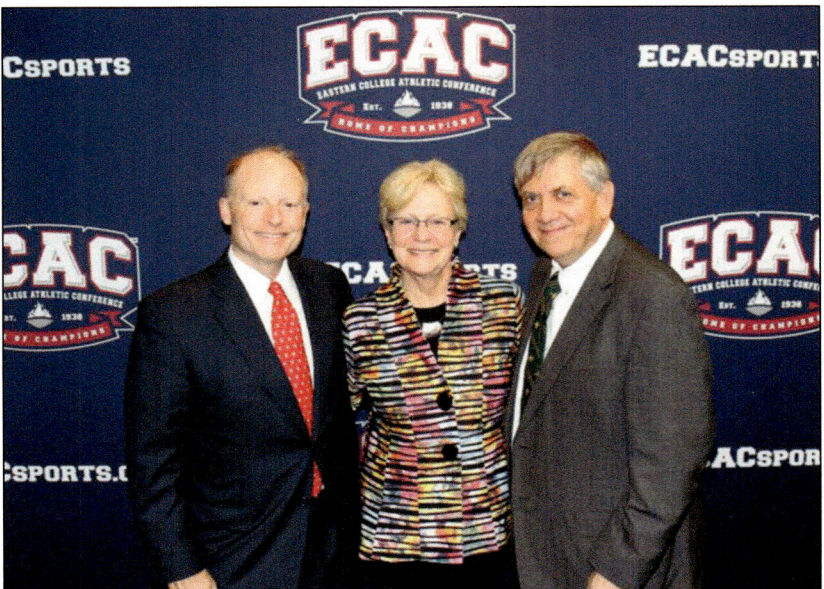

From the ECAC Hall of Fame induction in 2018, with two Harvard friends, Hobey Baker Award winner Mark Fusco and Harvard Associate AD Pat Henry. Mark and I were teammates on the Depot Cafe Bombers of Gloucester, MA. Pat and I worked in Harvard's athletic department together. (Photo courtesy of the ECAC)

In 1975 in Cortina d'Ampezzo, Italy, a clothing store had me pose along with my teammate Fabio Polloni. I think the mask with a mustache was the attraction. Three decades later, Fabio came over for a visit and we re-created the pose.

The beautiful Stadio Olimpico in Cortina a'Ampezzo was my home rink in 1974-75 and was the site of the 1956 Winter Olympics.

Perhaps my all-time summer camp staff (with apologies to John Binkoski, Andrew Huntoon, Garry Scott, et al): standing from left, Paul MacAuley, Bob Conceison, Bob Bartholomew, Rick Mills and Mo Randall. (John Giammatteo Photo)

The family poses at Frozen Fenway in January 2014. From left: Joey, me, Kathy, Grace and Bobb
(Photo courtesy of the Boston Red Sox)

e middle three stayed out on the ice for our regular Fenway hockey game.

My one team photo with the Budweiser Kings. Back row, from left: Wally Cox, Bobby Jackson, Rico Graham, John Monahan, Leif Rosenberger, Dennis King, Bobby Jefferson, Kerry Young, Chuck Lambert. Front row, from left: Tommy Colby, Tommy Mulvey, Bob Hayes, Tim Flynn, me, Bill Lamarche, Joey Flynn and Ken Muse.

The "Cardinal and Maize" of the Depot Cafe Bombers deserve a color page and here it is. Standing, from left: Ian Wood (in the back), Peter Fish, Jim Turner, Kirk Bransfield, Gene Kinasewich, John Gummere, Steve Scott, Tom "Red" Mechem, David Quinn, J.D. MacEachern, Jay Somers, Bob Carr and Ben Smith. Kneeling, from left: me, Stu Irving, Jay Valade, Tom Mutch, George Mechem, Mark Fusco and Ken Irving. (Elz Spofford Photo)

Little Known Goalies In History

Don Goalieone   Goalie Hawn   Ayahgoalie Khomeini

One feature of my half century of summer goalie camps was merchandise. Hats, tee shirts, coffee mugs. This original artwork was featured on mugs and shirts.

My daughter, Grace, became a goalie for her last two years in high school. This picture was taken at the MicroIce rink in North Andover, MA, where I got to work with Grace one summer.

This was the only Boston Bruins team photo I was in during my six full seasons with the team. This club lost to Edmonton in the 1988 Stanley Cup Finals. (Al Ruelle Photo courtesy of the Boston Bruins)

My infamous "ceremonial first pitch" in August 2013 at Fenway Park. (Photo courtesy of the Boston Red Sox)

with the Bruins committed to be there in 2010, with all the fanfare that would accompany their game, the directors eventually warmed to the idea. And so the focus was on who would play and what the financial structure would be.

Originally, Sam Kennedy had his heart set on Fenway hosting the Beanpot Tournament. I tried to convince Sam that this simply would not ever happen. The schools, let alone the Garden, would never agree to this. But Sam and the Red Sox didn't get to where they were by thinking small, and this notion would surface in scheduling talks over the next several years.

I believe it was Jack Parker, serving as both a coach and a BU administrator, who captured the moment. Jack made the case that for there to be other events down the line, the first one had to be a success. And the best way to guarantee a success would be to put your best product forward. And that would be Boston College vs. Boston University.

Not surprisingly, there was some pushback, particularly from those who felt that the Boston schools, with their Beanpot and everything else, received too much preferential treatment already. But, in the end, it was hard to argue against Jack's logic. That match-up was the marquee event in Hockey East and, if there was any doubt, it was blown away when all 38,000+ tickets for the game sold out in a matter of hours in the late summer of 2009.

As noted earlier in this book, I have been a passionate Sox fan, one whose first summer job was selling hot dogs and the like at Fenway Park back in the late 1960s. I was thrilled to be part of this and looked forward to diving into the details. And it was a treat to find the Red Sox staff so easy to work with, particularly Fred Olsen, our primary liaison. Here are some of my recollections from the first four Frozen Fenway events.

2010

• By the time the first Frozen Fenway was announced, we had added a women's game, UNH vs. Northeastern, that would precede the BC-BU game. The women would play at 4:00 and the men would face-off at 8:00. Since the ballpark only had two locker rooms, the batting cages were outfitted to be team rooms and the umpires room became the referees room. The women waited until the men took the ice for warm-ups and then went into the respective locker rooms for their postgame shower. The league bought them terry cloth bathrobes for the short walk to the showers.
• Because of concerns about the long walks over dirty mats from locker rooms to the ice surface, skate guards were purchased for all players.
• Access to suites, and the heat provided therein, became valuable. Individual ticket prices ranged from $5 down low to $75 up high. There was an inverse value from baseball season. Low seats at field level were great for baseball,

Top: Before BC met BU on Saturday in Frozen Fenway '10, a group of us enjoyed a Friday night skate. Brother Bob in the foreground and niece Michelle, my wife Kathy, me and nephew Michael. Below: The pregame festivities included BC and BU captains and three former members of the Red Sox who played high school hockey in Massachusetts. In the white jerseys, from left, Richie Hebner (Norwood), John Tudor (Peabody) and Bill Monbouquette (Medford). (Photos courtesy of the Boston Red Sox)

but since the boards and glass were constructed on a slightly raised surface, low seats did not allow much of a view for hockey.

• We had hoped to cash in on merchandise, but we struggled to get an event logo that would capture the features of Fenway we could market. Major League Baseball did not allow variations of standard MLB marks, so we could not use the Red Sox font or the bricks or the "Monster Green" associated with the Red Sox. In particular, I wanted to use the "Hanging Sox" logo with skate blades affixed to them. While the latter would eventually be approved years later, we were only able to put them on a limited number of game jerseys that were given to Hockey East and Red Sox staff.

• Many of those commemorative jerseys were on display on the night before our college games. As part of our agreement with the Red Sox, Hockey East would get to host a skating party for its staff, school personnel and sponsors the night before the games. In addition, the commissioner received an hour of ice for a pick-up game that included 40 of my closest friends, former teammates, family and peers. It became a staple of each Frozen Fenway opening weekend. Two memories from these Friday night skates: While dressing in the Red Sox locker room, David Ortiz walked in. "Hi, I'm David," he announced. The second memory was less upbeat. With a few minutes left in our first game, Jeff Mead, a former Arlington High School and UMass Boston player, took a slapshot and broke the ankle of Stu Irving, my good friend and 1972 Olympian.

• The Red Sox had a sharp event coordinator in Sarah McKenna with whom we worked on some of the pregame ceremonies. My recollection is that we clashed at first but then worked together for a pretty special pregame. Brian Leetch and Mike Eruzione served as honorary captains for BC and BU, respectively, each wearing their school game jersey as they skated on the ice. I arranged to have three famous athletes who had connections to both the Red Sox and hockey take part in the ceremonies. They were Bill Monbouquette, an All-Star Sox pitcher who had played high school hockey in Medford; John Tudor, a former Sox pitcher who won 20+ games (for St. Louis) and who played hockey at Peabody High School; and Richie Hebner, a phenomenal high school hockey player at Norwood High who was a hitting coach for the Sox after a long playing career, most notably with Pittsburgh.

• I had Monbo in my suite, sitting with my father-in-law, Bob Leonard. They had played against each other in high school, and I was able to find an old newspaper cartoon that featured both of them in a recap of a Greater Boston League Saturday. The cartoon was featured in the game program. I became friends with Bill, my favorite Red Sox player from the 1960s, when I met him at a women's Beanpot game at Harvard. I was walking my mother to our car after the game when this guy I did not recognize said hello to me. He identified himself and told me that he always got tickets to the men's Beanpot from Bill Cleary before he went off to spring training as a pitching coach. On Bill's recommendation, he was attending his first wom-

Clockwise from upper left: David Ortiz visits me in the Red Sox clubhouse; My sister Carol met Wally during that same event; Jack Parker and Jerry York before the 2010 BU vs. BC game; Cardinal Sean O'Malley shakes hands with Boston College captain Patrick Brown in 2014 as Sam Kennedy and I look on. The schedule had four Catholic schools playing so I extended the invitation to Cardinal O'Malley to drop the puck. (Photos courtesy of the Boston Red Sox)

en's hockey game. When he and his wife Josephine moved from Medford to Gloucester, we became good friends, his home just two streets from mine.
• A light snow fell throughout the men's game, providing great photo opportunities. It had a marginal effect on the game itself and actually added to the experience. BU defeated BC, 3-2, the Terriers going up 3-0 and BC clawing back, the Eagles' second goal scored shorthanded by future NHL star Cam Atkinson. Disappointed that day, BC would win the NCAA title that year. With attendance announced at 38,472 and thousands more watching on NESN and the NHL Network, Hockey East enjoyed tremendous exposure from Frozen Fenway I.

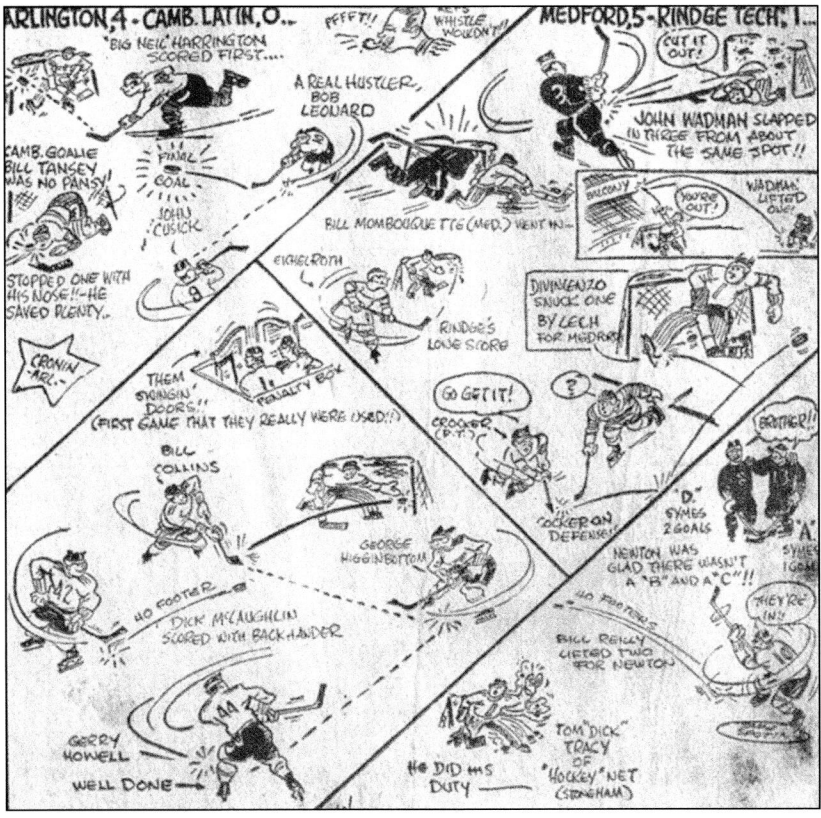

This cartoon from the sports pages of a Boston paper in the late 1950s was featured in the first Frozen Fenway program. It references future Red Sox ace Bill Monbouquette in the Medford-Rindge Tech section and my father-in-law, Bob Leonard, in the Arlington-Cambridge Latin summary.

2012

• With BC and BU the benefactors of the Year One schedule, we tried a different tack in 2012. We convinced the Red Sox to go with a men's doubleheader featuring four state universities. This allowed us to bring the second-biggest rivalry in the conference, UNH vs. Maine, to Fenway, with UMass and Vermont in the other game. This, too, sold out but took a little longer to do so.

• Once again, we took part in a press event at Fenway in August, this one coming on one of the hottest days of the summer. I remember this because the poor guy in the Maine mascot uniform collapsed during a photo shoot. I also remember very well how Sam Kennedy handed me a baseball around 1:00 in the afternoon. "What's this for?" I asked. "Oh, didn't I tell you? You are throwing out the first pitch tonight," he replied. I was reminded of this when I watched Dr. Anthony Fauci bounce a pregame pitch during the summer of 2020. When the good doctor's errant toss went well up the first base line, I said to my daughter, Grace, "Ha! He was even worse than me." Being the sympathetic child she is, she responded, "Dad, he's 78 years old." On that August day in 2011, a number of Hockey East coaches and captains had assembled for that press launch I had not thrown a baseball in many years and immediately went into a cold sweat. I knew what was likely ahead of me. Even before I did my "crow hop" and delivered the pitch, the likes of UNH coach Dick Umile, UVM coach Kevin Sneddon, Maine coach Tim Whitehead and UMass coach Donald "Toot" Cahoon had already started laughing. You can see them laughing in the photo that appears in this book's centerspread. What is not visible here is that pre-Photoshop, the image on the Jumbotron said, "Joe Bertanga," until my PR assistant, Pete Souris, edited it. When nine people in a row say, "Don't bounce it," what do you think is going to happen? Dan Wheeler, the Sox player who caught my throw on the short hop, brought me the ball and said, "Well, I bet if it was a puck you might have reached me." It's all fun now. But that day? I was never so nervous in my life.

• The 2012 schedule also included a men's game between Boston College and Northeastern on the second Saturday and a women's game midweek between Providence and Dartmouth.

2014

• The desire to keep changing things up continued in 2014 when we decided to do a pair of doubleheaders on consecutive January Saturdays. Two things happened here that started to challenge the universal support of these outdoor events. First of all, it was more difficult to sell tickets, and instead of the sellouts of 2010 and 2012, we had 31,569 on one weekend and 25,580 the second. And this time, the weather did not cooperate.

• The doubleheader played on January 4 featured Merrimack and Providence in the opener and BC and new Hockey East member Notre Dame in the nightcap. A snowstorm earlier in the week threatened to keep the Irish from getting to Boston. They ended up finding a charter and made it in time while Fenway staff was shoveling out the old ballpark. Unlike a football stadium, whose staff might have a reliable plan for such weather, Fenway was not used to clearing snow. Notre Dame also had difficulty getting out of Boston and extended its stay at the Sonesta Hotel. All of this combined to spike up our expenses, threatening to wipe out any profit we had planned to make. It was in this context that Sam Kennedy got all parties on the phone and proposed that the unbudgeted expenses be shared among all parties. Contractually, a case could have been made that it was all Hockey East's responsibility. But Kennedy's solution bailed us out. I mentioned this later to Red Sox president Larry Lucchino. "Sam looks for solutions," said Lucchino. "That's what he does." I always used this example when someone asked what a true "partner" does.

• Some observations about Notre Dame. The courtship of Notre Dame came when the old CCHA split up in 2013, some schools going to the new Big Ten hockey league, some to the new NCHC and some to the re-designed WCHA. Hockey East actually courted both Notre Dame and Miami, thinking that bringing in two schools with familiarity might work out well. Miami went to the NCHC and Notre Dame came to us. Given that Notre Dame left after four seasons, and that we picked up UConn, it was probably better that Miami had gone to the NCHC. Miami without Notre Dame would not have made much sense. The Irish gave us everything we had hoped for, winning games, qualifying twice for the NCAAs, and providing an attendance boost on some campuses when they came to town. Jeff Jackson, a coaching icon, added to our already-deep roster of great coaches. But the Irish also brought some negatives. When they qualified for the Garden, they sold barely a ticket, the reputation of their traveling football fans not inherited by their hockey brethren. During that 2014 Frozen Fenway experience, the school refused to produce merchandise with the official logos, marks that would bring royalties to Hockey East. Instead, they created their own logo, using "Frozen Boston" instead of the approved marks. That way, they could keep all the revenue. In the end, their move to the Big Ten was not totally unexpected. They were always the outsider, having to travel more than the other schools, not being readily visible in any historic listings of past champions or past all-stars, etc. With the Big Ten, they would be with other large universities and all teams would travel equally, providing more of an even playing field.

• The second weekend was without snow. But not without rain. Lots of rain. Northeastern played UMass Lowell in the first game and we got the game completed before the heavens opened up. Actually, we started the BU-Maine game with the hope of squeezing that in, too. I recall sitting in the visiting dugout with Red Sox staffers and a laptop, watching images of impending downpours on radar, planning ways to cut out time. Shorten the intermission. Reduce timeouts. Anything. It was a mess, and certainly when lightening struck, no conditions in which to be playing hockey. Maine would defeat BU, 7-3, and I can recall how well BU coach David Quinn took it all.

2017

• We broke from our every-other-year pattern by staging Frozen Fenway IV three years later. The primary reason was that the Bruins were again part of the Winter Classic in 2016 but this time hosting Montreal in Foxboro. Out of respect for the Krafts, the Red Sox opted not to host their own outside hockey in the same period. We also thought, given the slowdown in ticket sales for our event, adding another year in between events might be a good idea.

• We again scheduled two doubleheaders, the participants being BU-UMass and BC-PC the first weekend (moved to Sunday due to weather) and UConn-Maine and UNH-NU the following Saturday. In between, the Boston College women played Harvard on a rainy midweek night. With UConn's appearance in the event, all 12 Hockey East schools had played at least one game at Fenway Park.

• Attendance continued its downward trend. On the first weekend, we drew 19,547 and on the second 16,432. While a far cry from the 38,000+ of the first two years, these numbers still represented the biggest crowds to watch college hockey that year apart from the NCAA Frozen Four.

• Concern about ticket sales and playing for league points on potentially bad ice started to be voiced. Some of these latter games were actually non-league games played between league foes. There were some schools that seemed less interested in keeping the event alive than others. Still, we drew up plans for a fifth event, but it never happened during my remaining years at Hockey East. The Red Sox started hosting football in the fall and that, coupled with off-season construction at the ballpark, put off our plans. Covid-19 also intervened. The Sox, having taken ownership of the actual rink, still spoke of hosting hockey. But it would take some time. At the time of this writing, I was suggesting that outdoor hockey could come to Polar Park, the new minor league ballpark in Worcester. I'm ready to suggest a schedule and I might even ask if I can throw out a first pitch there.

The NCAA Frozen Four

The first NHL building to host the NCAA Division I Men's Championships (not yet called "The Frozen Four") was the Boston Garden, which made that history in 1972. Actually, that began a three-year run as the Garden was host in 1973 and 1974 as well.

During my Hockey East tenure, Boston hosted memorable Frozen Fours in 1998 (Michigan nipping BC, 3-2 in OT), 2004 (Denver outlasting Maine, 1-0) and 2015 (Providence shocking BU, 4-3). Boston University served as the host institution in the first two of those and Hockey East in 2015. There were also other attempts to bid and host that were denied.

Serving as the host facility came with staffing responsibilities but also a six-figure stipend that made it worth the extra effort. The staff worked closely with the NCAA and the Garden staff, the latter being our partners with our own conference championship, so there was a comfort level that made this enjoyable. Collectively, we felt we knew how to run a championship, though the Frozen Four was not completely analogous to our event.

As the Frozen Four locked in on NHL venues, the experience inside the arena had become quite scripted and universal. And so a host tried to make the experience outside the building unique and, toward that end, tried to make the city the star.

Traffic and congestion aside, Boston has so much to offer its hockey guests. I always felt that the Frozen Four should be played in Boston and St. Paul in every three- or four-year cycle. Try other places but always come back to these hockey hotbeds. Part of my position is that when the event is in Boston or St. Paul, thousands of regular fans, if they can get tickets, can drive to the games, avoiding the need for plane tickets or hotels. Reward the diehards who are in college hockey arenas every weekend all season.

As hosts, we tried to showcase Boston. The team reception the night before the semifinals was held at Fenway Park, with veteran broadcaster Sean McDonough as emcee and Travis Roy as speaker. (McDonough had broadcast Hockey East games on NESN early in his career.) The dinner for the NCAA and extended organizing committee was held at Ray Bourque's restaurant in the North End. Chosen to drop the puck for the final were legendary Boston coaches Len Ceglarski, Bill Cleary and Jack Parker.

The Hockey East staff, particularly Kathy Wynters, did a phenomenal job meeting all of our responsibilities, and we were rewarded in the best possible way when two of our teams, BU and Providence, met in the championship game.

Knowing your league would have the national champion before the puck drops makes for a very enjoyable night. The only uncomfortable moment, for some of us, came when PC's Tom Parisi flipped a long, high shot toward Terriers goalie Matt O'Connor with just under nine minutes remaining and BU ahead, 3-2. The 18,000 or so fans watched in a combination of amazement and horror as O'Connor caught the puck momentarily, dropped it between his skates and then inadvertently directed it into the goal. Few were shocked that the Friars turned this to their advantage, Brandon Tanev scoring the game-winner with 6:17 left in regulation for PC's first NCAA crown. When it was all over, no one was happier than Kathy Wynters, Providence College Class of 1982.

Friendship in Belfast

Robert Fitzpatrick's vision of ice hockey in Belfast drew plenty of skepticism. The Boston College-educated Fitzpatrick is the CEO of the Odyssey Trust in Belfast, Northern Ireland, and he was the driving force that brought NCAA hockey to his city.

Among the holdings of the Odyssey Trust are the Belfast Giants and the arena in which they play. The Giants are somewhat of a phenomenon in Belfast, a city many know for either: a) the Catholic-Protestant "Troubles" or; b) the port from which the Titanic was built and launched.

In this city of historic strife, the Giants represent hope and friendship. It is not by coincidence that the fans enter the arena clad in the neutral teal colors of the Giants and not the partisan colors of the once-warring factions.

For hockey to grow beyond the Giants in Northern Ireland, the Giants need to succeed and the Odyssey needs a second rink. That is a simplification, but it explains some of the motivation behind Fitzpatrick's moves to develop a U.S. college hockey event in Belfast.

Five years before the puck dropped for college hockey at the Odyssey Arena, Fitzpatrick landed an even bigger catch. The Boston Bruins, en route to a preseason exhibition in the Czech Republic, stopped in Belfast to play the Giants. This was Part I of "they said it couldn't be done." The Giants even scored the first goal in what was eventually a 5-1 Bruins win on October 10, 2010. And it started a quest for college hockey.

Both Northeastern University and UMass Lowell had relationships with schools in and around Belfast. A conversation with them was the natural starting point and serious talks about the two schools playing each other began in 2011, the prime participants being Peter Roby and Dana Skinner, ADs at Northeastern and UMass Lowell, respectively. But it wasn't until a meeting at the Parkman House in Boston on October 9, 2014, that the notion of a four-school tournament began to take shape.

Boston and Belfast had a "sister city" relationship and the idea for a college hockey tournament abroad was, from the start, more than just a sporting event in a new venue. The vision was a bringing together of these great cities and their people in a business, athletics and friendship undertaking. Thus the meeting at the city-owned Parkman House, located within a wrist shot of the State House. Attendees at that 2014 meeting included representatives of local schools, local government, the Odyssey Trust and a few movers and shakers who could bridge the interests of all.

Fitzpatrick envisioned a tournament bringing schools from both Hockey East and ECAC Hockey, and so I was invited along with my ECAC counterpart Steve Hagwell. Because of the city-to-city relationship, it was hoped that at least one Boston school would participate annually. It is important to note the word "annually," as from the start, this was not presented as a "one off."

From that first meeting, Fitzpatrick made it clear that he wasn't looking for exhibition games. He pressed us to commit to providing "meaningful games," competition that would show NCAA hockey at its best. It fell to Steve and me to work our schools and get them on board to play league games on the first night of the event and then guaranteed crossover competition in the consolation and final games. These would be the first actual NCAA games, not exhibitions, played abroad.

What might have been more of a logistical challenge was mitigated by the presence of two former Boston University (and Giants) hockey players who worked with Fitzpatrick. Shane Johnson and Steve Thornton were members of BU's 1995 NCAA championship team who, after stellar careers with the Giants, moved into administrative roles.

If I recall correctly, it took some convincing in the first two years to get teams to commit to playing these meaningful games some 3,000 miles away from campus in the middle of the season. But that is indeed what we were able to announce on Friday, April 10, 2015, a group of us standing beside the Bobby Orr statue on Causeway Street in the shadow of TD Garden. It wasn't just the statue that was the draw. We chose the date and site because the 2015 NCAA Frozen Four was on its off day in Boston, and we wanted to take advantage of the media who would likely be in the vicinity.

The field for what we called "The Friendship Four" was Northeastern and UMass Lowell from Hockey East and Brown and Colgate from ECAC Hockey. The conference rivals would meet on Friday, November 27, with the crossover games on Saturday. The dates, Thanksgiving weekend, were chosen for a couple of strategic reasons. Thanksgiving break allowed for the teams to spend a full week in Belfast, mitigating jet lag and allowing the athletes to see the city and interact with its people, most notably children, through school visits. That Thanksgiving weekend was traditionally set aside for inter-league play was also a plus.

Some recollections on Friendship I:
• We were able to secure television coverage with nominal financial help from the schools and conferences, NESN providing most of the exposure.
• Our hosts covered all school expenses, which would remain the case for the first few years. Eventually, schools covered plane tickets but the event hosts still absorbed all other costs.
• As would be the case going forward, each game was a separate admission, with hundreds of screaming school children making up the bulk of the after-

noon crowds and a healthy turnout of paying customers for the nightcap.
• Thursday being American Thanksgiving, all of us in support roles looked
for a special way to celebrate and found the perfect venue on the second
floor of McHugh's Pub. The self-proclaimed "Oldest pub in Belfast" and
not the only one to make the claim, McHugh's was perfect. Former UNH
All-American Ralph Cox, who was serving to bring together various support groups behind the scenes, had arranged for us to take over that second
floor, approved a set menu and even found local musicians to entertain. Ralph
would come to be known as "The Ambassador." I vowed then that if all went
according to plan, I would never eat Thanksgiving dinner at home again.
• The results: On Friday, Lowell nipped NU, 3-2 in overtime, and Brown
blanked Colgate, 5-0. Colgate's troubles continued on Saturday when the
Huskies enjoyed a 7-1 romp in the consolation game before Brown and the
Riverhawks engaged in a wild 5-5 OT affair eventually won by Lowell in a
shootout.
• The winning team received a unique prize, an old school bell, presented
by Robert Fitzpatrick to UML captain Adam Chapie. Momentarily at a loss

**The first Friendship Four tournament was announced on the off day of the 2015
NCAA Frozen Four in Boston, just outside TD Garden. (Photo courtesy of the Odyssey
Trust)**

Top: Boston Mayor Marty Walsh (far right) presented many of us with hats when he visited Belfast in 2019. The others, from left, are Steve Hagwell, me, Robert Fitzpatrick, Ralph Cox and Eric Porter. (Photo courtesy of the Odyssey Trust)
Bottom: After some encouragement from Fitzpatrick, victorious UMass Lowell captain Adam Chapie rings "The Bell" for the arena crowd. (William Cherry photo courtesy of the Odyssey Trust)

upon being handed the bell, Fitzpatrick barked, "Ring it!," leading Chapie to circle the ice with his teammates, ringing the bell in triumph. Thus, a new college hockey tradition was born.

• The only sour note came after we returned home. When UMass Lowell lost its first two post-Belfast games to UConn, Riverhawks coach Norm Bazin suggested in the media that the trip to Belfast might have had something to do with the defeats. Knowing we still had the task of convincing others to commit to Friendship II and beyond, this was tough to read. Conversely, Northeastern coach Jim Madigan had nothing but praise for the experience. The Huskies, after the Friday loss, had a record of 1-11-2. Starting with the win over Colgate, NU went 21-2-3, culminating with a 3-2 win over, wait for it, Lowell, in the Hockey East Championship. Madigan credited the Belfast experience with bringing his team together.

Over the next four years, the Friendship Four welcomed Boston University, Clarkson, Colgate (again), Connecticut, Maine, Massachusetts, New Hampshire, Northeastern (again), Princeton, Providence, Quinnipiac, RPI, St. Lawrence, Union, Vermont and Yale.

In addition, women's hockey was added in 2019 with a pair of games between Clarkson and Northeastern, followed a year later by two games between Merrimack and Quinnipiac. These games were billed as "The Friendship Series." In all, 19 different institutions sent teams to Belfast in five years to enjoy the competition and the incomparable friendship of the hosts and their city.

The sixth iteration of "The Friendship Four" fell victim to Covid-19. It was to include teams from Atlantic Hockey for the first time. As college hockey, and the rest of the world, emerges from the shadow of the virus, plans are still alive for a continuation of this event in the fall of 2022.

NESN's dropping of Hockey East in 1997 turned out to be a short-term problem. After a two-year hiatus, NESN and Hockey East re-connected and the partnership remains as strong as ever as I write. I should say, however, it went through some rocky times.

When Hockey East returned to NESN in the 1999-2000 season, the job of negotiating an agreement fell to me. On one hand, we had a great product that fit perfectly into NESN's Bruins-heavy winter schedule. On the other hand, we didn't have a lot of leverage. NESN was where we wanted to be and there weren't a lot of other suitors knocking on our door.

And so we took what we could get, and my inexperience in this area showed in the early agreements. Maybe I am being hard on myself here, but in retrospect, we had terms in those agreements that were not in our best interests.

Where it might have been myself and a single NESN executive negotiating early deals, it quickly became a team of Hockey East negotiators sitting in on later talks. Hockey East created a Television Committee comprised of administrators with experience and knowledge of a changing landscape. We brought in media consultants, like Tag Garson of Wasserman Media Group and Dan Gale from Leona Media Group. And our attorney, Maura Sheehan, played an increasingly important role in bringing things to a favorable conclusion. In fact, Maura became involved with any number of thorny contractual matters over the last half of my time at Hockey East.

Broadcast issues became more complex and, for the most part, more favorable to Hockey East. Two converging developments changed everything over my final two years with the conference. First, schools started to upgrade their own production capabilities on campus to produce improved streaming of all their games. Second, the demand for content among new streaming services made our product all the more valuable.

The game-changer came when schools started to produce broadcast-quality games so that the days of backing up "the truck" next to the rink and spending $25,000 a game were over. NESN and CBS Sports Network, for example, could just take the games directly from the schools and bring a quality product into homes across the country. And other entities competed for these rights.

In my final year with Hockey East, the conference negotiated the most lucrative media deals in conference history. I state that as a fact but not to take credit. Most of the credit goes to my then assistant, Brian Smith, and a team of administrators and consultant Dan Gale who put the NESN and CBS deals together.

There were other benefits to the schools upgrading their technology. The quality of video coming from the schools had uses beyond streaming on game night. Highlight clips shown on school and league web sites, and through social media, enhanced the ability to tell our stories and put the spotlight on our athletes. It also improved our ability to discipline athletes, and others, when their behavior crossed a line.

Each NCAA hockey conference has the ability to issue some form of "Supplemental Discipline." The intent of such policies is to address situations that occur on the ice that aren't adequately covered by the rule book. So, yes, the book provides for a five-minute major and a game disqualification for any number of dangerous actions. These include, but aren't limited to, fighting, spearing, butt-ending and the like.

But in a time when there is a renewed focus on concussions and head injuries, a conference (and the NCAA) might wish to send a message to players and coaches, and to fans, that contact to the head is particularly dangerous, and when such action takes place in an egregious manner, the conference may go beyond the five minutes and disqualify (DQ) or suspend a player for an additional game or games.

Each conference does some variation of the same. Maybe it is the commissioner doles this out. Maybe it is the supervisor of officials to whom this falls. Or maybe there is a committee. Invariably, whoever has this responsibility looks at video, consults with peers and then issues the discipline.

When I was with the ECAC, we were the last conference to institute a formal protocol for such a process. And that came when the NCAA applied some pressure to the ECAC to join the others in this area. I recall some resistance from administrators who suggested schools would get together and simply "do the right thing" if players misbehaved. All these years later, it seems like such a quaint throwback to older times.

In Hockey East, men's player-on-player discipline fell to the supervisor of officials; when the behavior in question was that of a coach or referee or other non-uniformed party, I got involved. In fact, that was the men's policy. For women's hockey, it was all me. But, I should add, these things were rarely done solo. There was always consultation.

Over the years, the discipline could range from a warning or mild reprimand to the rare multi-game suspension. More often than not, a single game was the penalty of choice. Sometimes, this was the result of that egregious hit described above. Sometimes it was because no call had been made on the ice and this was righting a wrong.

There were other factors. The right call might have been made on the ice, but perhaps it happened with seconds left in a game. What justice comes from a major and game misconduct if the perpetrator only served a few seconds? Maybe the player had been warned earlier in the year and this was a second example of dangerous play.

As noted, the upgraded video capabilities improved the quality of available video. I can recall the days when a coach would call on a Saturday morning and I would drive to meet him on the side of a highway so he could hand me a VHS tape. Then I would have to find a machine and a TV to view the situation.

Jump ahead a few years and I might be dining with my wife on a Saturday night and get a text while the game was still in progress, and there, on my phone, was a state-of-the-art video clip for me to review in real time.

Some situations were pretty clear cut, others not so. I suppose on the spectrum of discipline providers, I was maybe in the middle. I didn't second guess myself often, but there were a few of those cases. I recall one from a women's game when a Vermont player and a Northeastern player were down on the ice, their legs entangled. There was some kicking and eventually the players were free of each other. I studied the video for a long time and came down on the side of no discipline, as both players were trying to get free.

The following week I found myself at Matthews Arena and ran into NU women's coach Dave Flint, someone for whom I have great respect and, I believe, the feeling is mutual.

Dave asked me if I had a second and showed me a photo of the bruise his player received from the last kick. He respectfully offered his opinion that I "missed" on this one. Looking back, I think he was correct.

When players were issued suspensions, the league office would issue a brief public statement. At one time, these were longer and included a quote from me. With time, we reduced the statements to a simple acknowledgment that player X would miss the next game due to an incident that happened in game Y and that he or she would next be eligible to play on date Z.

Some administrators and coaches opposed our making any public statement, asking what purpose that served. It was always my position that these actions happened in public, and it was in the conference's interest to be public in showing that we care about such incidents and that there is accountability for the player.

Coaches were also subject to supplemental discipline. These situations were always a little more sensitive than dealing with players as I had to interact with these coaches on a regular basis and knew many of them as longtime friends.

In my experience, there was a small handful of coaches you had to deal with in any given year, but those two or three guys could drain you emotionally. It often led to the false sense that "the coaches" were a problem. More often than not, it was a fairly small subset of coaches, with the majority being perfectly fine.

Often, the troublesome coaches fell into one of the following categories: a) a coach in the last year of his contract; b) a coach who felt he had a special team, one that had real championship potential; or 3) a coach who was a perfectionist (most were) who just couldn't deal with a certain on-ice official or perhaps a certain opponent.

More often than not, the supervisor of officials would be on the receiving end of calls or texts or emails, usually with video attached. The source of a coach rising to "irritant" stage may not have been one big incident but rather the never-ending string of complaints and calls and texts, the latter coming at all hours of the day and night.

I would get involved when the coach's behavior spilled into the public on game night, and I felt some punishment was due. My late mother used to ask me how I could take action against coaches who were friends of mine. It wasn't anything I enjoyed. You hoped the coaches would understand that it was part of the job and not personal.

One example of how well this can turn out is my relationship with Northeastern University men's head coach Jim Madigan. Jim had an emotional streak that he would be the first to acknowledge. I believe I suspended him twice, and after the second time, his athletic director, Peter Roby, called a meeting for Jim and myself to attend in the AD's office.

It was a good hashing out of things, and I don't think I ever had another issue with Jim. And more than that, I think I might have enjoyed the best relationship of any of the Hockey East coaches in my closing years with Jimmy. In my first year away from the league, it was Jim Madigan who went out of his way to stay in touch and see how I was doing more than any other Hockey East coach.*

While most of the coaching incidents occur during the game, there is the occasional example of bad behavior after the game, particularly at the postgame press conference. These press briefings are a routine part of the game. Sometimes, in the regular season, the media might have to find the coaches outside their respective locker rooms. But with the improvements at most rinks, and always in the postseason, the media are brought to a dedicated press area and the host SID or conference officer runs a professional press conference.

Some coaches stand out as always being gracious at these events. I always thought Jerry York was the best. He always began by giving credit to his opponent, whether in victory or defeat. Joe Marsh, who enjoyed a phenomenally successful career at St. Lawrence, had the ability to be gracious, candid and uniquely funny. In defeat, he would often take personal responsibility for the loss. And in tournament settings, when players might join the coach on stage, I never saw players so eager to praise their coach than when it was Joe and a few of his stalwarts up there.

But, alas, not everyone handled the moment so well. I can almost excuse the coach who is up there after a tough tournament loss that ended the season, and, in the case of seniors, their careers. But, I have to say "almost." You are a professional. It is part of your job. Step up and handle the challenge as expected.

I had one unique postgame situation that I found interesting. It happened in one of my later years at Hockey East and involved UMass coach Greg Carvel. I went back a long way with Greg. A Canton, NY, native, Greg was an outstanding player at St. Lawrence from 1989-93. A finalist for a Rhodes Scholarship, Carvel applied for the ECAC intern program, the one that I had enjoyed in 1976. (He led UMass to the 2021 NCAA title while I was working on this book.)

By 1993, the ECAC intern program had expanded to multiple interns, all working the entire academic year. At the time, I was ECAC Hockey Commissioner and lobbying for an assistant. The lobbying was not successful. So when I saw Carvel applying to be an intern, I switched my lobbying efforts to his candidacy. That, too, failed.

Jim was named Director of Athletics at Northeastern in June of 2021 and his long-time assistant, Jerry Keefe, became the Huskies' new head coach.

Three of my good friends from Hockey East were together in Naples, FL, in April 2021 when the hockey community got together to say goodbye to the Naples Beach Hotel and Golf Club. From left: Hockey East sales director Tim Flynn, Northeastern University head men's coach Jim Madigan and former Providence College women's head coach Bob Deraney (named head men's coach at Worcester State in 2021). (Jennifer Ziegelmaier Photo)

As to my discipline story, I was driving on a Saturday morning when my assistant, Brian Smith, called to tell me that Carvy had been critical of the referees the night before. When I asked what he said, Brian responded, "You can hear the whole thing. I'll send you the MP3 file." Technology certainly changed over the years.

What I heard wasn't particularly egregious but still worthy of a call to Greg. Upon taking my call, he said, "Go ahead and suspend me if you have to." I explained that I didn't want to suspend him or any coaches, but I needed to warn him that he couldn't continue to do that.

Then he said, "By the way, do I have to go to these press conferences? Is that required?"

After I confirmed that, yes, it was part of his duties as a coach, I asked him why he didn't see this as an opportunity rather than an obligation. He explained that he didn't trust himself to always say the right things.

Now this was a bright guy, an experienced guy who had spent time as an NHL assistant coach. I suggested that he look for positive things to say. He had a free opening with the media to talk about whatever he wanted. Talk about your special teams. Talk about your freshmen. Praise the third line forward who played a tight checking game. Just stay away from commenting on officials. Bob Johnson could lose a game, 8-1, and spend 20 minutes describing the great goal his team scored.

Early in my Hockey East tenure, I had to deal with a number of situations involving Boston University coach Jack Parker. I had known Jack for a long time in a variety of roles. My first recollection of Jack was when he played at BU when I was just starting high school. In our street hockey games, we all took on the names of college hockey players, usually Beanpot stars like Jack.

He had also been the assistant coach at Medford High School, one of my rivals when I was at Arlington High School. I was the goalie when our coach, Ed Burns, first lost to the same team twice in one season. That team was Jack's Medford Mustangs, and we lost 2-1 and 1-0.

But I later learned that I had something else in common with Jack. When my grandfather, Joe Marchetti, passed away in 1973, Jack showed up at the wake. I was surprised at the time because I wasn't really that close to Jack. When I commented to my mother about this, she explained the real reason he was there.

When my mother was 18, she was chosen to dance with the famed Radio City Music Hall Rockettes in New York. This was in 1936. Being so young, she wasn't allowed to move to New York on her own so her mother, my grandmother, went with her.

Back in Somerville, my grandfather and my aunt decided to move in with another family, that being Jack Parker's mother's family. And so Jack was attending Joe Marchetti's wake on behalf of his mother and her family. Like I said, I knew many of the coaches well and that could make handing out discipline a challenge.

So what led to my suspending Jack in February 2000? It was my third year with Hockey East, and Jack had developed a reputation for challenging on-ice officials in one manner or another. In that season, there were three incidents involving Jack and officials, no single one of which would likely have led to any discipline on its own. But combined? I decided I should do something.

The first incident came at a December tournament at Minnesota Duluth when I heard from WCHA Commissioner Bruce McLeod. Bruce told me that Jack's language toward a WCHA official was pretty harsh and inappropriate. I recall speaking with Jack and believe part of the conversation focused on one of the officials being a Minnesota-Duluth alumnus working Bulldogs' games. Our policy at the time was to not assign officials to work when their alma maters played.

The second incident involved Jack putting his hand on referee Jim Villandry's jersey in an effort to get his attention. Jack insisted he was just trying to speak to him and the contact was simply to get his attention as he skated away.

The third situation took place on a February Friday night in Providence, a snowy night that caused the Terriers to arrive later than usual at Schneider Arena. Having made that trip on Fridays since then, I know how long it can take even without bad weather.

Jack was having issues with one of the referees that night, Scott Hansen I believe. And in protest to the issue at hand, Jack kept his team in the locker room between periods, delaying its entry to the ice for the start of the next period. Knowing the rules, as Jack certainly did, he brought his team out just before he would have had to suffer a forfeit.

Sitting at home in Gloucester, I was getting reports from Providence by phone and decided that this was enough. Three incidents, all showing some level of lack of respect to officials, in my mind. And so I made a decision to suspend him for his next game, which was the following night at home against the same Friars. Jack and I spoke later that Friday night and he tried to convince me to change my mind. I told him that he could appeal to the three-person Executive Committee of administrators. He said he preferred to appeal to me. But I did not change my mind.

As it turned out, I was hired to work the televised broadcast of Saturday night's BU-PC game at Walter Brown Arena. Working alongside play-by-play announcer Bob Kurtz, who had called Red Sox games on NESN, I took my position at center ice, something I had done often at BU, usually when Mike Eruzione wasn't available. In that role, I had the pleasure of working with the likes of Don Orsillo and Dave Goucher.

What developed that night seems somewhat comical now but wasn't at the time. At some point in the game, we were made aware that Jack was sitting in the press box at the end of the rink to our right. And he appeared to be talking, by phone, to BU assistant coach Mike Bavis, who was on the Terriers bench.

Bob Kurtz, and the guys in the truck, thought this was hilarious. They put up a split screen of Jack in the press box, phone in hand, and Bavis with his headset on the bench. And Kurtz started to direct his remarks, on air, to me. "Well Mr. Commissioner, what do you have to say about this?" And he went on for some time.

I can remember watching the local news on Sunday night and I believe it was Ed Harding at WCVB, Channel 5, who had all kinds of fun with this story. I wasn't laughing and arranged to get a copy of that night's broadcast to share with the Executive Committee. The ADs took me out of the mix, knowing I would have to deal with Jack on other issues, and they decided to suspend him on the grounds that he hadn't actually served his initial suspension by being in the rink and communicating with his staff.

Jack took the position that nobody had explained to him what he could and couldn't do, and over the years, I have found this to be the defense of others in this situation. It actually happened within a month of my writing this in the junior hockey league in which I now work. And so we had to put down in writing, in very specific language, what it means to be suspended from a game.

Jack and I survived that incident and went through other rocky moments before our respective tenures at Hockey East were completed. I want to believe there was always respect for each other. I know that I badly mishandled another situation when Jack refused to shake hands with an official before a Beanpot game. I made a big deal out of it and authored a number of over-the-top emails that I shared with far too many people. In the process, I took an issue that had some level of legitimacy and turned it into a referendum on my judgment. It was not one of my my better moments.

When Jack retired, I went to the press conference. Approaching him after the formalities were done, I told him I came for two reasons. The first was out of respect for his career. The second was because I wanted to make sure he didn't change his mind. (I later wrote a tribute on Jack for the American Hockey Coaches Association newsletter which I have re-printed toward the end of this book.)

One note about Jack's sense of humor. When Jack's mother died, I went to the wake and offered my condolences. As I began to walk away, he called me back. "Joe," he said. "I need to talk to you about a ref." I was stunned. Then I realized he was joking. "Thanks for coming," he added.

When I reminded him of this recently, he said, "The best part was when (BU radio announcer) Bernie Corbett came to the wake. After he said how sorry he was, I said to him, 'Bernie, I feel sorry for you. You just lost half your audience.'"

Of all the discipline-related situations I had to address, two stand out among all others. They were serious and more challenging than the rest.

When the 2002-03 Hockey East regular season came to an end, Boston College was tied for first with New Hampshire but, having failed to beat the Wildcats during the year, lost the tie-breaker and so the Eagles were the #2 seed for the tournament.

That meant BC would be hosting seventh-seeded Merrimack. The Eagles took two out of three from Merrimack during the year, and when all the games were played out, Boston College would be winners of twice as many games as Merrimack (24 for BC, 12 for MC).

Weeks earlier, the two teams had played a regular-season game in which one of Merrimack's best players, Marco Rosa, had been injured. Rosa took a hard hit from Boston College defenseman Andrew Alberts that knocked him out. As he fell to the ice, he broke his wrist and was lost for the season.

At 6´ 5´´, Alberts was a solid, physical defenseman who would go on to play in the NHL. While some on the Merrimack side thought it was a dirty hit, those on the BC side pointed out that it is difficult for someone with Alberts' height to completely avoid head contact when lining up a shorter player for a clean hit. Alberts was not a dirty player.

Regardless of your position on that play, it certainly provided a tense background for the quarterfinal match-up between the two programs. Also factoring into the equation was the David and Goliath feel to MC vs. BC. Merrimack, a small (then) NCAA Division II school in suburban North Andover, MA, often felt disrespected and was now going up against the biggest and arguably most successful school in the conference.

Well aware of this background, I assigned myself to the MC-BC series as site director because I was afraid something might happen. For most of the opening game, my fears were unfounded as the game was without incident, BC leading 2-0 with just over six minutes remaining in the third period.

Then, as BC killed off the end of a penalty, there was a loose puck flipped toward the Merrimack end. Warriors goalie Joe Exter decided to race out to beat BC forward Patrick Eaves to the puck, Eaves coming with pretty good speed. They arrived at the puck at the same time, Exter going low, Eaves seemingly trying to vault over Exter.

When I saw the play live, my first reaction was that Exter was the aggressor and that he took Eaves out by going low. What happened is that as they collided, Exter's helmet was knocked off and as he went down, his head hit the ice hard. He started convulsing and the sight of his distress set off a reaction on the already fragile Merrimack squad.

Merrimack players swarmed on Eaves and fights broke out all over the ice. Eaves, among others, had to defend himself and engaged in the fisticuffs while referee Jeff Bunyon and his crew tried to control the situation. It was everything I had feared when I put myself on that game.

Exter was taken off the ice in a stretcher, was put in an induced coma for over a week, but made a full recovery. As I write, he is an assistant coach at Michigan State and just completed his term on the Board of Governors of the American Hockey Coaches Association. Eaves went on to a long NHL career after BC.

Eaves was heavily penalized that night but not, as was commonly reported, because Hockey East took action against him. Under NCAA rules, a game disqualification means you sit the next game. On your second DQ, you miss two games. On your third, three games and so forth. He had received a DQ for spearing in the fall and was given two for what happened in that Merrimack game. The first was for the collision with Exter and the second for the ensuing fight. Since these were DQ's #2 and #3, he received, by the NCAA rule book, five games.

The following memories remain vivid all these years later:

• As conference commissioner, I worked for both BC and MC and had to be sensitive to what was happening on both campuses. The two teams had to return for Game #2 the next night, so I made sure to visit each school early on Saturday to speak to both teams about the importance of keeping their emotions in check.

• Game #2 was uneventful, thankfully. BC won 2-1, the game staying close long enough to keep both teams focused on playing hockey.

• Then there was the week between quarterfinals and the championships at the Garden. Boston College was concerned about the effect on Patrick Eaves and how he would be perceived if Exter did not recover from his ordeal. At that time, the NCAA rule book still used the term "intent to in-jure" and if Eaves was saddled with that term and Exter died, how would he be perceived? BC began an effort to vindicate, or at least protect, Eaves.

• Having lost Marco Rosa earlier and now seeing their goalie go down, emotions were particularly raw at Merrimack and they bristled at any talk of diluting the penalty to Eaves. They suggested that any attempt to make Eaves a priority while their goalie lay in a coma would be an insult to the Merrimack community and another example of BC having its way.

• When the tournament banquet took place the following Thursday night at the Royal Sonesta hotel, I noticed that Eddie Swift was there, sitting at the BC table. Swift, a former Princeton goalie of my vintage, was writing for *Sports Illustrated* at the time. The magazine assigned Swift to this story and the piece he would author was titled, "Two Victims." It was welcomed at BC, a national story that portrayed Eaves as a victim alongside the injured Exter.

• As the article explained, Boston College and the Eaves family took issue with the calls made on the ice. Specifically, they wanted the officials and the conference to acknowledge that a mistake was made in the initial major called on Patrick Eaves. Suggesting as much, Swift wrote, "The referee, Jeff Bunyon, was 100 feet and two zones away, but he raised his arm to signal a penalty."

• With this as background, I can recall how my work week went following the incident. First, I consulted with lawyers to understand any liability the conference could face. Next, I summoned the on-ice officials to my office. I wanted to understand their thought process in making the calls they did. A referee often has choices as to what can be called in a given situation. There is a matter of matching the right call to the offense committed. But there is also, in the midst of injury and multiple altercations, the matter of game management. There can be legitimate debate over the first major, which was initially called roughing and then changed, before the sheet was signed, to charging. Complicating the situation was the presence of a replacement scorekeeper at ice level that led to the game sheet having errors. This was

unintentional but an element of sloppiness. I never considered criticizing the officials. They made a judgment call under duress. I was interested, however, in taking some burden off of Patrick Eaves. I asked if the second DQ, for fighting, could have been a roughing. They responded that Eaves and his opponent were trading punches and that refs had always been advised to call "fighting" when it was that obvious. Then I asked all three officials if they thought Eaves had intended to injure Exter. When all three said, "No," I decided to issue a press release on our findings, emphasizing up front that we found no reason to believe that Patrick Eaves meant to injure Joe Exter.
• When both Boston College and Merrimack expressed displeasure with my statement, I figured we had gotten it right. BC didn't think it went far enough. Merrimack didn't understand why we would be so moved to give BC and Eaves this attention.

Like the Eaves-Exter ordeal, the second situation remains vivid in my memory. It was, perhaps, the single most upsetting of my 23 years with Hockey East. For a number of reasons, I can only discuss it in broad strokes.

This situation also occurred in a playoff game and involved a racist slur directed from one player to another during a break in play. A linesman caught the tail end of what was said, but because it happened when one player skated through a group of three or four opponents, he could not confirm who the speaker was.

During my final years with Hockey East, and in my first year out of college hockey, volunteering in Massachusetts Hockey discipline hearings, I came across numerous examples of players — and coaches — using inappropriate language during competition. In most cases, the person using the language would acknowledge, after the fact, that they were wrong and would be sincerely remorseful. On the rare occasion, the perpetrator would try to suggest it was just "trash talk."

The NCAA Men's and Women's Ice Hockey Rules Book has a very specific penalty that can be issued for offensive language. In the case at hand, no call was made on the ice. And so, I had to investigate but was unable, with certainty, to identify the speaker, the school in question also unable to determine who uttered the remarks.

When we made a public statement, acknowledging that such an incident had occurred, we stopped short of identifying the offending party and, thus, did not issue any discipline. The statement said that without confirmation from eyewitnesses as to who was responsible for the remark, we did not feel we could suspend or otherwise punish anyone.

It was not a popular decision in many circles. I even had to hear it from my own family, who thought I should have taken punitive action. They reminded me that the player on the receiving end of the language had identified the player. Still, with that player denying it and the linesman (and institution) unable to confirm, I chose not to go forward with supplemental discipline.

A few weeks later, I was attending the NCAA Frozen Four in Buffalo and while walking the concourse, a gentleman wearing a hockey jersey stopped me and asked if he could speak with me. Seeing that his jersey was that of the school that endured the offensive language, I knew what was coming and agreed to chat.

He mentioned that he worked at a small private school in the Boston area where they take respect for diversity quite seriously. And then he expressed his disappointment with the way I handled that situation. I told him that I understood why he felt that way, gave him my summary of what happened but offered little defense. His school's hockey community had every reason to be upset. And I was starting to second guess my actions.

It wasn't unusual for fans to approach me at games and I frequently enjoyed it. I have always considered myself a fan and this interaction came with the job, even if it wasn't always flattering.

More often than not, these encounters are lighthearted. I was scheduled to be in Orono for a Friday night game in February 2010 where, between periods, I would present former Hockey East commissioner Stu Haskell the prestigious Hockey East Founders Medal. As luck would have it, I had suspended Maine's talented forward Joey Diamond just days before my trip to Orono.

When I was announced, the Alfond Arena crowd responded with a chorus of boos. I made the presentation and walked back up the aisle to my seat. At the top of the aisle, there was an oldtimer in a satin Maine baseball jacket and when I said to him, "Well, that went well. No gunfire," he responded, "Not yet."

Regarding the suspension of Joey Diamond (whom I got to know later on and enjoyed the relationship): Many years after the suspension, my son, Bobby, was in a bar in New York and was asked to show identification. The bartender looked at his license and asked, "Are you related to the commissioner?" When Bobby said that he was, the bartender said, "He suspended my brother once, Joey Diamond." They both had a laugh over it and before the night ended, my son received a free shot.

A year or so after that unresolved on-ice language incident, an old friend took me to lunch at his summer club. The news that Hockey East would not be offering me a new contract had just broken and I think the lunch offer was a friendly response to the news. As we walked to our cars after lunch, he turned to me and said, "Hey, I've been meaning to ask you something. Do you think how you handled that discipline situation might have had something to do with your contract not being extended?"

The question came out of the blue, but I couldn't blame him for asking.

And my short answer was, "I don't know."

With the attention given here to some uncomfortable memories, I don't want to leave the impression that I did not enjoy my Hockey East experience. In fact, most of the 23 years were highly satisfying, thrilling and maybe not fully appreciated at the time. I have fond memories of the people and the venues, savoring the routine of the overall experience as much as any given season, game or moment.

Trips to BC meant running into any number of alumni, friends and fans on the concourse. That included former Red Sox manager Joe Morgan who, upon meeting me, launched into a critique of Hockey East referees. BC also meant spending time with Tom Burke, Tom Peters and John Hegarty, three of my favorites in the league. And the men's and women's coaches were always respectful to me. Sometimes the visit was for a day-night doubleheader, with the women at 2:00 and the men at 7:00. Having the much- coveted "Conte Loop" parking pass was special, my car being parked within 10 paces of the arena entrance.

Trips to BU were split between Walter Brown Arena and Agganis. I loved the former, primarily because it was the only rink where I didn't lose to BU as a player, tying once and winning once in the arena's first two years of existence. Agganis had the best pregame meal and it also meant I would likely get on BU radio with Bernie Corbett, another cherished memory. For women's games, I could see my fellow goaltender Brian Durocher, the BU coach.

Like BU, trips to UConn meant two different buildings, Freitas Ice Forum on campus for the women and the Civic Center in Hartford for the men. These trips allowed me to see two of my favorite coaches, Chris MacKenzie and Mike Cavanaugh.

The Maine trip was usually scheduled for October, so I could get ahead of the worst of the weather. I loved walking around Alfond, checking the history, which included a photo of my friend Jim Tortorella in his goalie gear as an undergraduate. Catching up with the late Red Gendron was always time well spent. Same with seeing trainer Paul Culina and journalist Larry Mahoney.

I remember searching out Nonni Daly, former associate commissioner of Hockey East, in my early years. In letters, she referred to me as "Garlic" and herself as "Gaelic." Later, as Facebook friends, we reveled in our shared politics. I recall bringing a Pat's Pizza back for Tom Caulfield, our Sonesta Hotel contact and a former manager of the Maine hockey team.

Trips to Burlington, VT, and Amherst, MA, took on special meaning when son Bobby and daughter, Grace, attended UVM and UMass, respectively. The Vermont trips were especially memorable as I had so many close friends living in or near Burlington. There was my old boss at Harvard, Dave Matthews, who lived in Stowe. My fellow Arlington goalie, Garry Scott, had an exemplary career with the Vermont state police. Whether with him or Bruce Bosley or Dave Smallwood, we would dine before the game at Al's French Frys or after the game at the Upper Deck Pub at the Best Western. Maybe there would even be an appearance by former UVM coach Mike Gilligan.

For a couple of years, I joined the Thursday night skate at The Gut, playing with, for the most part, younger UVM alumni. The organizer was a contemporary of mine, Willie MacKinnon, a former Catamount star I first knew as a Dedham High School hockey player and against whom I played in 1973. A picture of me getting beat 30 seconds into that game hung on the Gutterson Fieldhouse wall for years.

I have to mention another memory from that game. We won, 8-4, and going through the handshake line, the UVM goalie said, "Well, it wasn't much of a night for goalies." To which I responded, "Speak for yourself. You're the one who let in eight!"

I also recall a memorable summer weekend when I took my sons to Burlington to participate in the Travis Roy Wiffle Ball Tournament. The event has raised significant funds for the Travis Roy Foundation. The year I attended, I got to play on the same squad as former Red Sox pitcher Bill Lee.

Fittingly, when I embarked on a brief "Farewell Tour" during my last year in Hockey East, UVM was one of the first stops and probably the most heartfelt of them all. Most of the people mentioned above were on hand and the event was catered by Al's.

The Tsongas Center at UMass Lowell was a great place to watch a game. I'd run into AD Dana Skinner, former coach Bill Riley and my former assistant Pete Souris. I'd do in an interview with Jimmy Connelly, say hi to broadcaster Bob Ellis and eat far too many of the tiny brownies that were dusted with powdered sugar.

You learned early that driving to Providence was easier on a Saturday than Friday, unless you went down early on Friday and scheduled a dinner on Federal Hill. More often than not, I'd opt for the simplicity of grabbing something at LaSalle Bakery, just down the street from Schneider Arena.

I also looked forward to seeing former Boston Bruins goaltender Ross Brooks when he ran Schneider Arena. Brooksie once told me a story about him being a back-up for Rochester in the AHL, when the coach told him to go into game that the Amerks were losing, 6-1, after two periods.

He started to skate toward the crease when he stopped, skated back to the bench and asked the coach, "Just curious. Do you want me to win it or just get a tie?" After a shared laugh, I asked, "So how did you do?" "Lost, 8-1," he said with a grin.

Scenes from "The Gut." Top: I get beat 30 seconds into the 1973 Harvard at UVM game, while teammates Kevin Hampe (left) and Mark Noonan look on. This photo graced the walls of Gutterson Fieldhouse for many years. Bottom: Nearly a half century later, I return on my Hockey East "Farewell Tour" and receive a nice UVM game jersey from Vermont head coach Kevin Sneddon, former coach Mike Gilligan and athletic director Jeff Schulman. (Photos courtesy of UVM)

Northeastern was a favorite trip, partly because of my history playing in the wonderful Matthews Arena, partly because my niece, Michelle DiStefano Collett, was an All-ECAC goalie for the Huskies, partly because of my fondness for coaches Dave Flint and Jim Madigan, and all of it in spite of the parking being the most challenging in the league.

Toward the end of my run, I found that I enjoyed trips to Merrimack and UNH more than the rest. The drives were not taxing, parking wasn't a problem and I had a comfort level with most all of the school personnel. I could also couple visits to my brother near UNH and my sister near Merrimack in the process. There were also years where I had a special relationship with one or more of the coaches at those schools — Merrimack's Mark Dennehy and UNH's Dick Umile come to mind.

The people make the experience. Throughout the book, I have tried to acknowledge all that Kathy Wynters did for the conference, and for me (see more below). My PR staffers were also special, starting with Ed Saunders and then on to Noah Smith, Brion O'Connor, the inimitable Pete Souris and finally Brian Smith. And I can't forget their cohort, Dan Parkhurst, who did a superlative job with the Hockey East website.

I'd also like to give a shoutout to the supervisors with whom I worked: Brendan Sheehy, Dick DeCaprio, Dan Schachte and, briefly, Brian Murphy on the men's side, and Bobby Quinn, John Gallagher and Dave Lezenski on the women's side. All of these guys did a superb and wildly underappreciated job. I can say the same for many of the on-ice officials I got to know. One of my biggest disappointments was the cancellation of the 2020 men's championships when Hockey East Founders Medals were set to be presented to Dick DeCaprio, Kathy Wynters and on-ice officials Tim Benedetto and John Gravallese.

Let me also acknowledge some of the regulars who brought Hockey East games into homes via television or radio. Of course, Tom Caron was a favorite on NESN. So versatile, always prepared and pleasant to hear. Tim Neverett did some TV for a while. Messrs. McDonough and Norton were already acknowledged.

The campus radio guys were a big part of the culture. I looked forward to the between-periods interviews from the likes of Bernie Corbett (BU), Dan Hannigan and Larry Mahoney (Maine), Brock Hines and Donnie Moorhouse (UMass), Bob Ellis and Jim Connelly (UMass Lowell), Mike Machnik and John Leahy (Merrimack), Pete Webster and Dan Parkhurst (UNH), Rob Rudnick (Northeastern) and Mike Logan (Providence). Apologies to any I missed.

I would be remiss if I didn't single out my experience with Women's Hockey East. Of all the constituencies, the women's coaches were probably the most supportive of me over the years, and I like to think that was mutu-

While at Hockey East, I advocated for women's participation in our special events, like Frozen Fenway and the Belfast Friendship Series. Top: At Frozen Fenway '10, I drop the puck between Colleen Coyne (left) and Shelley Looney before the UNH vs. NU game. Below: I present the Player of the Game award to Merrimack's Courtney Maud when the Warriors played two games against Quinnipiac in January 2019 in Belfast. (Photos courtesy of Hockey East, top, and William Cherry/ Odyssey Trust, below.)

al. The fact that many of them were goalies (Bob Deraney, Brian Durocher, Dave Flint, Erin Hamlen and Matt Kelly to name a few) probably helped.

I sincerely promoted the interests of the women's programs, whether in advocating for the very existence of the league, pushing to include them at Fenway or in Belfast or simply trying to treat them the way the men were treated whenever possible. One of my proudest projects was suggesting that a student-athlete be given the opportunity to design a perpetual women's regular-season champion trophy. Two students from Merrimack's team, Jess Bonfe and Madison Morey, answered the call and got academic credit for their inspired design.

In promoting women's hockey, I certainly had help with the Hockey East staff, none more important than Kathy Wynters. It was Kathy who did most of the heavy lifting with all of our special events, for men and women, but there may have been a little extra with her efforts overseeing the Women's Beanpot Tournament and the Women's Hockey East Championship.

These events moved from campus to campus, and for one four-year stretch, we ran the tournament out of a town-owned rink in Hyannis. Kathy did it all, right down to the flowers on the tables and signage in the locker rooms. Her ability to multi-task was legendary. And I was often the beneficiary, as the commissioner would get credit for things that she actually did. (I believe most people knew who really did the work.)

It was at her urging that the directors named the women's championship trophy after me. I wish I had the time and presence of mind to push to name the regular-season trophy after her. Maybe there is still time.

There are the memories of great Hockey East players. Brian Gionta, Jason Krog, John Muse, Connor Hellebuyck, Johnny Gaudreau, Jack Eichel, Cale Makar, Marie-Philip Poulin, Alex Carpenter, Alina Mueller, Aerin Frankel, Jen Huggon, Katie Burt, Megan Keller, Kendall Coyne and so many others. I won't forget watching them perform, limited by the commissioner's inability to clap and cheer them. Unless it was in non-league play.

Finally, I miss the routine of the year. Every year. Starting the day after Labor Day, when the slow pace of summer gives way with a jolt. You return to a work week that is full and are immediately under some pressure, a month of meetings ahead and women's games just three or four weeks away.

There are referee meetings where rules are reviewed. Coaches meetings, often noted for how little men's coaches wish to speak. AD meetings, the September meeting being the first of three and, arguably, the least consequential.

Then the local hockey community assembles for Media Day at the Garden. It is a quick and fun get-together with few speeches, a nice meal and, for many years, a chance to sit with Steve Nazro and Jack Grinold, two of my mentors.

Then six months of games begin and the weekends unfold like I

Clockwise from upper left: I present the Bertagna Trophy (Women's Hockey East championship trophy) to Boston University players Marie-Philip Poulin, Kayla Tutino and Shannon Doyle along with coach Brian Durocher. This photo was taken at the Hyannis Youth and Community Center where BU won four straight titles; the Women's Hockey East Regular-Season Trophy, designed by two members of the Merrimack College women's team; My final puck drop was appropriately performed with Kathy Wynters at our final co-directed tournament, the 2020 Women's Hockey East Championships hosted by Merrimack. The centers: Paige Capistran of Northeastern and Catherine Crawley of UConn. (Photos courtesy of Hockey East)

previously described, with my goal to see 60+ games annually. And then came "Tournament Time." We used to tell intern candidates, who we would interview in the spring, that they should be prepared to work an extreme amount of hours in mid-March. The two tournaments swallowed us all up but when they were over, we took great pride in what we accomplished. I always thought that the athletic directors had little idea how much work so few people churned out in the month of March each year. It really was impressive, the amount of detail we all went into to deliver the best banquet, the best program, the best awards, the best hospitality, the best atmosphere and, in short, the best tournament experience for the schools.

For me, it was a personal thing. My family moved into the Sonesta Hotel for the weekend, a practice uninterrupted until the kids went off to college. The only photo I own of my mother with Grace was taken in my suite at the Sonesta in March 2001, six weeks before my mother died. Grace was five months old.

The Thursday night awards banquet started the weekend. Arriving at the Garden two hours before Friday's first semifinal, I had people to see and protocols to launch. If I had done my job, I could relax once the puck was dropped, knowing we had put all the needed people and procedures in motion. The games, of course, provided the best memories.

For Friday, you really wanted a clean and quick first game. Alas, we

College hockey has always been the beneficiary of fair media coverage. Two of the best guys to cover our game have been John "Jocko" Connolly (left) of the *Boston Herald* and the late Bob Monahan of the *Boston Globe*.

had a couple of triple overtimes on my watch, causing the second semifinal to start late. You hoped that your #1 seed advanced, though there were also years when you focused on getting more teams into the NCAAs.

On Saturday, you looked for a close, one-goal, well-played final. And as the scores from other conferences came in, you started asking the "experts" among the media, often Jimmy Connelly, what the final Pairwise Rankings would be. For many years, you also spoke with my two favorite scribes, Bob Monahan from *The Boston Globe* and Jocko Connolly from *The Boston Herald*, in the Garden media room.

As the championship game wound down, there was a little drama that played out many years. Everyone involved with the postgame awards ceremony assembled in the media room. A member of the Lamoriello family, usually Timmy, would arrive to present the championship trophy named after his father, Lou. Then Tim Flynn would show up to present the MVP Award named after his father, Bill.

We named the All-Tournament Team after Steve Nazro in one of my final seasons, but Steve would be in the room anyway, along with volunteers Bruce Bosley, Bob Olivari and Joel Weisblatt, and, often, the Herald's Jocko Connolly. We watched the game on TV, the NESN broadcast a few seconds delayed. The time left on the game clock was displayed next to the TV and this created tense moments when it was a one-goal game.

More than once, the trailing team had pulled its goalie, was pressuring its opponent in the offensive zone, and we would see the game clock stop. We couldn't hear any crowd noise, so there would be seconds before we knew what caused the whistle: goalie tying up the puck or trailing team tying up the game?

The 2000 final was one of the more memorable. The triumvirate of Bertagna, Flynn and Lamoriello was walking down the corridor to present Maine the trophy when we heard the crowd erupt. BC had scored with 40 seconds to go, tying the game at 1-1. As we walked back to the Media Room, expecting an overtime, Maine's Niko Dimitrakos scored with three seconds left to give Maine a 2-1 win and a championship.

The postgame events also brought some of the lighter moments of the weekend. In one of my final appearances, I was standing on the ice waiting for Northeastern's Jeremy Davies to come and receive his All-Tournament Team award. After some delay, teammates called for him to join me. When he arrived at center ice, he looked at me and, in all seriousness, said, "Hi. So, ah, what's this about?"

UMass Lowell goaltender Connor Hellebuyck, a future Vezina Trophy winner with Winnipeg, recorded three shutouts in his four Garden games. When asked how it was that he got these shutouts at the Garden, Hellebuyck responded, "Well, that's where we played the games."

Another specific post-tournament memory involved Shawn Walsh. Shawn would routinely call the office on the Monday after his team participated in the tournament to offer his thoughts on how to make the event better. He might have an idea on overtimes or who plays in which semifinal game. But they could be very obscure suggestions as well.

One year he called to talk about where the schools' fans were placed in the Garden. "Joe, I understand why the tickets are behind our benches, but I think it would be great if they were placed on the other side of the ice, so when our teams come out of the locker room, all pumped to play, that they can look up and see our fans rising to greet them as they take the ice." Yes, he thought of everything.

Finally, when I think of the Garden and all those tournaments, I think mostly about Steve Nazro, one of my mentors and a great friend. He, along with Sam Kennedy of the Red Sox, showed what true partners do. Yes, there are contracts to be followed in many of our business relationships. But partners want both sides to succeed, and they don't let contractual language get in the way of looking for solutions to problems. Sam and Steve understood that.

Here I present an All-Tournament Team award to a future NHL star, this time to UMass Lowell goaltender Connor Hellebuyck. Hellebuyck, who would win a Vezina Trophy with Winnipeg, had three shutouts in four Garden games. (Steve Babineau Photo courtesy of Hockey East)

In September 2016, the Hockey East directors announced that I had been given a three-year contract extension that would take me through the 2019-20 season. It was the ninth contract I had signed with Hockey East since joining the conference in July 1997.

In February 2019, I decided to reach out to the Hockey East Executive Committee to start a discussion on my future. We still had more than four months before they had to notify me of their plans and it seemed like a good time to raise the issue.

While I was aware they could decide it was time for a change, I thought I might get one last agreement, even if only for a year. When I called, I mentioned my desire to stay on and to start a conversation on how long I might stay.

To my surprise, I was informed that the directors had already decided that my current contract was the last and I would not be offered an extension. I was not prepared for that and asked if they could tell me why. I never did find out exactly why things came to an end when they did, and, as is often the case in such matters, I assume there were a variety of reasons.

The TD Garden brought together these three Arlington-bred athletic administrators. I was part of Garden events that unfolded in each of six decades on Causeway Street. In the middle, Tom Peters, who spent 26 years at Boston College but worked at Boston Garden before entering college athletics. And at right is Steve Nazro, VP of Events at the Garden for many years and a good friend to so many of us who made our way through the Boston sports scene. (Photo courtesy of Boston College)

Back in 2005, about a third of the way into my 23-year tenure, the directors commissioned a strategic plan carried out by a New York University professor named Bob Boland. I can remember his presentation at the AD meetings in Naples, FL, when he gave his findings from interviews with scores of Hockey East staff. He said, "The best thing about Joe Bertagna is that he is a hockey guy." Then, after pausing for effect, he added, "And the worst thing about Joe Bertagna is that he is a hockey guy."

What I took away from this is that people in the league saw value in my being their commissioner when hockey-specific issues dominated a given week or month. But, at the same time, Hockey East was a business and, increasingly, there was the business of hockey that had to be addressed. And so, as far back as 2005, some people were thinking that maybe a "hockey guy" isn't the best person to be dealing with issues like marketing, branding, sponsorships, new media, etc. Issues that would overtake the hockey issues facing the conference.

I also think the relationship between myself and a growing number of directors had become strained. I could place blame for this on both sides, but now, with some distance from our parting, I need to own this. I say this because, if for no other reason, they were my employers and I was the employee.

When the end came, my relationship with a number of the directors was not particularly positive. I had issues with some of the people to whom I answered, and when these issues surfaced, I made little effort to hide my feelings. I grew less deferential to my bosses and it probably showed. When I thought they crossed a line, I was quick to confront them and let them know how I felt.

And perhaps there was another factor affecting my relationship with individual administrators. I saw myself working for this single entity, Hockey East, and I was always trying to identify what was in the best interest of that entity and the group of schools as a whole. Somewhere along the way, I stopped seeing myself as working for each of the individual schools that made up the conference. And this made it easier for me to confront individual administrators or coaches if I thought they weren't acting in the best interests of the conference as a whole. It wouldn't surprise me if I learned that those administrators and, to a lesser degree, the coaches, got tired of the confrontations.

When Hockey East was in the middle of its search for a new commissioner, I thought they would hire either a marketing type or, more likely, one of their own, someone less likely to be so frequently confrontational. When they hired veteran UNH associate director Steve Metcalf, a solid, experienced and popular administrator, my thoughts were confirmed.

Chapter Seven —
Alphabet Soup: AHCA, HCA and NCAA

"The National Collegiate Athletic Association (NCAA) is a U.S. based organization whose primary purpose is to govern and integrate sports within institutions of learning in a balanced manner that the sportsmen and women get an opportunity to excel in both."
— NCAA Mission Statement

Early on in this writing process, I realized that I couldn't deliver a strict chronological account of my time in amateur hockey. Too many jobs overlapped at any given point in time. So I decided to devote one chapter to those national organizations for whom, or with whom, I worked while simultaneously employed by one college hockey conference or another. There were three of these, though USA Hockey, primarily referenced elsewhere, has also been part of my professional life.

American Hockey Coaches Association (AHCA): Formed in 1947, the AHCA was founded to bring coaches together to discuss issues of the day, share best practices and, through a series of awards, recognize individuals who made unique contributions to the sport. The AHCA has served as a conduit between coaches and the NCAA, most directly through an annual convention held each spring in Florida. The awards ranged from those honoring career accomplishments to annual Coach of the Year and All-American recognition.

Hockey Commissioners Association (HCA): Originally formed to promote the common interests of Division I men's hockey in 2005, a counterpart for women's hockey was formed a decade later. The conference commissioners would meet in person a handful of times each year, more so by conference call, to identify ways to advance Division I hockey, while working closely with coaches and, when appropriate, with the NCAA to identify potential sport-specific legislation.

National Collegiate Athletic Association (NCAA): The common administrative body for intercollegiate athletics, the NCAA impacts college hockey in three primary areas: national championship tournaments, on-ice playing rules and legislation that addresses overall by-laws, either Association-wide or sport-specific. When referring to "the NCAA," one might be referencing the national office in Indianapolis, the staff who are assigned to ice hockey or the culture writ large that often seems to be at odds with the singular interests of the hockey community. Let me establish right up front that I had nothing but respect and admiration for the many staff liaisons who worked with hockey over the years.

These organizational summaries do not do justice to the actual impact each of them has on college hockey. So, I will try to remedy that by serving up some detailed examples of the roles each of them played annually during my time in college hockey. I think this can be done by using the three NCAA "columns" to start the conversation: tournament, rules, legislation.

NCAA Tournaments

There was a time when the NCAA tournament was a simple affair. Two teams were chosen from the West and two teams were chosen from the East. For decades, it was held on a college campus. Oh, I'm sure there were arguments and gripes as decisions were made over the phone or in the proverbial smoke-filled rooms. But the event wasn't always the big deal it has become.

The first NCAA championship took place in 1948 at the Broadmoor Ice Palace in Colorado Springs, CO. In fact, the first 10 NCAA championships were held at the Broadmoor. It wasn't until 1957, when the University of Minnesota's Williams Arena was the host, that it was played anywhere else. And it never returned to the Broadmoor.

Today's men's event involves 16 schools, its field chosen primarily by a computer, and, since 2007, it has been played at an NHL arena, save for the 2010 games at Detroit's Ford Field. It is the highlight of the season for many and, given that more than 25% of all Division I men's programs qualify for the tournament field, almost everyone starts the year thinking they have a chance to qualify.

On the women's side, only eight teams make it, given the smaller number of schools that sponsor Division I women's ice hockey. Still, these eight make up almost 20% of the women's hockey membership.

Both the men's and women's events have benefited from the addition of playing conferences whose sponsorship of the sport came relatively late and without all the bells and whistles of established programs. For the men, this happened when the Metro Atlantic Athletic Conference (MAAC) began play in 1998 with Canisius, Fairfield and Iona as MAAC institutions, along with associate members American International, Connecticut, Holy Cross, Quinnipiac and Sacred Heart.

A year later, Bentley and Mercyhurst joined the MAAC, followed the following year by Army. For the most part, these schools did not fund their hockey programs to the extent most Division I programs did, particularly in the area of scholarships. But this influx of new Division I programs allowed the men's tournament to expand to the 16-team format it still enjoys. When Fairfield and Iona dropped the sport in 2003, the remaining teams emerged as the Atlantic Hockey Association.

The women's path was a little different. Its Division I event is actually called a "National Collegiate" championship because to sustain an eight-team field, with only 30 or so D-1 programs, it needed to provide access to Division II schools like Saint Anselm, St. Michael's and others.

By 2019, a new Division I hockey conference was born, the New England Women's Hockey Alliance. This brought the number of tournament-eligible programs to 42, and while the women's field remained at eight, it staved off those inside the NCAA who had begun to question how the sports sponsorship numbers could even justify eight schools.

The growth of these events, with huge crowds and ESPN coverage, has taken them from something that affected only a few teams in those early years to a goal of almost every program at the start of a season. Teams scheduled strategically to boost their chances, so they believed, of having a great Pairwise Ranking (PWR - a strength of schedule indicator) at season's end.

One casualty of this pursuit of a postseason berth was the end of inter-divisional play. There once was a time when a Division I team might maintain a local rivalry with a nearby Division III opponent. But the days of Colgate playing Hamilton or Vermont playing Middlebury are long gone.

Conferences, always competing for bragging rights, touted their NCAA tournament success above most other metrics. In that regard, with apologies to the ECAC and Hockey East, my former employers, the crown goes to the Western Collegiate Hockey Association. Following the 2021 events, the WCHA men boasted 37 of 74 NCAA men's crowns and a phenomenal 17 of 20 for the women. No other conference comes close.

While it is easy to relegate Atlantic Hockey to the other end of the success spectrum, that might be unfair. Particularly to their coaches. School administrations may not devote the same resources to Atlantic Hockey programs, but the Atlantic coaches have done a tremendous job at ice level making their teams increasingly competitive over the years.

When I started to research some numbers to back up this assertion, I thought I'd find a few upsets in the opening round of the NCAA Regionals, like the Holy Cross win over Minnesota in 2006. But I was surprised to learn just how many times the Atlantic entry, more often than not the #16 seed drawing the #1 overall seed, either won or, perhaps, lost a one-goal game.

Since the NCAA field expanded to 16 teams back in 2003, Atlantic teams have won seven times and lost by a single goal five times. Here are the #16 vs. #1 results in four of five years, starting in 2015:
• 2015: RIT 2, Minnesota State 1
• 2017: Air Force 5, Western Michigan 4
• 2018: Air Force 4, St. Cloud 1
• 2019: AIC 2, St. Cloud 1

My first NCAA Tournament was in 1971 when I was Harvard's back-up goalie. Having won the 1971 ECAC Tournament, we qualified along with the BU team we defeated in the semifinals. BU was 28-2-1 that year, its overall record punching a ticket to Syracuse ahead of the Clarkson team we beat in the ECAC Championship. The West sent Denver and Minnesota.

My memories of that weekend in Syracuse are somewhat disappointing as we coughed up a one-goal lead, while on the power play, in the final minute of our semifinal game with Minnesota and lost in overtime. Future coaching great Dean Blais had three goals for the Gophers.

Before our consolation game with Denver, coach Cooney Weiland told me that he wanted to start our senior goalie Bruce Durno and that I would go in after five minutes or so. When the first whistle after the five-minute mark blew, I asked Cooney if I should go in. "Quiet," he barked. "Watch the game."

So I sat on the bench with my mask buckled and never got the call. Durno was spectacular, stopping 44 shots in a 1-0 loss to a Denver squad that included future NHLers Ron Graham in goal and Peter McNab up front.

Another memory from the game was a fight between the Pioneers' Brian Morenz and our Dan DeMichele, both players ejected from the game. As their fate became known, Cooney was heard to mutter, "DeMichele for Morenz? I can live with that."

Like every college hockey fan, I have memories of great NCAA teams and great Frozen Four games. I think I have attended every championship weekend since 1983, when Harvard lost the final, 6-2, to Wisconsin in Grand Forks, ND.

Among the special memories:

1985: RPI finishes a 35-2-1 season with a 2-1 win over Chris Terreri's Providence Friars in Detroit.

1989: Harvard, after losing NCAA finals in 1983 (see above) and 6-5 in OT to Michigan State in 1986, wins its first national title, 4-3 over Minnesota in OT in St. Paul. I did color commentary on Harvard radio with Bill Newell. Later I wrote the script for the highlight video that chronicled the year. I remember working with Joe "Video Joe" Curnane in producing this. Joe got the idea that George Plimpton should narrate it. I asked Joe, "How will you find George Plimpton?" He had it all figured out. "He's in the New York City phone book," said Joe. So we called him, he agreed to do it if we found a studio in New York and he ended up recording it in one take.

1993: This was the game when Shawn Walsh changed goalies at the start of the third period, down 4-2 to Lake Superior State in Milwaukee. Expecting the Lakers to dump the puck a lot with a one-goal lead, Walsh took out the talented Mike Dunham for the better puck handler, Garth Snow. The Black Bears, led by Jim Montgomery (three goals) and Paul Kariya, outscored LSSU, 3-0, in the third to win their first NCAA title. Maine finished 42-1-2 and joined the discussion for best team ever with the 1985 RPI squad (see above) and the 1970 Cornell team (29-0-0.)

1996: This was the ill-fated tournament when a workman drilled into a cooling pipe prior to the start of play in Cincinnati. While all teams had to deal with the sloppy ice conditions, the speedy Vermont Catamounts couldn't show off what Marty St. Louis, Eric Perrin, Tim Thomas and the rest of the Cats could do. After a tough 3-2 double overtime loss to Colorado College, UVM coach Mike Gilligan won over legions by taking the high road in the postgame press conference, refusing to make excuses for the loss.

1998: Michigan, behind goalie Marty Turco, defeats Boston College in overtime, the winning goal beating another future NHL goalie, Scott Clemmensen, from an improbable angle.

1999: In my second year with Hockey East, I am a proud commissioner when I accompany three HE semifinalists to Anaheim and watch Maine defeat UNH, 3-2 in overtime. After the game, I go into the Maine locker room to congratulate the Black Bears. Shawn Walsh sees me enter the room and signals for me to wait a second. He then tells his team, in front of me, "Boys, league officials may not like what I have to say," prompting one player to shout, "Fuck 'em!" "Winning the Hockey East regular-season and tournament titles mean nothing to us," says Walsh "This is all that matters. Now, the commissioner has something to say." Mustering any professionalism I could, I congratulated the team and then left the room to go down to the UNH locker room to see my friend Richie Umile. A few weeks later, Maine AD Sue Tyler took me aside and asked why I was heard saying that

I felt sorry for UNH after the game. I told her that they had just lost the national championship game and asked why wouldn't I feel sorry for them? She responded, "Why wouldn't you just say you were happy for us?" I decided not to share my Maine locker room anecdote with her.

2001: BC and North Dakota are in overtime. I can't watch from the stands. Too nervous. I go up to the concourse in Albany and watch the game on a TV monitor. I see BC's Krys Kolanos beat a Sioux defender and cut in alone on the diminutive Karl Goehring. But before he can finish the deke, I hear a roar from the crowd and only then realize what I am watching is on a delay. I figure out he has scored and BC is the champion seconds before I see the puck go in the net.

2004: At the Garden, Maine is enjoying a 5-on-3 with a pulled goalie in the final minute of play but even at 6-on-3, can't get the equalizer in a painful 1-0 loss to Denver.

2005: This is the year the WCHA had all four semifinalists. I wasn't going to mention it except I can't forget the number of times that my friend, WCHA commissioner Bruce McLeod, asked me if I had seen the tee-shirt he had made up with all four WCHA school logos. I seem to recall that had I been asked one more time, I planned to do something to him with one of those tee shirts that could have been considered aggravated assault.

2009: With the full Bertagna family in tow in Washington DC, we watch BU stun Miami, pulling its goalie, down 3-1 with more than three minutes to go, tying the game and winning on a fluke goal in overtime. I was happy for BU and sad for my friend, Miami coach Rico Blasi.

2013 and 2014: My HE teams fail to win, but I am happy for Steve Hagwell and my ECAC friends when, in consecutive years, Yale and Union win national titles. I remember my 15 years with the ECAC when we we finished out of the money 13 times.

2015: The BU-PC Final in Boston. This was covered elsewhere in these pages.

I'm sure I could conjure up all sorts of non-competition NCAA memories but would need to check to see if the statute of limitations have run out. Beers at Murphy's in Providence, on Wisconsin AD Elroy Hirsch's tab. Bocce tournaments in hotel corridors across the country. Re-visiting haunts in Milwaukee from my Marquette University/Milwaukee Admirals days with Tim Danehy. Attending April baseball games on the Friday off day in various cities, more than one of them in sub-freezing temperatures. (I can still remember the look on the faces of the poor guy trying to sell ice cream in St. Louis when it was barely above freezing.)

I have many fond memories of dining with a group of friends known as "The Puck Posse," a group of hockey fans, most with some connection to the

I join members of the "Puck Posse" who attended the 2015 AHCA Convention in Naples, FL, when Bruce Delventhal was presented the John "Snooks" Kelley Founders Award. From left: me, Stu Horn, Bruce Delventhal, Bill Harris and Glenn Craft. (Jennifer Ziegelmaier Photo)

greater Albany area. They joined the AHCA for many years under the guise of being youth hockey coaches, primarily to gain access to the few prime Frozen Four seats the AHCA sold to its members.

Beyond the games, the Frozen Four brought the college hockey community together — East meets West — breaking down geographic barriers that once threatened the civility between competitors. I particularly liked the tradition of running into the likes of John Gilbert, Jess Myers, Neil Koepke, Paula Weston, Wally Shaver, Dave Fischer, Mark Bedics and others in the media room.

This camaraderie was never better than during "Friday Night at the Frozen Four," when the Hobey Baker Award and other trophies were handed out at or near the arena hosting that year's games.

This event, like the tournament itself, had grown over the years. I remember when Mark Fusco of Harvard was announced as the 1983 Hobey winner in a small function room in Grand Forks, ND. A handful of writers and broadcasters were the only ones on hand, and when Mark was announced, the writers from out West quickly walked out of the room. "A Harvard guy?"

The event eventually drew thousands of fans, large contingents of media members and representatives of competing schools. The Hockey

Humanitarian Award was added to the festivities and later the event served to announce the AHCA All-American Teams, the Mike Richter Award, given to the top goalie in the country, and a couple of awards given out by the Hockey Commissioners Association. The Hobey presentation became a nationally televised event.

The women's Frozen Four and the Division III championships don't have an equivalent of the men's Friday night. But all of the Frozen Four events serve as the backdrop to the announcement of the All-American teams and other AHCA awards.

One of my favorite award ceremonies came in Tampa in 2016 when the AHCA's Lou Lamoriello Award was added to the Friday festivities. The award, named after the former Providence player, coach and AD, recognizes a former college hockey player or coach who goes on to a uniquely success-ful career as an adult. The 2016 recipient was General Mark Milley, then the Secretary of the Army and later the head of the Joint Chiefs of Staff.

I had known Mark growing up, even before he went to play hockey at Princeton. So when his motorcade showed up at the Tampa Theater, I was the designated greeter. "Joey Bertagna," he bellowed as he stepped out of the limousine. "How are ya?"

Moving to the green room where others involved with the evening's festivities were waiting, he met Harvard's Jim Vesey, who was about to receive that year's Hobey Baker Award, and Michigan coach Red Berenson, who had a player among the finalists.

General Mark Milley, Secretary of the Army, greets Red Berenson in Tampa in 2016, as Bruce Delventhal (behind Red) and I look on. Milley, a former Princeton University hockey player, won the AHCA's Lou Lamoriello Award that year.
(Photo by Brian Blanco courtesy of the Hobey Baker Award Foundation)

"Red Berenson? I didn't know you were still alive," said Milley to a grinning Berenson. He then had some fun with Vesey, suggesting he pass up a pro hockey career and consider a military assignment with Uncle Sam.

I have to acknowledge I don't have the same depth of memories for the Women's Frozen Four. Their championships always took place on the same weekend as the men's conference finals. I had to be in Boston to direct the Hockey East men's event but, along with Kathy Wynters, would always book a flight to wherever the women's final was on that Sunday. If a Hockey East team made it to the championship, Kathy and I would be there.

That resulted in some hectic trips, to Erie in 2011 and Minneapolis in 2013. The most memorable of all of these, and most painful of maybe any tournament game I ever witnessed, came in 2016 when UNH was hosting the Women's Frozen Four in Durham. Boston College took a record of 40-0 into the championship game against defending champion Minnesota. The Eagles gave up a goal just 13 seconds into the game and never quite recovered, losing 3-1 and denying Hockey East its first national champion.

The NCAA Ice Hockey Rules Committee

I'm not sure why I have had a long fascination with playing rules, but I believe it has something to do with how my commissioner job changed over the years. As issues moved away from the game itself and more toward marketing, branding and selling, I am sure I pined for more involvement with the actual game itself.

Serving on the NCAA Men's and Women's Ice Hockey Rules Committee, which I did on two separate occasions (1993-95 and 2013-18), filled this need. Both of those stints ended with my serving as chair of the committee. At the same time, as a USA Hockey At-Large Director, I have served on the USA Hockey Playing Rules Committee for nearly two decades and continue to do so.

The NCAA rules process was pretty simple, given we started any given year with an existing book. Originally, the Rules Committee edited the book annually but for a number of reasons, went to a two-year edition starting around 2005. Cost of printing may have been one reason. But there was also an interest in not having rules added one year and scrapped a year later, without being given a real chance to survive. Hockey voluntarily went to the two-year book before the NCAA mandated it for all sports in 2007.

The committee would meet via conference call during the year, the bulk of the calls addressing issues that would come up during the playing season. Sometimes a new rule had been passed without all its ramifications anticipated. So the Secretary-Editor of the book had to issue guidance, with input from the Rules Committee and NCAA staff liaison.

The Secretary-Editor was an important and influential figure, one who had to know the book well and issue appropriate clarifications. Former coaches Bill Cleary of Harvard and Sid Watson of Bowdoin were legendary figures in this role. In my time, former on-ice official Steve Piotrowski, who became Supervisor of Officials in the CCHA and then the Big Ten, did a masterful job, so much so that his stay was extended beyond the recommended number of terms.

Others not on the committee played key roles, too. Ty Halpin was an NCAA staffer who served as the liaison to the Rules Committee. He was a tremendous asset who became a good friend. And perhaps no one knew the rules book better than Tom Lynch, a longtime administrator for NIHOA, the National Ice Hockey Officials Association. Tom had the time and the skill to know when a rules change inserted in one section of the book had references in other sections, all of those pages in need of edits.

The Rules Committee would meet with the nation's coaches at the annual AHCA Convention each spring and then convene at the NCAA Office in Indianapolis in June. The sessions at the convention could be, shall I say, "spirited." The annual meetings, on the other hand, were more disciplined and on point.

I loved the June meetings. For three or four days, you would meet with a cross-section of the sport, everyone, taking their responsibilities seriously. Yes, each person represented a constituency but, collectively, you were there to serve the game. By NCAA mandate, the Rules Committee had representatives of all three playing divisions, both genders, and a mix of coaches and administrators. Also invited to attend but not cast votes were representatives from the NHL, the National Federation of High School Associations (sometimes), NIHOA and an active referee and an active linesman. There might also be a Supervisor of Officials on hand, like WCHA veteran Greg Shepherd. Each of the non-voting attendees would make significant contributions to the discussions.

At the start of the meetings, we were reminded about basic tenets of rules writing. How the safety of the athletes was first and foremost. How we had a need to balance offense and defense. How the wording had to make the intent of the rules clear and easy to understand. I think the writer in me liked the challenge of choosing the exact word to provide that clarity.

The addition of active on-ice officials was a great development. Often, we would turn to them for advice on how something was worded. Did this make it easier or harder to make a call? Should this be a major or would it be better if you had the option of a major or minor?

Administrators might provide input on any rule change regarding equipment, or the arena, that had cost implications. For example, we discussed goal pegs one year and wanted to mandate a certain peg that involved drilling into the arena floor. The administrators were quick to point out that not all schools played in rinks they owned, and as a result, not all schools could comply with certain conditions placed on rinks.

The NCAA also had a process whereby all sport-specific rules changes had to be vetted by a standing committee that made sure matters of finance or safety were appropriate. An example of the latter would be the committee's multiple efforts, during my first term as chair, to do away with full face masks (and replace with half-shields). Eventually, we were asked to stop submitting that proposal, unless we could accompany it with data proving our contention that the full mask made the game more dangerous, despite its prevention of eye injuries and facial lacerations.

As technology became more pervasive in our game, more time was spent on the use of video replay. As only Division I schools utilized video replay protocols, I always felt for the Division III reps on our committee who had to sit through hours of discussion on video issues that never touched on their level of play.

Of all the outside contributors, the NHL representatives were, to me, the most fascinating. Whether it was the late E.J. McGuire or his successor Mike Murphy, the inclusion of an NHL rep was a huge benefit to the process. We never got the feeling they were looking down on us in any way. They came equipped with reports on what the NHL was doing, what was being adopted, what was on their radar farther down the road and, at the same time, they were genuinely interested in what we were doing. They even acknowledged, on the rare occasion, that they took some wording or interpretations from us and incorporated such things into their game.

Three issues stand out in my time, issues that spiked passionate dialogue among coaches across the country and committee members.

Standard of Play: By the early 2000s, it was apparent that the game was suffering from an increase in what was commonly called "clutching and grabbing." Players both with and away from the puck were being impeded and restrained, either by stick use or along the boards, perhaps, by being held.

It wasn't something that just came upon us. I can recall an NCAA rules event around 1990 when video clips from recent years were shown to a function room full of coaches. When it became apparent that many of the clips showed Lake Superior players holding St. Lawrence players in the 1988 NCAA Final, won by the Lakers, a single voice was heard in the darkened room. "Hey, can we play this game over?" It was SLU coach Joe Marsh.

By 2003, it had only become worse. Other NCAA championship games, the most important and most viewed contests of any season, displayed hooking and holding and, of particular concern, defenders wrapping their hands around opponents along the boards. It was in this context that CCHA commissioner Tom Anastos led a movement to do something about it.

My recollection is that Anastos articulated the problem and began a wider discussion. The commissioners and their supervisors, for the most part, were certainly on board, as was the NCAA's Ty Halpin and Miami University head coach Rico Blasi, chair of the Rules Committee for the 2003-04 season.

I was eager to support the effort and to lend my hand to writing up whatever "directive" the Rules Committee would issue with the 2004-05 rule book. And so, working with Ty Halpin, we produced an "Open Letter to the Hockey Community," which announced a new standard of play. Here are some key excerpts from the document that was sent out in September 2004:

Purpose: The stated purpose of this initiative is to allow all players to benefit from the rules book and how the book is called. While the so-called "let them play" philosophy has become deep-rooted and the concept of penalty selection is universally accepted, these philosophies need to be amended. The traditional approach – "let them play" – has allowed too many infractions to go without a penalty being called and the result is a different game. The result is, in our opinion, a less attractive game.

Target Areas: We have a general target: allowing all players the right to meet their offensive and defensive responsibilities without being held, hooked, or otherwise obstructed. While we hope to see increased offensive opportunities from this initiative, there is evidence that attacking players are also frequent offenders in the area of obstruction (e.g., face-off picks).

We also have identified three specific target areas:
• Offensive players coming through the neutral or offensive zones being unfairly/illegally held up while they make a legitimate attempt to get or remain open for a pass from a puck-controlling teammate.
• Offensive players coming through the neutral or offensive zones being unfairly/illegally held up while they attempt the legitimate pursuit of a loose puck.
• Players along the boards, on or away from the puck, being unfairly/illegally restrained.

The document pointed out that we were not adding new penalties but that this initiative sought to encourage the calling of already existing penalties with more consistency. At its core, the directive sought to allow offensive players to use their skill without being impeded by illegal tactics. The following spelled that out.

*In all of the areas above, we feel that a player, who, through the use
of physical skill and/or anticipation, has a positional advantage on an
opponent, shall not lose that advantage through the illegal use of hands,
arms, or stick. Any player in pursuit of a puck or open lane shall not lose a
perceived positional advantage by the illegal use of hands, arms, or stick by
an opponent. If a player is deprived of that advantage by an illegal act (e.g.,
hook, hold, interference, etc.), the appropriate penalty must be called.*

*A "positional advantage," in other terminology, might be called
"a step," as in: "He/she had a good step on the defender, but the player
hooked just enough to catch up."*

I remember speaking with veteran referee John Gravallese at the time
this was being written up. I asked him why penalties were not called in
some of these situations. He said, "We sometimes don't call it because the
guy fights through the hold or the stick." Our response was, "Why should
the player have the burden of 'fighting through it?'"

We then described very specific tactics that we wanted to remove from
the game.

• *Using a free or open hand or arm to restrain an opponent, along the
boards (pinning) or in open ice;*
• *Using a free or open hand to grab any part of an opponent's uniform (tug-
ging), equipment, or stick;*
• *Tying up an opponent by illegal use of hands, arms or stick, rather than by
body position;*
• *Picking or screening a player who does not have possession of the puck,
and, in the process, preventing the player from moving to open or unoccu-
pied ice in any zone; and*
• *Placing the stick between an opponent's legs, preventing his or her right to
participate in the play.*

The final component of the letter was called "Weathering the Storm."
We knew that to make this effective, there would be a dramatic increase in
penalties called early in the 2004-05 season and that everyone had to brace
for it and not succumb to pressure.

My friend Ed Swift reported on this very outcome. In the November
22, 2004, issue of *Sports Illustrated* entitled, "Giving Hooking the Hook,"
Swift reported that, "Through the first five weeks of the season college
referees have called an average of 19.4 penalties per game, up 35% from a
year ago." We got through it and the game was better off for it.

Reduced Manpower Overtime: In recent years, few rules issues proved more controversial than the various efforts to address overtime formats. Historically, college hockey has had myriad overtime formats, more so in the postseason when a winner needs to be determined. (See: "total goals" and "mini-game.")

For decades, regular-season games that were tied after 60 minutes reverted to a single five-minute, sudden-death overtime. If the game remained tied at that point, it went into the books as a tie. At various times in more recent years, some conferences experimented with shootouts after the sudden death overtime, solely to provide a winner for league standings. The game was still considered a tie for the NCAA and coaches' records.

By 2014, other elite levels of hockey, most notably the NHL, were introducing some form of reduced manpower overtimes. Studies showed that 3 vs. 3 overtimes were almost twice likely to produce a winner as a 5 vs. 5 OT. The NHL, the IIHF and even junior hockey all used some form of reduced manpower overtime.

While I was in my second stint on the Rules Committee, we began allowing leagues to experiment with 3 vs. 3 play for counting in league standings only. The NCHC started using this with the 2014-15 season, followed a year later by the WCHA.

By 2016, coaches and fans alike were expressing a desire for college hockey to have one overtime system across the board. A few dynamics were developing. Where 3 vs. 3 was used, most people really enjoyed it. That its use was discretionary created confusion. For example, Colorado College and Air Force both played in Colorado Springs, CO. CC used the 3 vs. 3 and USAF did not.

At the same time, most of the schools that did not use it were militantly opposed to being forced to use it. Hockey is a 5-on-5 game, they argued. Stronger programs get more skilled players than others, some said. Let people do what they want but don't force us to go along.

Opposition, for some unknown reason, was particularly strong in the East. Coaches from both ECAC Hockey and Hockey East were close to unanimous in their opposition. One stated concern was the chance of a team missing the NCAAs because of games decided by so few skaters.

This discussion was accompanied by discourse on the value of a tie. Ice hockey was shown to be the only NCAA sport where ties still existed. Some coaches wanted to see a winner and 3 vs. 3 overtime resulted in more games having a winner than 5 vs. 5. Other coaches observed that there were "good ties," as when an underdog goes into the building of a heavy favorite and comes away with a point.

As chair of the committee in 2016, I felt that we had to show some vision, look where the game was heading and try to be progressive. At the same time, there were considerable numbers against mandating it. So how do we bridge these camps? People who used it, loved it. And fans across the country, as well as coaches, were clamoring for one system across the board.

Despite Hockey East coaches being unanimously against change, I championed what I thought could be a compromise, 4 vs. 4, which also could be a bridge to 3 vs. 3 down the road. The committee endorsed this proposal, it was put in the book after our June meetings and was then subject to a 60-day comment period.

It didn't take long for opponents to use that opportunity to mount a strong campaign against 4 vs. 4. The rules committee reconvened and we voted to withdraw the proposal. Looking back, I regret that I didn't hold our ground. Change was inevitable and when the 2019-20 rule book came out, two years after I left the committee, 3 vs. 3 was the law of the land.

There was still controversy. Opponents got some satisfaction when the Championships Committee agreed to weigh the results of a 3 vs. 3 win with a 55%/45% split (67%-33% for the women's tournament), so the winner wouldn't get all the value of such a win in the computer program used for the NCAA Tournament. But somehow, the coaches didn't fully realize that the results of those games would be the result that would go on their individual win-loss records. After the first season of 3 vs. 3 wrapped up, a national discussion took place on how coaches records would be listed in this new rule. As I write, it has not been fully addressed.

Video Replay: I will spend less time on this topic as it still needs to be addressed. The desire to "get it right" is shared across college hockey and the advent of video replay has certainly increased the collective ability to do so. When it was introduced to college hockey, the list of situations where it could be employed was fairly short: pucks scored illegally (high stick or kicked), whether the puck indeed crossed the line, whether the whistle had blown and whether time had expired. I may have missed one, but the section took up less than a full page in the book.

It didn't take long for this to expand. Video can be used to put time back on the clock, to confirm the right player in an altercation was penalized, to see if a major occurred, to determine if there was goaltender interference, to see if there were too many men on the ice when a goal was scored and to check if the play that led to a goal was offsides.

To one side in this discussion, all these things represent progress in the quest to "get it right." But to the other side, say those of us sitting at an NCAA postseason game, waiting for each goal to be "cleared" before it can be put on the board, waiting for yet another big hit to be reviewed for a possible major, the flow of the game is being taken away. Add the TV timeouts that seem longer in the postseason, and it makes for a very uncomfortable, and lengthy, experience.

Some modest efforts have already been made to stem this phenomenon. Take offsides. In the postseason, where every goal is reviewed, the time it would take to go back and check every zone entry was an obstacle for a quickly flowing game. On my watch, we amended this by ending any chance for an offsides review if the defending team gained possession of the puck. Once that was observed, no further review was allowed. It was a start. But more needs to be addressed in this area.

NCAA Legislation

The first two "columns" have worked well for college hockey. And part of this is because "hockey people" get to work with NCAA staff as members of the Championship Committee and the Rules Committee. That is, we get to have some say on how our tournaments are administered and how our on-ice rules are created and amended.

That leaves the third area in which we deal with the NCAA. The thick NCAA Manual, which comes out each year for each NCAA division, covers the overall rules of the NCAA. These are the rules that govern amateurism, eligibility, transferring from one school to another, recruiting, length of season, scholarships and the like. Most of these are association-wide, but there are still sport-specific components to these rules, like how many scholarships a given sport is allowed or how many paid coaches a sport is allowed.

Early in my administrative career, voting on such issues took place at the annual January NCAA Convention, each institution getting one vote within its division. All schools got to vote even when a proposal was sport-specific. So, for example, the 60 or so institutions that sponsored Division I ice hockey might be unanimous on a hockey matter but that was no guarantee the measure could pass. The other Division I schools could vote on the same proposal.

So, let's say hockey wanted to add a graduate assistant or a third assistant coach. And let's say the hockey schools supported this unanimously. Non-hockey schools might look at that and say, "If this passes, my lacrosse coach and my soccer coach will be next in line trying to use this to expand their staffs. No way I am supporting this."

I won't even attempt to explain how legislation gets into the system today. I will offer this. If you belong to one of the "Power Five" conferences, the ability to propose and move legislation is far easier than it is for: a) other multi-sport conferences; and b) a single sport conference, like five of the six Division I men's hockey-playing conferences. If you are basketball or football, you have a better chance of influencing your legislative destiny than if you are any other sport.

One exception to this is if a given sport wants to propose something that would be more restrictive than existing NCAA rules. You want to reduce your scholarships? That could probably pass. You want to increase staff size, probably not.

The subjects of amateurism and recruiting have long dominated NCAA by-laws discussions. Go back six decades to when my friend Gene Kinasewich, Harvard '64, battled for eligibility over some expense money received in Western Canada prior to college. Today, the competition between "major junior" hockey in Canada and the U.S. college system remains somewhat unique within the NCAA. College coaches have strong competition for the young hockey prospect, and not just the Canadian prospect.

This reality hangs over so many discussions about recruiting calendars and when players can be contacted or evaluated or offered scholarships. The Canadian juniors are not burdened with the limitations the NCAA places on college coaches, and in recent years, they have taken advantage of that and stepped up their efforts to go after U.S. players.

The colleges are not without weapons of their own. As the number of U.S. players has grown in the NHL, along with the number of former college players in positions like NHL coach, GM or director of player personnel, college coaches have found it easier to make the "best of both worlds" argument. Get a top-notch education for free AND have a path to the NHL.

Another recruiting issue involves the transfer rule. Hockey has long been one of a handful of NCAA sports where a player wishing to transfer from one Division I school to another, or "up" from a Division III school to a Division I school, had to sit out his first year of residence at his new school. The player could practice and could take advantage of the NCAA allowing an athlete five years to complete four years of eligibility, but could not play that first year at the new location. In 2021, legislation was passed that made it much easier to transfer, eliminating that "one year in residence" stipulation, so a student-athlete could finish one season at one school and start the next somewhere else. Coaches are bracing for aggressive recruiting of players on exiting rosters.

Right before I went to print, the United States Supreme Court forced the NCAA to change its policies on athletes earning money off their "name, image and likeness." This is going to open up opportunities for athletes but also bring more agents into the world of college sports in ways never before imagined.

My friend Donald "Toot" Cahoon was working at Princeton University when he came across a wonderful photograph of the 10th Annual Convention of the American Hockey Coaches Association from March 23-24, 1956. The picture, measuring 26 inches wide and 12 inches tall, shows 53 gentlemen, some standing and some seated, in a ballroom of the Hotel Ken-

Top: These are a few of my AHCA heroes. Upper left photo is of Minnesota Duluth coach Mike Sertich and upper right photo is of Bowdoin coaches Terry Meagher and Sid Watson. All three men served as officers of the AHCA. (Top left: Jennifer Ziegelmaier Photo; top right: Bowdoin College Photo)

Bottom: This is just a snippet of a terrific photo taken at the 1956 AHCA meeting in Boston. While we have been unable to identify all the gentlemen, we can confirm that you will find the following people in this photo: Jimmy Bell, Amo Bessone, Rube Bjorkman, Bernie Burke, Len Ceglarski, Bill Cleary Sr., Harry Cleverly, Will Cloney, Leonard Fowle, Jim Fullerton, Herb Gallagher, Ned Harkness, Eddie Jeremiah, Jack Kelley, Snooks Kelley, Bill McCormick, Murray Murdoch, Al Renfrew, Jack Riley, Bill Stewart, and Cooney Weiland. Three of the AHCA's major awards are named after Jim Fullerton, Eddie Jeremiah and Snooks Kelley.

The Stanley Cup visited the AHCA Convention in Naples, FL, one year and a group of retired coaches gathered around. From left: Al Renfrew (in the background), Amo Bessone, Lefty Smith, Charlie Basch, Fernie Flaman and Bill McCormick. Flaman, who captained the Boston Bruins and coached at Northeastern, found his name on the Stanley Cup as a member of the 1951 Toronto Maple Leafs. (Jennifer Ziegelmaier Photo)

more in Boston, the hotel where Ted Williams used to live during baseball season. The photo includes some of the greatest contributors in the history of college hockey.

Ned Harkness, Snooks Kelley, Amo Bessone, Murray Murdoch, Herb Gallagher, Vic Heyliger, Jack Kelly, Cooney Weiland, Al Renfrew, Jim Fullerton, Eddie Jeremiah. They are all there.

The work of the AHCA was fairly simple in the early years. As they do today, coaches contributed to the NCAA Tournament and rules talks. They began choosing a Division I Coach of the Year in 1951, Eddie Jeremiah of Dartmouth, and they first honored a Division III Coach of the Year in 1970, Sid Watson of Bowdoin receiving the first Edward Jeremiah Award.

Prior to 1957, All-American teams existed but the process by which they were chosen could be sketchy. As previously noted, the first 10 NCAA championships were played at the Broadmoor in Colorado Springs. Viewing copies of the *Colorado Springs Gazette* from those years, I found references to "this year's All-Americans, as chosen by the managers of the four NCAA semifinalists."

The first "official" AHCA All-Americans date from 1957 and over the years grew to include Division III teams, women's teams and in most cases, separate East and West squads (except for Division I women).

For many decades, coaches would join the AHCA as individuals, and high school coaches made up a significant part of the early AHCA, so much so that the Board of Directors had a high school representative for many years. Many of us who have served the AHCA have heard stories of former UNH coach Charlie Holt and his wife, Nancy, handling membership mailings from their kitchen table. For years, the banner hung at the AHCA Convention was one sewn together by Nancy.

By the late 1980s, the work of the Association, like everything else, grew more complicated and time consuming, and there was a desire to move the in-season administrative responsibility from active coaches volunteering to do the various jobs to a paid part-time administrator.

It was in 1991, with Boston University coach Jack Parker serving as AHCA President, that the Board decided to create the position of AHCA Executive Director. I guess I can now share how this ended up being me. Jack asked me if I would be interested in the job. I was working part-time for the ECAC at the time and thought I could mesh the two jobs easily.

So, he told me to write up a job description and, in doing so, describe myself. So I did. *Applicant should have a background in coaching and administration, with proven organizational skills and talent in writing ...*

The AHCA posted this job description, I applied and the Board said, "Hey, this guy's perfect." And I got the job. Today, 30 years later, I'm still there.

At the time I took over, membership was still done on an individual basis and membership numbers were somewhere under 300. I don't know whose idea it was, but when we changed to one check for a school's entire staff, membership spiked immediately. With the addition of women's hockey and, later, the American Collegiate Hockey Association (non-varsity teams) and some junior leagues, membership passed 1,200.

The growth of the membership led to an expansion of the annual AHCA convention in Naples, FL. What was once an all-men's event changed with the addition of the above groups. Some coaches balked at the changes women and club teams brought, some still do. But the ability of the AHCA to survive depended on growing the membership, and the ability of the convention to thrive was a direct result of this growth. For example, as more Division I programs had school-wide deals for equipment and apparel, the annual trade show managed to prosper when vendors could still sell to the expanded constituencies. And the AHCA continued to turn vendors away from packed ballrooms.

I enjoyed the opportunity to work with all divisions, men and women, East and West, that the AHCA afforded me. Working closely with Bruce Delventhal, the AHCA Secretary-Treasurer, I juggled a number of duties, many

I was proud to be a leading voice in ushering women's coaches into the AHCA and have continued to support the efforts of a strong group of coaches of women's hockey, both male and female. The first women to attend the AHCA Convention were Kelly Dyer and Heather Linstad. Above, from left, Jodi McKenna, Digit Murphy, Katie Crowley and Cara Morey. (Jennifer Ziegelmaier Photo)

of them related to awards, their history, their promotion, etc. The newsletter, *Stops and Starts*, allowed me to indulge my love of history and writing.

It was in *Stops and Starts* that I provided an annual of breakdown of the geographical sources of NCAA hockey players, sorted by gender and division. I would often do a study of where goalies came from and how tall they were. The latter was a reflection of how short goalies were increasingly rare.

One trend in which I took a particular interest was the decrease in the number of Division I players produced by my home state of Massachusetts, along with the entire six-state New England region. Comparing rosters from

Maine's Shawn Walsh was one of the most successful and, often, controversial coaches in NCAA history. His legacy lives on through the work of "Hockey Coaches Care," the relief fund of the AHCA, that received funds from the Shawn Walsh Foundation when Walsh passed away in September 2001. I like this photo as I often saw Shawn with one foot on the dasher, either speaking to a player, as he does here, or trying to get the attention of a referee. (Photo courtesy of the University of Maine)

2000 and 2020, here is what we found. Massachusetts went from 205 D-I men's players to 107. New England went from 326 to 175.

By contrast, we took a look at the growth in players from non-traditional sources. Looking at Arizona, California, Florida and Texas in that same study, we found an increase from 17 players in 2000 to 94 in 2020.

The AHCA Board of Governors contained a rotating number of coaches representing all constituencies in the college hockey world and they were the key to making the AHCA work. In particular, those who agreed to serve multi-year terms as president went a long way in providing leadership for the organization. The women were particularly fortunate to have strong leadership among those who volunteered to put in extra time.

We had one celebrated transition of power when it was time for Maine coach Shawn Walsh to move up to the president's job. At the time, Walsh had been embroiled in some NCAA rules issues and as he was about to move from First Vice-President to President, some voices were heard suggesting that Shawn should not be the AHCA head.

I had mixed feelings. Yes, the AHCA president should have a good reputation for fair play and obeying rules. The president also should be a worker, with energy and vision, who would take the job seriously and with passion. A compromise was worked out by the Board whereby Shawn would be delivered a message by delaying his ascension to the top and, instead, nominating him to repeat as First VP. Mankato coach Don Brose was a non-controversial replacement and when it came time for the slate of officers to be proposed at the convention, it was Ron Mason of Michigan State, Shawn's father-in-law, who made the proposal. It was accepted and Shawn eventually became president a few years later.

A couple of other observations about Shawn. He was one of the greatest coaches in the history of college hockey. He recruited well, he was a good in-game coach and his teams got better as the season went on. Oh, and he frequently flirted with rules violations. I will add that he just wasn't particularly popular among many of the coaches against whom he competed. Yet he was voted Coach of the Year many times by Hockey East coaches because they respected his coaching ability.

I had some moments with Shawn but overall, I got along with him. The AHCA sponsored a couple of different senior all-star games over the years. The latter ones sputtered as so many of the game's great players either left school early or, by the time they were seniors, signed minor league contracts as soon as their last game was played. All of this made it difficult to assemble rosters for these events.

One year, we did put together a pair of games against seniors of the Canadian university system. One game was in Detroit and one in Toronto. When I named Shawn to coach the NCAA team, I heard some criticism immediately. Shawn was separated at the time and his children were living in Michigan. I thought it would be a good idea to let him coach and visit his family at the same time. From a hockey decision, I knew Shawn would dive into the assignment, like he dove into everything, and would do a good job.

Shawn passed away in September 2001, having lost a battle with kidney cancer. At the time of his death, the Maine hockey community forwarded funds to the AHCA that had been raised for Shawn during his cancer treatment. Those resources helped bolster the AHCA's relief fund, "Hockey Coaches Care," which continues to help members of the extended hockey community today.

The site of three decades of conventions was the Naples Beach Hotel and Golf Club. In April 2020, the AHCA Convention was canceled due to Covid-19. In 2021, the convention went virtual but there was a "Farewell to the Naples Beach Hotel" event, given that the facility was being torn down and replaced with luxury condos and a smaller luxury hotel.

There were great memories of not just the business conducted but the fun and games. The banged-out trade show was always a great way to mix business and pleasure. It always started on a Thursday night, following a cocktail party that raised money for "Hockey Coaches Care." Bruce

Delventhal and the officers ran the event, balancing fun and some serious fund-raising goals.

Then there were the speakers, like everything else we did, some being educational and some more entertaining. One of the more memorable moments from our years of providing "professional development" came when veteran coach Barry Smith gave a talk on "Locker Room Dynamics." Smith, a former Elmira College coach who had great success as an NHL assistant, often alongside Scotty Bowman, was giving the talk that could, to some degree, be reduced to keep the guys that don't like you away from the guys who haven't made up their minds.

The talk went on for some time and then Smith asked if there were any questions. A hand went up in the back of the room. It was longtime Lowell coach Billy Riley. He was wearing a straw hat, sporting a multi-day growth on his face and one of his eyes appeared to be twitching. If there had been a parrot on his shoulder, he would have made a fine pirate.

"What do you think of the 'More-So Theory?'" he asked.

With that, the coaches from out West turned and looked at Billy with great interest. The coaches from the East dropped their heads into their

Billy Riley (right) receives the 2000 John MacInnes Award, with his longtime goalie coach Mike Geragosian. Gera and I ran goalie camps together for many years. (Jennifer Ziegelmaier Photo)

hands, sensing a set-up.

"I'm not familiar with that theory," said Smith.

"That's the notion that if you recruit a kid who is an asshole in high school, he will only be 'more-so' when he gets to college," said Riley. Needless to say, the only thing the assembled coaches took away from the hour-long talk was the "More-So Theory."

It was also at the convention that the most passionate discussions among coaches took place. Maybe it was about how teams were selected for the national tournament. Maybe it was a proposed rule, like the overtime issue. More likely it was about recruiting and some "gentlemen's agreement" that, by nature, was impossible to enforce.

This seems to be a good time to share a story about a situation involving just about all the groups I introduced at the start of this chapter. It is about coaches warning administrators about aggressive recruiting from Canadian juniors. It is about voicing these concerns at the AHCA Convention and to the Hockey Commissioners Association. It is about chafing at NCAA regulations. And it is about USA Hockey, through its relationship with the NHL, providing a solution to the coaches' dilemma.

At the turn of the century, there were five NCAA Division I conferences sponsoring ice hockey and the commissioners from those conferences formally organized the Hockey Commissioners Association in 2003 to provide structure to our deliberations.

By 2008, this group was: Bob DeGregorio of Atlantic Hockey; Tom Anastos of the Central Collegiate Hockey Association (CCHA); Steve Hagwell of ECAC Hockey; Bruce McLeod of the Western Collegiate Hockey Association (WCHA); and myself representing Hockey East. Through monthly conference calls and a handful of annual in-person meetings, this group worked to go beyond the interests of its individual league memberships by identifying initiatives that would benefit the sport as a whole.*

Among these initiatives was the establishment of the annual "Ice Breaker Tournament," an NCAA-exempted event that allowed four schools

---

This group eventually became six when the Big Ten got into the college hockey business in 2013 and in the aftermath of its announcement, a new conference was formed, the National Collegiate Hockey Conference (NCHC) and the CCHA dissolved. Starting in 2021-22, the men's WCHA will no longer exist as seven institutions announced that they would leave the WCHA and come back under the previously retired "CCHA" name. NCHC commissioner Josh Fenton, outgoing WCHA commissioner Bill Robertson and Big Ten advisor Red Berenson made major contributions to men's Division I hockey administration in the pandemic year of 2020-21. Former University of Minnesota head coach Don Lucia was named commissioner of the new CCHA, starting in 2021.

to start the year in a prestigious tournament in which the two games each school played didn't count toward the 34-game limit imposed by the NCAA. This exemption was obtained through targeted legislation, another area in which the commissioners as a group have been successful over the years.

In a broader sense, the commissioners often met to discuss the future of the game and how new initiatives could be identified and funded. For many years, the commissioners, individually or as a group, would visit the offices of the National Hockey League, usually during the off-season, to meet with Commissioner Gary Bettman or his deputy, Bill Daly. The visits were as much social as functional, but they did eventually peak with a formal presentation to the NHL general managers in Naples, FL, in February 2008.

Working with the other commissioners was one of the best experiences I had in my time as an administrator. Everyone understood the issues that each other faced and how the growing partisanship affected our jobs directly.

Every time we had an issue with a coach or AD, they had a rooting interest in how the issue would help their on-ice success. We, on the other hand, didn't care about who won a given game or who finished first. Their inherent partisanship made it virtually impossible for them to be objective. They want to move a league game because they could get a better opponent. We say no. It affects others adversely. They want to see their opponent suspended for a bad hit. We show the video to other commissioners and all agree the play doesn't even warrant a minor. They want a ref pulled off a game and we say no. We are always the people who are in the way of a school getting something it wants.

Here are a couple of examples of what we had to deal with. A coach calls us before he is about to go on the road to start a quarterfinal series. He can't believe we have assigned a certain ref. I should know that he has had issues with that guy and he wants him pulled off the game.

He calls Monday. He calls Tuesday. His AD calls Wednesday. He calls Thursday. Friday comes and he wins the game. On Saturday, he calls to see if he can have that same referee for Game Two.

A veteran coach arranges to meet me in my office at 5:00 p.m. on a Tuesday. He lost an overtime game the previous Saturday, the winning goal coming after an icing had been waved off. The coach explains to me that he has a system where his team has certain goals that, if met, increase his chances of winning. Outshoot the opponent. Win more face-offs. Don't give up any goals in the first and last minute of a period. Take fewer penalties than your opponent. Score first. And so on.

The coach tells me if he hits most of these marks, he rarely loses. If he hits all of them, it is impossible to lose. He believes that. And he hit all the marks in that last game. So he has concluded that the missed icing is solely responsible for the loss.

Top: Four hockey commissioners in Venice in the fall of 2019. From left, Bob DeGregorio, myself, Tom Anastos and Steve Hagwell. Bottom: Longtime WCHA Commissioner Bruce McLeod addresses the AHCA audience upon receiving the Jim Fullerton Award in 2004. (Jennifer Ziegelmaier Photo)

I call a former linesman who was at the game. I ask him about the icing being waved off. He says when he saw it live, he thought, "Great call. The defender made no effort to get back to play it." I send him video of the play. Upon seeing it four days later, he says he isn't sure. Could have gone either way.

The objective person agrees with the call in real time. With the benefit of video, it is 50-50. But for the coach with a rooting interest, that one call clearly cost him the game.

This is what commissioners deal with all the time. People whose objectivity is skewed by their rooting interest. I would also see this in the weekly national polls I did for the AHCA. Some coaches would invariably rank their own team five or six places higher than anyone else who voted.

I think this common experience helped create a bond with our group of commissioners. When you think about it, who else doesn't cheer for one team or another when watching a league game? We might be the only ones in the building, along with the on-ice officials, who don't care who wins or loses.

For some time, the Division I men's coaching body had been appealing to the commissioners for help in combatting what had become newly aggressive recruiting of young hockey players by Canadian junior hockey. This message to the commissioners reached a somewhat fever pitch at the annual convention in Naples, FL, first in April 2008 and then in a more urgent manner in April 2009.

Between these two conventions, it was learned that the NHL was about to announce an annual grant to USA Hockey of $8 million. When the commissioners were made aware of this, they reached out to Gary Bettman and were told to negotiate directly with USA Hockey, as this grant was designated for "the growth and development of amateur hockey in the United States." The message was clear: USA Hockey will respond positively to you and, if you have difficulty, come back to us. But we don't think you will have difficulty.

A series of negotiations took place between January and June 2009. When talks slowed down, a sub-committee of NCAA coaches, frustrated by the lack of significant progress, offered a more confrontational approach. The commissioners asked the sub-committee to be patient and let the process continue.

After a few more meetings, and with those coaches' threats articulated at a key moment, an appropriate offer was finally made and accepted by the commissioners and remains the basis of the agreement as of this writing some 12 years later.

Dubbed "College Hockey, Inc.," the new marketing arm of NCAA Division I ice hockey was immediately in need of a defined mission statement and internal structure, as well a staff. In the summer of 2009, work began on incorporating CHI and finding an executive director.

The commissioners set up a series of interviews at a Logan Airport hotel in Boston and attracted an acceptable, if somewhat pedestrian, stack of résumés when a new candidate emerged mid-process. Paul Kelly, a Boston-based attorney and former federal prosecutor, had recently parted ways with the National Hockey League Players Association, where he served as its Executive Director. The commissioners felt fortunate that Kelly had expressed interest in the position and invited him to interview.

He seemed to possess everything the commissioners sought. He was coming from a high-level executive position within hockey, he was relatively young, intelligent and good on his feet. He had energy and, significant to launching a new venture, a high profile in the sport of ice hockey. He was offered a two-year contract and on November 24, 2009, he was introduced at a press conference held at Harvard University.

Kelly did a great job launching CHI, using his many skills to put CHI on the map as he traveled extensively, pursued an active speaking agenda and brought instant credibility to the organization.

Early on in his tenure, the exact point in time difficult to pinpoint, Kelly began to develop a special relationship with a group of high visibility head coaches, about a dozen of the most successful and visible coaches in the game. Many of these coaches had won national championships, and combined they had won nine. But they were equally strong as spokesmen for the game, not prone to staying on the sidelines when issues were raised.

As Kelly moved from Year One to Year Two (2010-11), the relationship between Kelly and the commissioners as a group – and certainly between Kelly and myself – began to change. Coaches with long and positive relations with the commissioners began to share information about Kelly being openly critical of the commissioners and, to a lesser degree, critical of USA Hockey.

Specifically, Kelly was suggesting that the commissioners were impeding his ability to do his job, a message that began to drive a wedge between some coaches and the commissioners. We, the commissioners, were concerned that Kelly was starting to see the coaches as his first constituency, not the commissioners who: a) hired him; and b) had to oversee CHI, consistent with the agreement that the HCA had with USA Hockey. USA Hockey trusted that the commissioners would be professional in their supervision of this new entity and the money being provided. The commissioners were given explicit guidelines as to expectations on their supervisory role.

We addressed these rumors directly with Kelly on more than one occasion. He always responded by declaring that the reports were false and that he understood that he answered to the commissioners and not the coaches.

In addition to the nature of his relationship with the coaches, the commissioners also had concerns over what appeared to be Kelly's desire to change his role and to expand the areas under his job title. It appeared to some of us, myself included, that he was not content in simply serving as the chief executive of the marketing arm of Division I college hockey. I believed that he wanted to be to college hockey what Gary Bettman was to the NHL. He wanted a greater role in the day-to-day administration of college hockey, something that the commissioners were not prepared to give up nor would the nation's athletic directors, for whom we worked, allow.

Through written communication and multiple in-person meetings, the commissioners continued to remind Kelly about respect for the chain of command and the importance of keeping to the job description we had created for him. And each time these issues were raised, he always denied any wrongdoing.

All of this came to a head in February 2012 when Kelly revealed in an email to a sitting athletic director that he indeed wanted to change his duties, be the administrative head of college hockey and no longer answer to the commissioners. The email was copied to one of the commissioners and began a process that ended up with Kelly and the commissioners parting ways.

One phenomenon that is worthy of note: Even when the commissioners could show the nation's coaches that we had been misled by Kelly, the staunchest of his supporters remained unmoved. In their minds, they, not the commissioners, were responsible for the existence of CHI. In my opinion, this group did not appreciate all that the commissioners did, and still do, for the interests of college hockey and its coaches. Maybe, as described earlier, the coaches see us as the people always saying "no" to them and this leads them to believe that an independent advocate for their interests is preferable.

Following Kelly, CHI got on stable footing with the hiring of Mike Snee as its second executive director. An affable and skilled Duluth native and University of St. Thomas graduate, Snee has been a remarkably steady leader from his first day, a passionate hockey man, one with no agenda other than CHI's mission statement. He has been a star.

And he has been aided from the beginning by his deputy, Nate Ewell, who actually started at CHI during Kelly's tenure. The two have made sure that CHI has lived up to its original intent, and everyone — coaches, administrators and commissioners — have sung the praises of this staff with nary a complaint.

Chapter Eight —
Starting Over

"It was a game that pleased no one, this 24-24 tie between the Harvards and the Princetons on the final Saturday of October. Oh, it was a beautiful day for football and the thrills and big plays were many. But the fates were cruel for it was a game that at one time or another, each of the teams had owned. But in the end, when it mattered, it belonged to neither."
— *"News & Views," Harvard Varsity Club, October 1978*

The spring of 2020 was an odd one. I was able to maintain some sense of normalcy through the Hockey East Women's Championships, hosted by Merrimack College in the first weekend of March. But then things took a downward turn.

The Covid-19 pandemic was just ramping up and it was during the second week of March that the Hockey East men's championship was cancelled, along with most other sporting events in the country. Shortly after that, one of our two college-age kids brought the virus home and four of us got sick, me the worst. Bobby, the only member of the family not living at home, was spared.

While I was recuperating, Steve Metcalf took over at Hockey East and, from a distance, I assisted with the transition. It was odd to go through the spring without the normal commissioner duties, particularly the preparing for the athletic directors' meeting that took place in June of each year.

At the same time as I was pondering my future, my son, Joey, was graduating from college and he, too, was concerned about what was in store for him. I'm sure that on more than one occasion, I offered advice along the lines of, "Pursue what you know, with people who know you." It was what I had done so many years ago, my first few work experiences being: a teacher at my old high school; an intern at the athletic conference in which I played hockey; and the sports information director at the college I attended.

Strangely, while I re-lived that past and tried to help Joey, I was looking at a similar situation for myself. But I was counting on the benefit of a lifetime of experiences and contacts over five decades on which to call. Actually, as it turned out, many of those contacts called me.

Before those calls started to come my way, I thought about re-creating myself completely. Back in 2014, I had started to reflect on my life in sports and that's when the idea for this book started to take shape. I always saw myself as a writer, and with 38 years as a college hockey administrator coming to an end, I thought I would finally become the writer I always thought I could be.

The quoted copy that appears at the start of this chapter comes from a game story I wrote for the Harvard Varsity Club's newsletter more than 40 years ago. It appeared in *News and Views* following the tie game between Harvard and Princeton on October 28, 1978. I'm sure I was quite pleased with myself at the time, even more so when I received a call from Kevin Mannix, a sportswriter at the *Boston Herald*, a day after the newsletter was mailed out.

 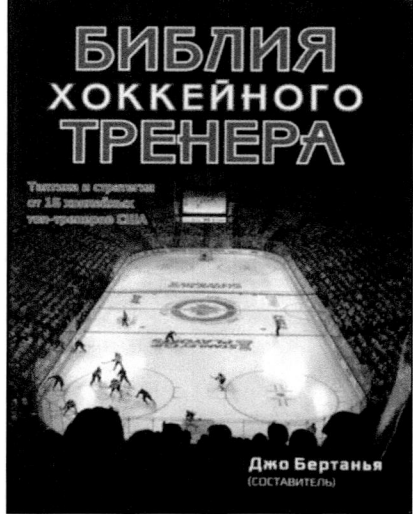

In 2015, I edited this collection of instructional pieces, most of them submitted by college coaches. It was published in Russia as well as in North America.

"I'm just calling to tell you how much I loved this game story," said Mannix, as he read aloud the aforementioned paragraph. I'm sure I was riding high the whole day.

While my primary jobs as an adult have been hockey coach and administrator, I have always had an urge to write: to either chronicle the people and moments of my hockey life or, on occasion, to have some fun in or out of the sports world. Toward this end, I took every opportunity within whatever "day job" I held to write stories. Perhaps it was in a program for some special event or in *Stops & Starts*, the newsletter of the American Hockey Coaches Association, or, perhaps, as a guest contributor to *U.S. College Hockey On-line* or for *College Hockey News*.

There were actually times when I was a *real* writer. I have written and self-published two books on goaltending, edited *The Hockey Coaching Bible*, a collection of instructional pieces by a variety of acclaimed coaches, and produced a photo history of Harvard University athletics, *Crimson in Triumph*. And, of course, there is this book that you are close to finishing.

I don't know if I should admit this but the most satisfying job I ever had was not in athletics. It was the year-and-a-half that I spent producing newspaper parodies. My team wanted to be *The Onion* before *The Onion* ever existed.

It was the summer of 1980 and I was working in Harvard University's sports information office when I got the idea to do a parody of the *Boston Globe*. During that summer, I would tell anyone who would listen about these plans, and then one day, when I was explaining this to an acquaintance named Jay Elliot, he stopped me and said, "That's funny. I was just at this guy's place in New London, NH, and the bathroom in his office had wallpaper with pages from a *New York Times* parody, *Not the New York Times*."

I remember purchasing *Not the New York Times* in 1978. I recall the front page story of Pope John Paul I dying shortly after assuming his role, the headline being, "Pope Dies Yet Again." I remember actor/writer Tony Hendra as the Pope ("John Paul John Paul) in a front page photo. And I recall that it came out during a newspaper strike in New York, great timing to catch people's eyes when the lookalike appeared on newsstands.

Jay, who was working for a scholastic magazine at the time, offered to introduce me to his publisher friend, Larry Durocher, and I followed up with plans to drive to New London and meet him. First, I did a little research on Larry. A native of Belmont, MA, a town adjacent to my hometown of Arlington, Larry never attended college but had been hugely successful as a publisher and direct mail marketing legend. He had been publisher of the *Boston Phoenix* and *Rolling Stone* magazine. He flew a plane for Bobby Kennedy during one of RFK's political campaigns. He raised money for liberals and conservatives alike. Somewhere in my research, I discovered we had a common friend in Pulitzer

Prize-winning political cartoonist Paul Szep.

The meeting with Larry went well and by the fall we had brought in a third partner, a Dartmouth alumnus named Dennis Jolicoeur, whose family owned a small weekly "shopper" that was distributed in southern New Hampshire. They also owned the local Pepsi distributor license, the Pepsi trucks and the newspaper working out of the same facility in Manchester, NH.

I would be the editor of *Not the Boston Globe*, making sure we had 24 filled pages. Dennis provided financing and a place where we could print the parody. And Larry would be the publisher, ensuring that we had retailers who would sell it.

In those days, "cutting and pasting" literally meant cutting and pasting. My typed stories went to a woman who set the columns in a Compugraphic machine that spit out copy set to the *Globe's* specifications. I believe the primary font was 9-point Bookman, if memory serves me well. I would take the copy, cut it with an Exacto knife, run it through a waxing machine and then "paste" it on a large sheet of paper that included a grid to guide me. Images were shot with a large camera and spaces were set aside for them to be dropped in later.

I convinced a former UNH hockey player, Tom Osenton, to join me as co-editor. I went back a ways with Tom and the two of us shared the same skewed sense of humor that served this project well. He also provided me some relief when the brilliant Larry Durocher would dominate a day with stories and day trips to places that might, or might not, have had something to do with the work at hand.

Our first headline, "Reagan still asleep," came from my watching the *Today* show one morning, the lead story being one of the Navy's fighter jets shooting down a plane over or near Libya. Part of the reporting referenced President Reagan being asleep when it happened and the staff not feeling the need to wake him. We ran with that, concocting a story where Reagan had been asleep for days and Alexander Haig deciding not to wake him, etc.

I contacted a photographer who covered Reagan during a primary stop in New Hampshire. I asked him if he had any photos of Reagan with his eyes closed, perhaps blinking. He delivered exactly that and it ran next to our lead story.

The very first story I wrote for the parody was an obituary of the Pillsbury Doughboy, Poppin' Fresh. It began, "Poppin Fresh, known to millions of Americans as the Pillsbury Doughboy, died late Saturday afternoon as a result of a kitchen accident in Battle Creek, Michigan. The popular television personality was attending the annual Pillsbury Bake-Off when an overzealous fan poked the loveable figure in the stomach and sent him sliding along a counter top and into an unattended Cuisenart. Fresh died instantly."

I think my favorite line in the entire paper was the obituary's ending:

One of my many mentors, Larry Durocher, joins me with our first parody front page, featuring our "Reagan still asleep" headline.

"Services will be conducted at Stroh's Bakery at 11 a.m. on Tuesday where Mr. Fresh, according to his wishes, will be baked at 375 degrees for ten minutes."

Another story did a twist on Irish activists who were engaged in hunger strikes in Northern Ireland around that time. No, that's not inherently humorous. But our story was of an Italian protester who declared he would eat non-stop until a local food tax was lifted. I named him Lorenzo Luigi Fagioli, which would translate to "L.L. Bean."

When we hit the newsstands before Christmas of 1981, we had two immediate issues surface. First, some retailers were afraid that the *Globe* might be upset with our parody and they were reluctant to sell it. Larry had me visit the *Globe* and somehow I was to get a copy of *Not the Boston Globe* on the desk of publisher Davis Taylor, who was related to my friend and hockey mentor Tim Taylor. And, in fact, I delivered the paper as asked.

When the the *Globe* ran a light-hearted piece about the parody in the next day's edition, we had what we needed and retailers were free to sell the paper. The next hurdle was that people were grabbing the parody and leaving a quarter, thinking they were buying the real thing. Given that we were charging $2, the newsstands would lose money every time this happened. In our next edition, we ran a red banner across the upper right corner proclaiming, "Special Parody Edition - $2.00."

Eventually, I left Harvard and went to work for Larry. We did a second *Globe* and then regional issues in Minneapolis, San Francisco and elsewhere before deciding to create a fake tabloid called *The Daily Constitutional*. When we set out to parody an existing paper, we had to spend a lot of time matching things like column width, proper font, local columnists, etc. And when those papers were "broadsheets," like *The Globe*, we needed longer stories, stories that would challenge our ability to maintain the humor throughout.

By switching to our own tabloid, even though it bore a striking resemblance to the *Boston Herald*, it was ours, with our own "staff" and our own specifications. That a typical tabloid featured large photos and short stories played right to our limitations.

In time, the Jolicoeur family pulled the financing and the dream that Larry and I had of creating a subscription humor magazine in the form of a fictitious paper went by the boards. Larry and I became fast friends, me being the godfather to his two terrific kids, Angus and Kate. He even offered me a job going to work with him on unidentified projects. I declined and shortly after that, opportunities with ECAC Hockey came my way.

I have often wondered what my life would have been if we had been able to continue to develop these parodies and bring them nationwide. From what I have detailed in this book, it is clear what I would have missed. But it is intriguing to consider what might have been.

Yale president A. Bartlett Giamatti enjoys my first edition of *Not the Boston Globe*. The man with the white hair behind the paper is Frank Ryan, Yale's athletic director at the time and a former NFL quarterback. A photographer for the *Yale Daily News* sent me the photo, which I subsequently had Giamatti autograph. Somewhere in my files, I have a letter from Giamatti requesting additional copies of the parody. This photo dates from 1982. Seven years later, Giamatti became Commissioner of Major League Baseball, serving only 154 days before he suffered a fatal heart attack in August 1989. (Photo courtesy of the Yale Daily News)

I received a call from Steve Metcalf on June 30, 2020, one of many calls from my successor at Hockey East that came in the month of June. In passing, I mentioned that I was officially ending my time at Hockey East as of the end of work that day at 5:00 p.m. Steve took it on his own to contact all of the head coaches and administrators in the conference, and I was the beneficiary of a number of calls and texts wishing me the best. It was a nice gesture on Steve's part, given that Covid had prevented any closure a single farewell event might have provided.

By that time, the transition to my new life had started to take place and it was quite gratifying to realize that there would be life, plenty of life, after my four decades of conference employment. One by one, the building blocks of a new life started to be pieced together.

Goalie coaching had always been there for me and one of the first people with whom I spoke was Peter Ferriero. Peter directed a number of hockey programs out of Salem, NH, and I had worked for him, off and on, for the previous two decades. He ran the Top Gun youth program out of Salem and that's where my previous work for him had been.

Along with his three sons — Benn, Cody and Nathan — Peter also administered the New England Fall Prep League, a schedule of games that augmented the regular prep season, games intended to bolster the prep schools as they battled junior hockey to keep their hockey players. The Ferrieros also oversaw a summer training program, on and off the ice, called Real Speed Training. I would have the responsibility for goalie training for all of these endeavors.

While the goalie coaching alone was a benefit, I also enjoyed working with Peter, a no-nonsense advocate for the right values, a true hockey guy, in a culture that was being taken over by entrepreneurs.

In addition to these goalie coaching duties, I was able to renew my agreement to coach the goalies at The Governor's Academy in Byfield, MA. The director of athletics at "GA" was Claudia Asano Barcomb, a good friend I knew from her days as both a player and a coach at Harvard. Claudia and I served on the NCAA Men's and Women's Ice Hockey Rules Committee together and I always enjoyed her company. In addition to her AD duties, she was the girls' hockey coach, working alongside the previous girls' head coach, Babe Ceglarski. Babe was the oldest son of the late Lenny Ceglarski. The boys' team was coached by former Boston University player Brian McGuirk, assisted by Mike Delay.

With the first piece in place, I was pleasantly surprised when the Hockey Commissioners Association reached out to me, offering me a chance to remain involved with that organization. I had been there from the start and had handled the checkbook as its treasurer for 15 years.

In addition to retaining that responsibility, I was given new duties that brought me back to my SID days. I would handle the monthly press releases, choosing the player, rookie and goalie of the month, and I would oversee the publicity and voting for the Mike Richter Award, given to the best goalie in men's Division I hockey. The HCA had taken over the responsibility and this was right up my alley. Not only was it SID work and about goaltending, but it allowed me to renew my relationship with Mike, my old student. On my suggestion, we added a women's Goalie of the Year award as well.

Two building blocks were in place, each in an area of great comfort for me. Next, I received a phone call from Bill Collett, someone I knew a little from hockey but more so because his brother, Mike, was married to my niece Michelle. Both Mike and Michelle had played at Northeastern.

Bill was calling to see if I might have interest in working with the Eastern Hockey League, a junior league that operated along the Eastern seaboard, its primary mission being to prepare hockey players and place them into NCAA Division III programs. It had an excellent track record, putting some 170 players into Division III hockey annually.

Through a series of calls, we arrived at a place that worked for both the EHL and me. I would go to work for the EHL as its "Senior Advisor" and would start my new job on June 1, 2020. This position created opportunities for me to attend games, enforce league rules, get involved with the discipline

Covid-19 protocols were in effect when I presented trophies at the Eastern Hockey League's "Frozen Finals." Above I present the tournament Most Valuable Player award to Connor Bizal of the Boston Junior Rangers. Bizal committed to play college hockey at Buffalo State. (Dan Hickling Photo courtesy of the Eastern Hockey League)

process and, eventually, help administer a post-season tournament. All of these duties mirrored what I had done as a college hockey commissioner for the past four decades. I even ended the year by presenting the EHL championship trophy at its "Frozen Finals" in Pennsylvania. It marked the first time I had traveled by plane or checked into a hotel in about 15 months, due to the pandemic. It also allowed me to keep intact a streak of 35+ years of handing out a postseason championship trophy.

As was typical of hockey, at least in the northeast, a new hockey experience allowed me to cross paths with people from my hockey past. The East Coast Wizards team was owned by Scott Fusco, a Hobey Baker Award winner and 1984 Olympian. The Worcester Railers were owned by the Addesa family, with former RPI coach Mike Addesa serving as general manager. The general manager of the Walpole Express was Todd Stirling, whose father Steve was an All American at Boston University and later a college and professional head coach.

The EHL staff that was in place were also familiar to me. I had experience with supervisor of officials Gene Binda, who served in that capacity for three college conferences and I knew his son, Gino, who had once taken part in an NCAA Rules Committee meeting many years ago as an active on-ice official when I was chair of the committee. And the director of hockey operations for the EHL was Ken Hodge Jr. I knew Kenny beyond his years as a great player at Boston College and with the Boston Bruins. Not only did he provide color commentary for BC hockey on the radio for many of my Hockey East years, he would demonstrate at skating camps run by Paul Vincent when he was a young boy. I worked for Paul in one of those summers, maybe 40 years earlier, and that is when I first met Ken. My associate, Neil Ravin, who did it all for EHL, was once a Hockey East intern.

By the end of the 2020-21 season, my "Senior Advisor" position had, in effect, morphed into the familiar role of commissioner in just about every way except holding the actual title. That was addressed when the EHL Board of Directors met in early May 2021 and voted to extend me a three-year contract to serve as its commissioner. I humbly accepted and was pleased to be a commissioner once more.

I look forward to a "normal" season in 2021-22 as many of the EHL's special events had to be cancelled in my first year of service. The EHL hosts showcase events that bring almost all of its 18 teams to one site to facilitate college coaches who get to see so many prospects in one place. They also put together all-star teams who play exhibition games against NCAA Division III schools.

To complete the list of familiar hockey responsibilities in my first year after Hockey East, I continued to work with the American Hockey Coaches

Association, though we were unable to host the annual AHCA Convention in Naples, FL, for the second straight year due to the pandemic. The Naples Beach Hotel and Golf Club, which had served as the site of three decades of conventions, was sold to make way for luxury condominiums and a boutique hotel. With the wrecking ball set to come down on May 23, a group of 100 or so stalwarts converged on the property for a farewell in April 2021, enjoying three days of new drinks and old stories.

Two weeks after the farewell, the 2021 AHCA Virtual Convention unfolded and brought the hockey community together in a different way. A socially distanced way. But the AHCA was able to conduct its business and maintain its relevance. Special praise should go out to the coaches who organized and delivered our efficient virtual event. UVM assistant coach Steve Wiedler did all of the detail work behind the scenes in setting up the platform that hosted the convention, while AHCA officers and governors, like Casey Jones of Clarkson, Chris McKelvie of Bethel, Mare MacDougall Bari of St. Lawrence and Holley Tyng of Colby, made sure both men's and women's interests were considered.

In putting together a busy 2020-21 hockey season, my time was less in the familiar world of college hockey and more in myriad programs that fell under the USA Hockey umbrella. Both the Top Gun and EHL work clearly fell under the aegis of USA Hockey. So too did the increased time I spent with Massachusetts Hockey, which is was part of USA Hockey.

As noted elsewhere in these pages, I have been involved with USA Hockey for decades. Many of those experiences were as a goalie coach, working the first summer goaltending camps back in the 1980s and also being the beneficiary of high-end goalie coach appointments, like the 1991 Canada Cup squad as well as the 1994 Lillehammer Olympic Team.

On the heels of these experiences, I was appointed to one of two NCAA "Director" positions in 1995 and served in that role until the loss of my Hockey East commissioner job meant that I could no longer hold that NCAA position. Fortunately, I was voted the title of "Director Emeritus" during the 2020 virtual Congress and that was certainly appreciated.

From these USA hockey-related experiences, I developed relationships with people closer to home in the Massachusetts district of USA Hockey. And in the 2020-21 season, I began to expand my involvement with Massachusetts Hockey. Up to this point, my primary connection to "MA Hockey" was through its Hall of Fame. Inducted into the Hall in 2018, I had volunteered to emcee the annual dinner and also serve on the HOF Committee. In 2020, I became the chair of the committee.

As the season unfolded in the fall, I was asked to participate in discipline hearings for MA Hockey, some determining discipline for bad behavior, some being appeals of discipline meted out by a previous panel. This was, overall, a positive experience, despite the nature of some of the behavior we saw. It was positive because I got to work with some terrific volunteers who were motivated by fostering proper behavior in our local hockey community.

Brought before us were cases involving such things as dangerous play, verbal abuse of officials and widely inappropriate language between players or between coaches and on-ice officials. The latter was particularly concerning because USA Hockey had provided us with statistics showing that approximately 40% of USA Hockey on-ice officials walk away from the position annually. The two reasons most often cited are abuse from parents and coaches and limitations on how quickly they can advance through the ranks.

The disciplinary hearings usually begin with a notification that MA Hockey needs people to serve on a panel. The particular situation is usually identified in an incident report filed by an on-ice official. This provides a brief description of which specific USA Hockey playing rule has been broken, how it happened, where on the ice and when in the game. Often there is video that may or may not be helpful, given the quality of video in a town arena.

The redeeming qualities of this process are many. Often, the person accused of the inappropriate behavior regrets their actions and is sincerely apologetic. That takes the edge off the hearing.

The panelists, all with relevant experience in hockey, take their responsibilities seriously, asking thoughtful questions and looking not solely to punish but also to educate. Often the on-ice official who wrote up the incident report takes part in the hearings and offers a measured accounting of what took place. There is the occasional referee who gets emotionally dragged into a situation, perhaps escalating it, but more often than not, they make a strong case to back up whatever penalties they called in response to the situation.

Often one of the on-ice officials will be a young man or woman, perhaps still in their teens, who displays admirable maturity in answering questions and defending their actions. Sometimes the young official comes across as more mature than an adult coach.

Yes, there are hearings that do not go as smoothly as what I have described above. There is the parent who can't see that their behavior was wrong. There is the coach who tries to justify his actions because he "knows" the ref was wrong. Those who are unable, in a cooler moment, to see the error of their ways usually end up receiving a more severe penalty. And many of those appeal the decisions, very few appeals mitigating their punishment.

When discussing youth hockey, or any organized youth sports today, it is easy to think of some of the excesses that are reported from time to time. Too many games. Too much travel. Specialization at an early age. Poor sportsmanship. The bad and the ugly sometimes overshadow the good.

I even did a parody of a youth hockey family back in 2004 for *U.S. College Hockey Online*, through the form of a fictitious family Christmas letter. Called *Our Holiday Letter*, part of it parodied the college recruitment process, other parts the excesses of the youth hockey culture.

Some excerpts:

We are all so proud of Bryan. He was heavily recruited as a walk-on at State University and will be going there next fall. He made a verbal commitment to seven other schools, just to be safe, but State just seemed like a perfect fit. It has been a whirlwind year for Bryan, what with the three junior teams he has been on and his 23rd birthday and all.

Jonathan (19) loves St. Grottlesex Prep. It seems like the perfect place for him. Unlike the last three. He is turning a few heads with his scoring ability. As of last week, he was 22-0-22. The only disappointment for Jon was the fact that his teammates couldn't see fit to vote him captain. We were all shocked.

Billy just celebrated his 8th birthday in Minsk. Yes, that Minsk. We heard of this fabulous Russian coach who can turn even the weakest mite into a potential NHL star. Billy wasn't too keen on going, but we know he'll thank us when they start allowing mail.

As for us, the old folks in the house, we are just trying to make sure the kids grow up like normal kids and keep a sense of perspective in their lives. As many of you already know, we lost the lawsuit so Bob will have to stay away from the local rink for the next six months. (I still don't believe that "Zero Tolerance" thing is constitutional! And that ref was WAY too sensitive. All Bob wanted to do was speak with him in the parking lot. And he was NOT pushed. He clearly slipped on that ice and, well, we have to abide by the gag order and that's all I can say here.)

My final new assignment came in the spring of 2021, I was contacted by Erick Kainen, a former goaltender for Tufts University, who was looking for volunteers to work as part of USA Hockey's goaltending development program. Specifically, he was looking to fill a slot in Massachusetts. I was somewhat familiar with what USA Hockey had launched in this area and agreed to get involved.

USA Hockey had recently articulated two goals involving U.S. goalies. First, at the grass roots level, it wanted to see an increase in young hockey players wishing to try goaltending. To enhance this, USA Hockey came up with two much-welcomed developments. One was the use of "quick change" goalie equipment. A young non-goalie could put on pads, with

The first USA Hockey Goaltenders Development Camp had this crackerjack staff: standing, from left, Al Godfrey, Keith Allain, Cap Raeder and Dave Peterson; kneeling, from left, myself. and Mike Dibble. (Photo courtesy of USA Hockey)

Velcro straps, right over his or her regular shin pads, don a padded practice jersey and swap out gloves and stick for the goaltending equivalent. Voila! Instant goalie! Next, they encouraged the use of intermediate nets, so a new goalie stepping into the position for the first time would have a better chance to experience what it was like to make saves, the full-size net being reduced considerably.

The other articulated goal of USA Hockey was a bit more ambitious. It came up with the slogan "51 in 30," representing the target of the U.S. having 51% of all NHL goalies by the year 2030. Currently, the U.S. can claim just over 16% of those goalies.

It was very gratifying to reconnect with USA Hockey in the area of goaltending development. This is not the first time I have served in that role. I was asked to work the first USA Hockey goaltender development camp in the mid-1980s, the exact year of which escapes me. Back then, goalie-specific programs were few and that first summer goaltenders' camp was one of them. It was a treat to be asked to take part, primarily because of the staff that was put together. There were three western coaches and three eastern coaches and we all became fast friends.

The guys from the west were future Olympic head coach Dave Peterson, his fellow Minnesotan Al Godfrey, a successful high school coach and NHL scout, and Mike Dibble, a former Wisconsin goalie who would have been a candidate for the 1980 Olympic team if not for a knee injury.

Our eastern triumvirate was former UNH All American goalie Cap Raeder, future Yale head coach Keith Allain and myself. We worked hard during the day and enjoyed our nights out with the same passion, and bonded in the process. We did it again a year later, with former Michigan Tech goalie Bruce Horsch joining us, as did Ron DeGregorio, the future USA Hockey President who had played goal at Middlebury College.

I had known Cap and Keith for some time. Getting to know "Coach Pete" and "Uncle Al" was a treat. I recall when Al asked if any of us knew how to play cribbage, I eagerly shouted, "I do. I know how to play." An hour or so later, after I had lost about $25 in the game, Al said, "What other games do you know, Joe?" I still have the plastic cribbage board, holding a deck of cards, that Dave Peterson gave me that year.

It was during this period that I worked with both Dave and Al to produce a goaltending manual and an instructional video. It began two decades of video/DVD work, the final count being seven different videos I was able to produce. Beyond the one for USA Hockey, I did one as part of an ESPN instructional series, hockey being one of many sports included. I did one for a former student of mine, Tom Ormondroyd, who attended Holy Cross.

Finally, I was approached by Championship Productions of Ames, IA, which resulted in four DVDs on goaltending, three filmed at St. Mary's University in Winona, MN, and one many years later produced in Salem, NH. That DVD is still relevant. It was shot with one of my staff coaches, Mike Morrison, who had played at the University of Maine and in the NHL.

Titled *Goaltending Today: Traditional Values Through New Techniques*, the DVD featured me playing the "old guy" and asking Mike how the newer techniques of today came about. At the same time, there was a respect for the traditional importance of positioning, rebound control and reading plays.

My first memory of interacting with USA Hockey comes from 1970, shortly after my freshman season at Harvard, when USA Hockey was still the Amateur Hockey Association of the United States or AHAUS. In the spring of 1970, I was on a team that won the AHAUS National Juvenile Championship in Amherst, NY. Tom Walsh, father of Arlington goaltender Eddie Walsh, put together a team of Arlington players who would compete against teams from Chicago, Detroit, Ithaca and Philadelphia, all of them all-star teams from their respective regions. Arlington, with the exception of Ithaca, was the smallest town to send a team.

I must not have had much of an ego back then because I agreed to start the tournament and, if we were able to get to Sunday's championship final, Eddie would be summoned from home, where he had baseball games at Browne and Nichols School, and he would play for the title. As it turned out, I played well, so well that when we got to the final, Eddie was told that he could stay home and they would go with me. We beat Ithaca, 4-0, to win the tournament.

One other memory from this period involves the political turmoil of the time. The spring was one of anti-war protests, and on an afternoon when our juvenile team had a practice in Arlington, there were demonstrations on Boston Common that turned ugly when participants dispersed late in the day. Banks and other symbols of the establishment were subject to sporadic vandalism.

I recall taking public transportation from Arlington into Cambridge, as I returned to my freshman dorm in Harvard Square. The rest of the team were all high schoolers, me being an 18-year-old college freshman and still eligible for the tournament.

As I came up the old escalator in the middle of Harvard Square, I sensed something wasn't right. The sounds were different. Stepping off the escalator, I looked around and saw scenes out of some movie. There were lines of armed police, face masks, shields and batons visible. A car was tipped over. A trash barrel and its contents were set on fire. Most of the gates to Harvard Yard were locked, posing an immediate challenge, as my dorm, Matthews Hall, was just inside the Yard near where I stood.

I approached one of the policemen and told him I wanted to get to my dorm and asked what I should do. He said the gate on Quincy Street on the far side of the Yard was open and that I should go directly there and then to my room.

My room was located on the fifth floor, with a fire escape that looked into Harvard Square. Upon arriving, I was able to take in the scene. Police had started to advise demonstrators to "please peacefully disperse" through bullhorns and warned of action to follow. That action became the use of tear gas cannisters that were fired into selected areas. While I can't recall why the tear gas would have been needed inside the gates of the Yard, I know that shortly after it was deployed, the gas reached us on the fifth floor fire escape and everyone in the dorm was scurrying to close windows to mitigate the damage being done. Later that spring, college students died at Kent State University when the National Guard fired shots into a group of protesters.

As I have visited my hockey past through this project, I have come to value my USA Hockey connections even more. And I have particularly embraced the two high-level assignments that I referenced in Chapter Three when recounting my goalie coaching work at the 1991 Canada Cup and the 1994 Lillehammer Olympics.

There are a couple of special memories from those experiences that I would like to revisit here, experiences from which I took away some tangible artifacts that constantly remind me of those unique experiences.

My friend Art Berglund passed away in December 2020. It was during the 1991 Canada Cup experience that I got to know Art, the director of USA Hockey's international teams. Art could be gruff, the proverbial "bull in a China shop." But once he took you into his inner circle, he was a loyal friend for life. I loved getting the occasional holiday phone call or maybe a text. Some were punctuated with, "Rage on," or some other exhortation.

Back in 1991, I accompanied him in Montreal when he was on a mission to find a certain painting he wanted to buy. We went to a gallery that featured the works of Terry Tomalty, an artist whose paintings frequently included hockey in some way. This was a step or two above the cute depictions of little kids in Montreal jerseys playing on a makeshift rink with other little guys in Toronto jerseys that you see on calendars or as jigsaw puzzles.

He found what he was looking for, an oil painting that featured a downtown scene, with a billboard advertising a Canadian brand of cigarettes, and walking near the billboard is a young man with a hockey stick over his shoulder, a pair of skates dangling from the end of the stick. Art loved to point out that you could see kids playing "boot hockey" on a side street in the painting.

When Art retired from USA Hockey, I bought that painting and I look at it every day. At the time of the sale, Art included a note he had received from the artist, remarking how much he enjoyed knowing that his work resided with hockey people. Terry's son played college hockey at Dartmouth.

My other story comes from the 1993-94 Olympic tour. That was

Art Berglund, Dave Ogrean and me at the 1994 Lillehammer Games. (Photo courtesy of USA Hockey)

the last non-NHL Olympic team and the last to take part in a six-month pre-Olympic schedule of games. The schedule allowed me to travel to Finland, Norway, Sweden and Russia, places I had never visited and places to which I have not returned. The pre-Olympic travel was as memorable as the two weeks in Lillehammer, partly because of the merits of the tour, partly because of our poor showing on the ice in the Olympics. But I did enjoy living in a house one block from the main arena with Art and Dave Ogrean.

The trip to Russia in December 1993 had somewhat faded from my memory but working on this book brought back some very specific moments. We flew out of Newark and I recall that one of the Ferraro brothers missed the flight.

Chris and Peter Ferraro were outstanding forwards who were among six University of Maine players on the pre-Olympic roster. Eventually, Chris was cut, not making the official Olympic Team but being allowed by coach Tim Taylor to travel to Lillehammer.

I had first met the Ferraro brothers when I was running a goalie camp in Hingham, MA, a few years before they attended Maine. I was in need of shooters on a Friday, a day we normally would end the week with a contest, keeping score on breakaways and other drills. On this particular Friday, we were light on shooters and I was told there were some good age-appropriate players in the other rink we might approach.

Walking over to the second ice surface, I found the Ferraro brothers and explained what I needed. I specifically told them that the goalies were competing and they should try hard and play it straight. When they came over to do breakaways, one of them started in from center ice (I can't recall which one) and as he approached the goalie, he threw one of his gloves directly into the goalie's mask and then with one hand on his stick, deked the startled goalie and scored. Not exactly "playing it straight."

During the pre-Olympic tour, Tim Taylor had me separate the brothers when rooming lists were created, but they always swapped keys and ended up together. When one of them was late for that flight to Russia, the other one wanted to stay behind and wait for the tardy brother. Coach Taylor would have none of that.

I recall a scary landing in Moscow. I remember bad weather for a few days and Tim and John Cunniff ignoring the weather and keeping their consecutive streak of going for a run intact. I'm not particularly proud that I ate a very salty cheeseburger in a Moscow McDonald's. But I am grateful that I got to meet the great Anatoli Tarasov, the founder of Russian hockey, at the arena where we played in the Izvestia Tournament.

It was at that arena where I purchased two neckties that I still have, and wear, nearly 30 years later. I was wearing a hockey-themed tie at the rink, probably one with Snoopy or a Walt Disney character, when someone

I was able to visit Moscow in December 1993 when Team USA participated in the Izvestia Cup. Amid the purchasing of nesting dolls and sampling local vodka, I also ate at a McDonald's.

asked if I had a collection of hockey ties. When I told the person that I did, he asked me if I would like to add to my collection. He explained to me that the referee-in-chief created homemade neckties and sold them out of his briefcase. When I asked if he spoke English, I was informed that he was particularly fluent when somebody was about to give him money.

This turned out to be a two-fer. First, I was shown some beautiful ties from which I could choose to make a purchase. These were unlike any I had seen at home. Most hockey neckwear in the States had a single hockey character or a skates-and-sticks design repeated throughout the print area. These ties were like small tapestries with a single large hockey scene unfolding from top to bottom.

The second benefit was that this referee-in-chief turned out to be someone whose name was well known in hockey history. Josef Kompalla was one of the on-ice officials in the famous 1972 Summit Series played between Canada and the Soviet Union in September of that year. Canada won three of the four games in Moscow to salvage the series, 4-3-1. At Tim Taylor's summer hockey camp, we all watched the highlights of that series and knew the key players by heart.

In looking back on both my experiences with USA Hockey and my flirtation with writing over the years, I recalled a conversation I had with 1984 U.S. Olympic coach Lou Vairo, who spoke to me about a book idea he was developing. Lou's life in hockey has taken him to many places but, in particular, he wanted to tell the story of his relationship with the great Soviet coach Anatoli Tarasov.

It was during my Canada Cup and Olympic experiences that I began to forge a friendship with Lou. His personal story is unlike any other in the annals of elite hockey in the United States. Think about it. How does a guy from Brooklyn, who was never a very good skater, who played as much street hockey and roller hockey as he did ice hockey, become the head coach of the United States Olympic Ice Hockey Team?

While coaching some kids in Brooklyn, he realized he needed to know more about hockey to do the job well. Motivated by that, he began a quest for knowledge that — and it is not hyperbole to say this — changed how hockey was played in America. I'll let Lou tell how this story began, as only he can tell it.

"I knew some of the kids from our roller hockey days and there was no coach. I don't know what to call myself, just an organizer of the group. And I said, 'Jeez if I'm going to be a coach, I better do something.'

"So, I went to the library in Brooklyn near my home and found one book on coaching ice hockey. It was by Lloyd Percival, *The Hockey Handbook*. I took it out and I read it three or four times, from cover to cover, and that started me off in coaching and, specifically, trying to understand what a coach's role is. After all these years of doing it, I can tell you that you can sum it up in one word: leadership. That's what real coaching is. It is leadership. It's not who knows the best drills or the most drills. It is understanding what's available and then leading your charges with that information and doing so from your heart. I also believe you coach not analytically, but you coach from your heart, if you are a real coach. So that began my coaching career.

"One morning, I got dressed. Nice sport coat, slacks, shirt and tie and off to church I went. After church, my grandmother had a Sunday ritual where everyone would come over and eat, and I mean *everybody*. It was a lot of people. So, after church I stopped by her house and went in and greeted the family, had lunch, got bored, wanted to leave, but I didn't want to be rude.

"So, I asked her if I could go into one of the bedrooms. There was a Zenith black-and-white TV with rabbit ears and aluminum foil. She said, 'Sure,' and I turned on the television. In those days, it was all black and white, usually fluttering or with snow or some disturbance. All of a sudden, I turned to channel 13, ABC, the *Wide World of Sports*. Remember that guy who was skiing downhill and he gets all tangled up, beat up, and you think he would be dead? But he was fine, they say.

"There it was, a hockey game from Stockholm, Sweden. It was 1969, Stockholm, Sweden. I'm watching this hockey game and I had never heard of the world championships. I couldn't believe what I was seeing. The level of hockey expertise by both teams, the speed, the skill level, everything. It was astonishing. I was a big hockey fan. I had been to many Rangers games in my life and loved it. I knew every player in the NHL. But this was a different hockey and it was appealing to me. It stimulated my curiosity and I said, 'I have to learn how you play hockey like this. But how would I do that?'

"Well, a little while later they sent one of those trailers along the bottom of the TV, showing the Soviet bench, and it read, 'Coach Anatoli Tarasov.' I had never seen a name like that, so I had to carefully jot it down. It's a good thing they kept it on for 10 seconds. I watched that game and I was overcome with joy. I thought it was beautiful hockey. I put the paper with his name in my pocket, the game ended and I had some cannoli.

"A few weeks later, I brought that coat to the dry cleaners and as I was leaving, the lady said, 'Sir, you have a piece of paper with something written down, here in the pocket.' So, I walked over and picked it up from her and I said, 'Oh yeah, that's that Soviet guy, that coach.' So I went home and wrote him a letter complimenting him about his team and telling him how interested I was in how they do things.

"I addressed the letter: 'Anatoli Tarasov, Head Coach, National Ice

Hockey Team, Moscow, Soviet Union,' and took it to the post office. Now, at the time, I was making $60 a week installing air conditioners in New York City, working five or six days a week. So, when the people at the post office weighed my letter and told me it would cost $3.75, well, that's a lot of money when you are making $60 a week. But I had no choice, agreed to it, they put a million stamps on it and off it went.

"Months letter, I received a response. Back then, the only mail I ever got were bills. Electric bills. Gas bills. And here is this letter, on blue tissue paper. You can almost see through it. With 'Par Avion' on the outside. It is from Tarasov. It was typed in red ink and blue ink and green ink, in the Latin alphabet. Not perfect grammatically but how I might write in a foreign language.

"He was pleased with my letter but, of course, he had to say, 'When you compliment, you steal.' He accused me of wanting to steal from Soviet hockey and, of course, he was right. Really, I just wanted to do a better job of coaching these kids. That's the real reason I was doing this. Eventually, I got to meet him, spend hours with him, and form a friendship with him and his family. And it all began accidentally. You could call it destiny and it certainly shaped my life."

It was a few years after the exchange of letters that Lou got to meet Tarasov in person. The Soviets were playing the future U.S. Olympic team in January 1972 at Madison Square Garden. Lou took his young team to the game and, through a connection he had with the Rangers' Emile Francis, was able to meet Tarasov after the game. (The Soviets defeated Team USA, 11-4, that night, but the Americans would win the silver medal in Sapporo, finishing as runner-up to the gold-medal winning Soviets.)

Tarasov, as he had in his letter, invited Lou to visit him in Moscow and, a year or so later, he did just that. Former women's Olympic head coach Ben Smith tells a story of how Tarasov, "sitting with Lou in an apartment, a single light bulb hanging over the kitchen table," told Lou that if he wanted to come to practice the next day, he needed to come with 100 drills. Lou stayed up all night, creating those drills.

Fast forward: Lou moves on from New York, gets a job coaching the Austin (MN) Mavericks junior hockey team. ("I thought I was going to Texas"). He wins multiple championships, using the systems he learned from Tarasov. Coaches, hearing about this savant in Minnesota using all these new and exotic systems, travel to watch Lou's practices in an attempt to learn from his success.

Lou then brings his knowledge to 1980 Olympic coach Herb Brooks, providing vital information that helps create the "Miracle" of 1980, though he receives little recognition for his contributions. Still, he keeps working, adding to his reputation, and is named the head coach of the 1984 U.S.

Top: Lou Vairo, front row center, during a meeting in Duluth in 1979. Front row, from left: Anatoli Tarasov, Lou Vairo, Arkady Chernyshev; back row, from left: C. Pekorek, Dr. Ladislav Horsky, Ted Brill, unidentified, L. Zarkarovich.

At left: Lou Vairo today.
(Photo courtesy of USA Hockey)

Olympic Team. You can't make this up.

Of course, there was no second miracle. The 1984 team could never live up to the hype following the heroics of 1980. Averaging just over 20 years of age, Lou's team struggled right from the start, losing to Canada the day before the Opening Ceremonies in Sarajevo. It would finish seventh.

Lou returned home, worked for the New Jersey Devils for a couple of years, coached in Italy and eventually settled in Colorado Springs, working as Director of Special Projects for USA Hockey. His contributions to the game, embracing his chance meeting with Tarasov and implementing his systems into American hockey, changed the way our game is played. It is a well-kept secret.

In 2010, a journalist named Slava Malamood conducted an interview with the great Russian player Igor Larionov. During the interview, Malamood said to Larionov, "Could a player such as you go far in today's American hockey system?"

To which Larionov said, "Do you know who Lou Vairo is? Not too long ago, when the USA won the Junior Championship in Canada, I sent him an SMS. I told him that the USA won thanks to 'Tarasov-Vairo' hockey. From Tarasov, they learned improvisations, quick passing and the ability to play any position. From America, from Lou Vairo - heart and soul. Lou was very grateful to hear this. He almost cried. He called me and for half an hour he poured his heart out to me. Everything he learned from Tarasov has now come into fruition. I told him the time has come for us to now learn from the Americans."

It's time for me to re-connect with Lou and see if he still wants this story told. When we last spoke about the project, he suggested that such a book might have a bigger market in Russia than in North America. Well, as I noted earlier, I am already published in Russia. So perhaps this will be the next project, one that combines my longing to write with my love of hockey.

Sure, I still have my goalie coaching and my administrative duties with the EHL and with the college hockey commissioners. There is still a year or two left with my AHCA position. But I have never had a light schedule and don't want to start now. Spending time with Lou Vairo? Maybe make a trip or two to Moscow? I can't think of a better way to start my eighth decade, remaining in the world of hockey that has been so good to me and being the writer I always felt I could be.

Chapter Nine —
Tributes

I am reprinting a number of pieces that were previously published, stories that pay tribute in some way or another. Most honor the lives of coaches and these appeared in "Stops and Starts," the newsletter of the American Hockey Coaches Association. Two are tributes to Harvard Hockey friends of mine. One pays tribute to a building, the old Boston Garden. And one is simply my musings that I posted to Facebook after the passing of two legends, Gordie Howe and Muhammad Ali, in 2016.

Gene Kinasewich
("Crimson In Triumph," The Stephen Greene Press, 1986)

Often, when writing a tribute piece, my personal and professional lives collided. Such was the case when writing about my friend Gene Kinasewich for the book "Crimson In Triumph." Gene was about 10 years older than me so I didn't know him when he was playing in college, nor did I see him play then. But I knew bits and pieces of his story. I first met him when he worked Cooney Weiland's hockey school at the Boston Skating Club, where I also met Tim Taylor. I was a junior high defenseman attending the camp. Later, we worked together at Timmy's camp and played together for the Depot Cafe Bombers in Gloucester for many years. Shortly before he died, at an event in his honor at Harvard, Gene presented two autographed copies of Glenn Hall's autobiography: one to his Harvard goalie, Godfrey Wood; and one to me. It is one of my most prized hockey possessions.

At times, the affair was downright ugly. The talented hockey player with the number 13 on his Harvard jersey would be warming up in some opposing team's rink when the voices would be heard.

"Hey, Kinasewich, who's paying you to play tonight?"

They called him a professional. They ruled him ineligible, not once but twice. But he came back. Not once but twice. And his name was finally cleared after everyone heard the whole story.

Gene Kinasewich was born on August 8, 1941, in Edmonton, Alberta. He was the second-youngest of 13 children, orphaned when both parents died when Gene was 10 years old.

Juggling school with a job to help support the family, Gene found time to develop considerable hockey skills. This talent led him to the Edmonton Oil Kings, a junior A hockey team, where he played during the 1957-58 and 1958-59 seasons. With an eye on college down the road, Gene refrained from signing a professional contract. He did, however, accept expense money. For his first year with the Oil Kings, he received $450. The next year it was $702, for a total of $1,152.

Meanwhile, Gene's older brother Orie was attending Colorado College and describing his brother to Jim Lombard, a Colorado freshman who was from the Boston area. Lombard, who later transferred to Harvard and became the hockey manager, took an interest in the younger Kinasewich and helped steer him toward Harvard by way of Deerfield Academy.

Gene Kinasewich slips the puck between the legs of Boston College goalie Tom Apprille to win the 1963 ECAC Championship in overtime at the Boston Arena. (Charles Carey Photo courtesy of Harvard University)

Even before Kinasewich enrolled at Harvard, the Ivy League Eligibility Committee ruled that he, should he come to Harvard, would be ineligible to compete on the varsity hockey team. He had taken money as a hockey player. He was a professional.

Although he received scholarship offers from Colorado and Michigan, where he would have been allowed to play, Kinasewich chose Harvard. That's where he wanted to receive an education. And so he arrived in Cambridge in September 1960.

In September of the following year, impressed with the character of this young man from Edmonton, the Ivy League reversed itself and allowed Kinasewich a new hockey life. He was ruled eligible to play and helped lead Harvard to a 22-5 season that included the 1962 Beanpot championship.

But the administrators struck again in the spring of 1962. This time it was the ECAC Committee on Eligibility that denied Kinasewich the right to play because of "his receipt of excessive expense allowances, i.e., payments over and above out-of-pocket expenditures."

The same rule that handcuffed Kinasewich included a small passage referring to "exceptions" when circumstances were unusual. Gene's story was presented to the ECAC again, with Kinasewich himself invited to speak on his own behalf. A few games into the 1962-63 season, Kinasewich was allowed to play once more.

All of this adds special meaning to the events of that wondrous season. In a year of on-ice triumphs, none was more memorable than the final game of the 1963 ECAC Tournament at the Boston Arena, with Harvard and Boston College fighting for the title. In overtime. George Frazier, writing for *The Boston Herald*, told the story best:

"Now, on this midnight in this madhouse, you suddenly knew that this was how this had to end. Now you knew that there could be no other way — that any other ending would be an indignity. This way, so suspenseful and storybook that hearts stopped beating, was inevitable. This was the hurrah for man's hope — so fit and proper that anything else would seem trite and contrived. For if ever there was a moment of truth, this was to be it. And then, with the hands of the clock standing at four minutes and forty-nine seconds of the 'sudden death' overtime period, he shot the puck past the goalie into the net and the red light flashed on and the game was over. Any other way and all our bright dreams would have been smashed to smithereens."

Teddy Thorndike
("News & Views," The Harvard Varsity Club, 1987)

This piece could have been placed in the Harvard University section, but I decided to include it here. Nothing pleased me more to know that the Thorndike family appreciated this tribute. I wrote it for the Harvard Varsity Club newsletter, "News and Views," in 1987.

A note about the reference to the sophomores helping me out in my senior year. I was having trouble getting to sleep after games. The level of concentration it took me to get through a game made it hard for me to "come down" afterwards. It got to the point that I went home to Arlington to see my family doctor, Patrick Campobasso. He rummaged through a paper bag filled with drug samples and handed me a jar, offering little guidance as to how to take the pills.

One night, after a game, I was sitting with my roommates having downed a pill and a few Budweisers. I started to get out of my seat. The little push upwards sent me careening across the room. I had to grab a couch and then a doorway to stop.

I mentioned this incident to a few of the sophomores at practice the next day. Being somewhat more educated in pharmaceuticals, they said they would stop by and see what I was taking.

"You aren't drinking when you take these, are you?" asked one of them. "These are Quaaludes. Do not drink when you take these and only take what is prescribed. And, if you have any to spare, I'll take them off your hands."

I had never lost a teammate before. Not from high school. Not from college. But on Sunday, January 4, 1987, I found out that Teddy Thorndike had died two days earlier.

Teddy was a member of the Class of 1975 and a member of the Thorndike family, which has given so much to Harvard over the years. His grandfather, who passed away last year, was Dr. Augustus Thorndike, a pioneer in the field of sports medicine in this country and, for many years, athletic surgeon for Harvard. His uncle, John Thorndike '49, was a track letterwinner who more recently has provided leadership for the Friends of Harvard Track. And Teddy's cousin, Edie MacAusland Mabrey, served as Harvard's field hockey coach from 1979-84.

My memories of Teddy are from ice hockey. As a senior at Arlington High School in 1969, I first met Teddy when he scored the winning goal against me in Phillips Andover's 3-2 win over the Spy Ponders. Four years later, we were teammates. At Harvard, Teddy played right wing, mostly on a line with Leigh Hogan at center and Jimmy Thomas at left wing. It's easy for me to close my eyes and see Teddy coming down the right wing and taking a semi-slapshot, usually heavy, usually high. That's the first memory goalies have of their teammates. How and where they shoot.

Thorny was so very likable. A free spirit, people would say. Living in Kirkland House with Steve Dagdigian and Leigh Hogan, Teddy hardly had a monopoly on the free spirit business in that room. But he was unique.

It was easy to draw a grin from Teddy, a high-pitched chuckle accompanied by his head tilting back. And his way of doing things produced even more grins and chuckles from the people who knew him. Like the time he and Didge, after a performance they weren't pleased with, decided to give each other a haircut. One night, shoulder length hair. The next day at practice, like tennis balls.

My favorite Teddy story happened after I had completed my undergraduate days. It was at practice, and Bill Cleary was chewing out his assembled skaters near the boards, stressing some on-ice problem that needed attention. At the end of the sermon, the coach asked, "Are there any questions?"

Off to the side, Teddy was staring intently at the boards. "Billy," he said. "Look at that nail coming out of the boards. Somebody's going to come by and catch themselves on that and get hurt." The team muffled its laughter. The coach looked skyward. Teddy was not being a wise guy. He obviously hadn't heard a word the coach had said. And, at that point, nothing in the world was as important to Teddy as that nail. He was totally serious. Said, the coach, "Everybody skate around."

Athletically, Teddy was a natural athlete who became a good hockey player. Stunningly handsome and gifted with a strong physique, he had worked hard, on and off the ice, to develop his hockey skill, first at Andover, then Harvard, and then on the 1976 U.S. Olympic Hockey Team.

His love for the game carried over into coaching and last year he coached the Milton Academy boys varsity and this year he was to be an assistant at St. Sebastian's.

His friends will recall Teddy the person before they think of Teddy the athlete. This aging goalie will remember February 1973, after a painful defeat at Ithaca where Cornell took a big game by a big score of 9-4. It was to be a showdown of the top teams in the East. But after five minutes, it was 4-0 for the hosts, primarily because the Harvard goalie was nervous and struggling. When it was over, and the

(Photo courtesy of Harvard University)

team returned to Cambridge, the goalie was having difficulty dealing with the disappointment. He was close to tears. Then he received a visit from two sophomores named Thorndike and Dagdigian. The youngsters took care of the veteran and helped him get his act together.

That was 14 years ago. A lot of things have happened. A lot of things have changed. But last week, for a couple of moments, that goalie was close to tears again. And the one guy who could have cheered him up wasn't around to help.

The Garden Revisited

(Beanpot Program, New Boston Garden Corporation, February 1995)

This is one of my favorite pieces. The old Boston Garden was going to be torn down for a new building that, when it opened, would be called The Fleet Center. In the Beanpot Tournament program in which this story appeared, there was an ad promoting suite tickets for "The Shawmut Center." That name never happened.

On the first Monday of the tournament, I recall sitting in the Garden media room, at the end of the rink above the old stadium seats, when legendary Boston Globe writer Bob Ryan walked by. "Nice job," he said, giving me a thumb's up sign. Made my night. I have edited the piece from its original form to eliminate repetitive stories that appear earlier in the book.

We've seen this before. An aging veteran, provider of so many rich moments and memories, is reaching the end of the line. Tributes pour forth from the media, from the athletes and even from regular fans, as the final season plays out.

Usually, the veteran makes a last tour around the league, bringing his act to the people one final time. But this is different. This time, the people are the ones making the farewell tour. The veteran is a building. The veteran is the Boston Garden and the time has come to say good-bye.

The ramp. My earliest memories are of the ramp. On every one of my early visits to the Garden, I imagined what it would have been like going down the ramp in a go-cart. And when you left the building, you were usually so pumped up by the fun you just had, your head filled with so many wonderful memories. The adults you were with always walked faster and they seemed to pick up speed coming down the ramp. You had to hurry to keep up with them, but you didn't want to hurry. You didn't want the day to end. And then you were at the bottom of the ramp. And some kid was holding up a newspaper, yelling, "Final Reck-ud!" Then you were outside and it was cold.

When you were a little kid, it was a special treat to go to the Garden —

for the circus, or the Ice Follies or a Bruins game, which always seemed to be on a Sunday night.

Entering the Garden, you were always excited, anticipating what you were about to see. Leaving, you were filled with memories of what just took place. It's funny, but today I don't remember the actual events very well. I remember sounds and smells. I remember the old guy who sold popcorn. I remember that the interior of the building was a strange green, not the gold-ish yellow of today. I remember liking the small clocks in the promenade section. I remember Richard Dwyer, "Mr. Debonair."

At some point, the Garden became a hockey place for me. At first, it was this great big building that you'd visit once or twice a year and every-thing blended together. From Mr. Frick to Leo Labine to the elephants, it was just this special place to visit.

But then it became a hockey place. The Bruins games started to out-number the trips to the circus or the Ice Follies. I started to know all the names and numbers. I thought I looked a little like Don Head. The BOW (Bucyk-Oliver-Williams) line was great. Jerry Toppazzini scared me. I started to care about this game. And not just the Bruins. In fact, through my older brother, I became a Chicago Blackhawks fan. I knew about Hull-Hay-Balfour and Hull-Esposito-Maki, and I knew the Scooter Line, too. I thought Glenn Hall was the greatest. I still do.

I was told we were going down to the Bruins' locker room. We were going to get a stick from Fernie Flaman, the Bruins' captain. My dad was working as an engineer on a construction job in Beverly. It was going to be the biggest bowling alley on the North Shore. "Go-Go Bowling." And two of the principal investors were Boston Red Sox catcher Pete Daley and the hard-hitting Bruins defenseman Fernie Flaman.

I don't know how old I was. I don't remember the team they played or anything about the game. I just remember that door opening and seeing a guy in a one-piece set of long underwear giving my brother the stick.

When I was about 12, someone took me to these hockey games that weren't played on a weekend. And it wasn't the Bruins. The games were played on a Monday night in February. They were something called the Beanpot. Suddenly, there were all these other guys whose names and numbers I knew.

I liked BU. I knew that the defensemen, Gilmour and McLachlan, were cousins. One wore #4 and the other wore #11. And their goalie was good and didn't wear a mask. And when I played street hockey, I was Bruce Fennie when I was out of the net and I was Jack Ferreira when I was in the net. I was a defenseman when I played real hockey. But I liked being the goalie when I played street hockey. Later, I'd become a real goalie.

We used to bring a plastic puck to the games and a lot of times, after watching a period of the game, we'd spend the rest of the night at the top of one of the stairways, playing a mini-version of street hockey. We'd make a goal out of two crushed Coke cups or maybe a cup and the remains of one of those "Hood" three-flavor ice creams, the ones that had the little wooden spoon tucked inside the wrapping. I'd be the goalie. Always. Rolling around on those grimy floors. Then we'd get tired and go back up to watch the end of whatever game it was.

Something happened to me when my sister took me to see Arlington High School in the state tournament. For the first time, the people I was watching were people I knew. And when I later came to see my brother play, it occurred to me that I could play there too. The transition was beginning: the transition from observer to participant.

My time came in 1967 as a back-up goalie. I remember dressing in a makeshift locker room way back near where the Zamboni is stored. The shower had a pull chain device. And we had a long walk, partly over wooden pallets and eventually through the crowd near the concession area. Stepping on the ice, I was in awe.

I have all sorts of reasons to remember playing in the Garden, particularly playing in that high school tournament. It was the first taste of the spotlight. It was the first taste of significant accomplishment. When I played and struggled at the Garden as a college hockey player, I always looked back on how much easier it seemed in high school. We were supposed to win then. That's how we felt. We were too naive to think it could be any

(Programs courtesy of TD Garden)

other way. Just putting on the Arlington shirt made it so.

I thought about that later when I played so poorly against Boston University at the Garden. Not once, but three times. The power of tradition is strong. It was Arlington's tradition that fueled our confidence in high school. It was too much respect for BU's tradition that contributed to my failures in college. And that grew out of those street hockey games so many years earlier.

I also remember the Beanpot routine. Getting tickets. Leaving tickets. Playing early in an empty building. Sitting in the loge seats watching the early game when playing the late one. Wondering if we'd get one of the carpeted rooms down the hall (#11 and #12). And I don't know why, but I can vividly remember the walk to the ice. I can feel the skates on the hard floor.

Of all the aspects of the routine, that period just prior to the start of the game is most vivid. If the result of the game before yours was in question near the end, the thought of overtime delaying your own game was awful. You just wanted to hear that taped announcement saying, "On the ice for the start of the next period."

February 5, 1973. The crowd roared one more time. "Who scored?"

The Boston Garden in the 1940s. (Photo courtesy of TD Garden)

The manager ran out to find out. Usually, you could tell from the noise. This one was driving us crazy. First BC. Then Northeastern. Finally, BC in overtime. Mike Powers ended up with five goals for the Eagles, who won it by 9-8. Then it was our turn. Then came that announcement. Then we were playing and I recall a long shot off the crossbar.

After I got out of college, I tried a number of things, most notably teaching school, playing in the New England League and playing in Europe. There we were, teammates in Italy — former Terrier Paul Giandomenico and me from Harvard — sitting in Cortina d'Ampezzo during the 1975 Beanpot. Harvard had smoked BU in December, 7-2, and I got plenty of mileage out of it. BU took the Beanpot rematch, also by 7-2.

And that's what the post-player Beanpot experience is about. The former opponents are buddies. The Beanpot fraternity stays in the area, for the most part, and all that stuff about "bragging rights" is true. There is endless kidding and joking, with your neighbor, with the guy in the office, with the guy in the no-check tournament. I could easily spend a Beanpot Monday night in a series of five-minute conversations with acquaintances, start at five o'clock, finish at midnight, never see a single shot or goal and not repeat any conversation twice.

It used to be that the largest single contingent of Beanpot alumni would meet at "The Horse." It's not there anymore. There's a sports bar there. But believe me, there isn't a fancy, franchised, game-jersey-walled, multi-televisioned, collectible-adorned sports bar in the country that could ever hope to capture what former high school and Beanpot tournament alumni embraced at "The Horse" on the first two Mondays in February. That place made for rough Tuesday mornings.

My post-Beanpot playing years took on the added flavor of journalist when I got the chance to do commentary on a number of Beanpot broadcasts, teamed with the likes of Bob Wilson, Glenn Ordway, Bob Gamere, Greg Madden and today's sportstalk junkie's new cult favorite, Ted Sarandis. Doing a Beanpot with Ted was like accompanying some kid who just won a sports fantasy contest. The word "enthusiastic" doesn't say it all. Looking back, I'm surprised the Garden staff let him work without a net.

Well Bernie, you know the goalie better watch out down at this end when pucks are dumped in. The pucks seem to take more funny bounces behind this goal than the other one. Why, just this morning, I had to fill in for Reggie at Bruins practice. Oh, nothing serious. A bit of the flu. So I was out there with Cam and Raymond and the guys and I noticed that the pucks ...

It's really kind of embarrassing now when I think of it. But there I was, somewhere in the late 1980s, going on radio or telling just about anybody who would listen how I had practiced with the Bruins that Monday morning in February. For some reason, the idea of being on that very ice, stopping pucks — OK, trying to stop pucks — and then coming in that night to watch the Beanpot really had an effect on me. I mean, 20 years had gone by since I first stepped on that ice in high school. Then, at age 40 or so, I park behind the Garden, walk up that creeky, wooden service ramp, carrying my stuff and proudly telling the guy at the top, "I'm practicing with the B's. They need me."

The tiny room was kind of a player's lounge. Later, it would become the coaches' office. The equipment guys had brought pizza in there and the players who were not dressing for the game kept sneaking in to grab a slice of pizza. Assistant coach Mike Milbury came in and told the guys to get rid of the pizza. After all, we were in the middle of a game. Dutifully, the guys folded the pizza box, with a couple of greasy slices still in the box, and shoved it into the trash barrel.

Not 30 seconds later, the door to the lounge reopened and in walked Pat Riggin, that afternoon's back-up goalie. With all the skill of the experienced veteran he was, "Riggo" sniffed once, reached for the discarded pizza box, extracted an intact slice of pepperoni pizza and impressively scarfed it down, before stealthily leaving the room and returning to his teammates in the locker room. It was time for the third period.

My six years with the Bruins as goalie coach were terrific. They made

My favorite goalie while with the Bruins was perennial back-up Doug Keans. Garden fans also appreciated "Keansie," displaying his record when he was traded. (Photo courtesy of TD Garden)

the Stanley Cup Finals twice and I had the pleasure of working with the likes of Terry O'Reilly, Mike Milbury and Rick Bowness. Like my other Garden experiences, I remember a few games and a lot of the routine.

Before the game, I'd check in with the staff, just to let them know I was there. First, I'd say "hi" to Andy and Joe, the usher in red and the policeman in blue. I'd visit briefly with the goalies, more often than not Doug Keans, Reggie Lemelin or Andy Moog. Then it was upstairs to the Press Room. I'd greet Bill McNamara, grab press notes, say "hi" to Heidi Holland, grab a hot dog, watch Tom Johnson's nightly cribbage game from afar and then compare Boston's goals against total with the other teams.

During the game, I'd watch the action on the television in the coaches' room. Then, when a coach (usually Messrs. O'Reilly or Milbury) came in screaming about how badly the goalie played that period, I could point out how that first one went off Galley's skate and how the goalie couldn't possibly have seen the second one.

Mats Naslund had scored the game-winning goal from a real bad angle. One more loss to Montreal and the season was over. Terry said he wanted to speak with his rookie goalie in his office. So I followed a visibly weary and unhappy 19-year-old netminder into the Garden's cramped coaches' office.

"You just blew that game," said Coach O'Reilly. "But I'm coming back with you in the next one, because we need someone who can steal one for us and you're the only guy we have that can do that. So get some rest and be ready to play."

The goalie coach was concerned. "Terry, do you think that was the best way to say that. That he 'blew the game?'" The coach didn't give any ground. He told it straight and he believed the goalie could deal with it. A few years later when he beat us in the Stanley Cup Finals, that goalie, Bill Ranford, seemed to have found a way to deal with the responsibility of the job.

By 1990, my relationship with the Garden was reaching its final stage. I was in my fifth year with the Bruins and I was set to direct my seventh ECAC Championship Tournament. Through the efforts of a number of people, the two eastern college hockey conferences, Hockey East and the ECAC, had agreed to bring their postseason tournaments to the Garden under one title, "Hockeyfest," giving the majority of college hockey fans something they seemed to crave.

Sometimes, having the best intentions isn't quite enough. Working closely with the Garden's Steve Nazro and Hockey East's Kathy Walsh, I thought we had everything in place. Then the measles came to Orono, ME.

From fan to player to journalist to coach and beyond, I have difficulty identifying the single most memorable moment from approximately 35 years of going to the Garden. Certainly, being on winning teams for the high school and ECAC tournaments was special in a personal sense, but my relationship with the Garden goes beyond all of that. My friends, my self-esteem, my livelihood, much of my belief structure all stem, in no small way, from my involvement in sports.

The Garden has played a major role in this process. At the Garden, I first saw the phenomenon of an individual, working with others, using courage and skill and preparation, meet challenges in front of the community at large. At the Garden, I first experienced personal success outside of my immediate community of family and friends. At the Garden, I was able to witness people who were the best in the world at what they did. And watching more than one generation of people who were the best at what they did in their own particular time, I became a witness to history. In some minor way, I even felt part of the history.

May 1990. For the second time in three years, the lights have gone out in a Stanley Cup Finals game between Edmonton and Boston at the Garden. This time, the lights will come back on. This time, the game is into triple overtime.

Tension is everywhere. Garden officials and NHL officials are scurrying everywhere with Garden technicians, working frantically to remedy the problem. Fans are thrilled at what they are witnessing, but wrought with anxiety over the outcome. And then there are the players.

They have been working since September and since childhood for the prize that is within their reach. Years of training and discipline prevent them from feeling exactly how tired they are but, still, they are human. It is not without special effort that the most human feelings and thoughts are kept in the background at these times.

And in the midst of all of this, the Captain sat at his stall, wearing a comforting grin as he looked around at his teammates. "This is great," said Ray Bourque. "This is great." And the grin appeared in front of just about every stall. In the middle of everyone else's tension, one of the truly great athletes of our time recognized the greatness of just being there, just being part of it all.

Raymond Bourque never played in a Beanpot tournament, but he has played many a game in Boston Garden. Perhaps that is why he, vicariously, can capture so perfectly some of the essence of the Beanpot.

... just being there, just being part of it all.

Revisiting An American Hero: Jack Riley
("Stops and Starts," AHCA, 2004-2005)

Perhaps my favorite "Stops and Starts" piece, and longest, was a two-part feature on Jack Riley, longtime coach at West Point, 1960 U.S. Olympic head coach who won gold at Squaw Valley and member of one of the great hockey families in our country. I played in college with Jack's oldest son Jay, sons Rob and Brian followed Jack at Army, son Mark played at Boston College and daughter Mary Beth played at St. Lawrence. Jack and his brothers Bill and Joe are the only three brothers in the U.S. Hockey Hall of Fame. Jack's nephew Billy Jr., was a highly successful coach at UMass Lowell and Billy's son, Bill, now carries on the coaching tradition at Groton. Oh, and Rob's son Brett just completed his first season as head coach at Long Island University, a Division I independent.

I paid a couple of visits to Jack in his Marstons Mills home on the Cape, putting together a story at the urging of former Army standout Ed Hickey. This ran in consecutive issues of "Stops & Starts" during the 2004-05 season. Jack was 83 when I conducted the interviews. He passed away in 2016 at the age of 96. He was a great interview, though the day after our sessions, he would call me and tell me I couldn't use this story or that quote. And he asked me to clean up his "scurrilous language." On more than occasion, an intern in my office would answer the phone, put the caller on hold and announce to me, "Joe, you have a Colonel Riley of the Salvation Army on Line 1."

This story, appearing here as one long piece, was published on the 60th anniversary of the end of Dartmouth College's 45-game unbeaten streak. An edited version also appeared in the Dartmouth College alumni magazine.

When the 2004 presidential campaign heated up over the summer months, fueled in part by a review of the candidates' activities during the Vietnam War, the nation found itself assessing what the words "hero" and "heroic" meant. Could a true "hero" volunteer for combat in an unpopular war, appear to pursue subsequent commendations for his participation in that war, and then return stateside to condemn the country's involvement in said war? Is it heroic to "merely" serve stateside during a war? And what actions were more heroic: risking life and limb in combat or testifying before Congress on evils observed or reported from that experience?

The last public discourse on heroes occurred in the immediate aftermath of September 11, 2001, when the country re-discovered the heroic Everyman. He and she were firemen, policemen, co-workers and next-door neighbors. They did not have to seem larger than life. They could be teachers or coaches. Their very ordinariness became part of their appeal. We realized there are "Heroes" and "heroes," some performing on larger stages than others, some toiling without a spotlight or media attention.

It is, then, all the more fascinating to come upon an individual whose life story has been one chapter after another of both the Heroic and heroic. And, as is often the case, the most significant accomplishments in this life received the least attention. Such it is with the extraordinary career of Jack Riley.

From Boston to Hanover

In the fall of 1940, three talented hockey players arrived in Hanover, New Hampshire, and began a decade of dominance for Dartmouth College. Dick Rondeau first made a name for himself at the Mount St. Charles School in Rhode Island. He was a prolific goal scorer and would become Dartmouth's all-time scoring leader, despite a war-abbreviated career. The equally talented Bill Harrison, who hailed from Walpole, MA, would match Rondeau's points-per-game numbers but would leave school earlier and fall short of his overall records.

Then there was John P. Riley of Medford, MA, by way of the Clark School in Hanover, NH. In very little time, the names Riley, Rondeau and Harrison would roll off the tongues of college hockey fans the way baseball aficionados once recited Tinker to Evers to Chance. Riley still remembers the first time he ever skated with Rondeau, in a pick-up game on Occom Pond.

It is pretty clear that Dartmouth's legendary coach Eddie Jeremiah never considered separating this talented trio. That was evident from their first varsity tryout.

"In tryouts, Jerry used to divide the team in half using the alphabet, right down the middle. A to L or M. Something like that," says Riley. "But this time, he had one group A to G. That kept the three of us in the same group and we played together from the start."

While they undoubtedly expected big things of themselves and their team, it is doubtful this trio anticipated all that would happen to them, on and off the ice, over the ensuing years. A week before the first game of the season, Japan attacked Pearl Harbor. The impact of this event was not fully grasped by Dartmouth's young athletes.

"I remember saying to my roommate (Henry) 'Snookie' Hughes, 'Where the hell is Pearl Harbor?' We all thought that we would never go to war because of the distance. At the time, we were more concerned they would cancel our trip to Colorado and Illinois."

On December 19 and 20, Dartmouth split a pair of games with Colorado College in Colorado Springs, winning 3-2, and then dropping the finale, 3-1. Rondeau scored the game-winner on a third-period penalty shot in the victory. It was the first of his school-record 103 goals.

Next up were a pair of games with the University of Illinois, first in

Chicago and then in Champaign. On December 22, Illinois did something that no other college hockey team would do for four years and fifteen days. It defeated Dartmouth. The score read, "Illinois 4, Dartmouth 1 in overtime." (The overtime was not "sudden death," as indicated by the three Illinois goals in the extra stanza.) Riley, Rondeau and Harrison were kept off the scoresheet. It would not happen again.

The next day, December 23, 1941, the longest undefeated streak in college hockey history began, and, ironically, Jack Riley did not play.

""In the game before, I broke two fingers," recalls Riley. "Johnny Krol took a shot that was coming right at my head. I put my hand up to prevent getting hit in the head and the damn thing broke two fingers."

Down 4-2 in the third period, Dartmouth rallied to tie the game and won it on a Rondeau goal with just 30 seconds left in the 10-minute overtime. "The Streak" was born.

Returning to Hanover, the young men of Dartmouth had to face the reality thrust upon them by Pearl Harbor. The Draft Board mailed notices to all eligible young men. Physicals were ordered. Fulfilling hockey dreams seemed doubtful.

"At the time, the mayor of Medford, Ernest Martini, thought it wouldn't be too good if I didn't get drafted," Riley recalls. The Riley family was well known in Medford and in nearby Boston. Jack recalls helping the mayor in

Some people insist that the three Riley brothers — Joe, Jack and Bill above — all played at Dartmouth at the same time, citing this photo. They did not. This photo was taken at an alumni game. (Photo courtesy of the Riley Family)

his campaigns. Jack's mother, the former Elizabeth Cunningham, ran the most prominent fashion house in Boston, "Driscoll's," where everyone in high society purchased evening gowns and formal wear.

"Every year, before the Harvard-Yale football game, there would be 10 limos lined up in front of the store," recalls Riley. "What do they say? 'The Cabots talk only to the Lowells and the Lowells talk only to God.' They all went there."

Recalling that time, Riley says, "I got my notice and was supposed to report to Boston. But we all still wanted to finish our season."

Enter Whitey Fuller, the former sports information director at Dartmouth, now a lieutenant commander in the Navy, stationed in Boston. He gave Jack and 30 other Dartmouth students another option.

"Whitey said to me, 'Jack, how'd you like to become a Navy pilot? It's a way to finish the season and get to be in the Navy.' I thought, I'm afraid to fly, let alone be a Navy pilot."

But this is exactly what 31 Dartmouth students did, 29 of them athletes, in becoming the Indian Squadron. Their proactive enlistment took precedent over the Draft Board's edict and it bought time for Jack Riley. They would all eventually report to Squantum Air Base, just south of Boston, on June 4, 1942.

By the time Riley returned to the Dartmouth line-up on January 7, 1942, The Streak had reached four and counting. Still feeling the effects of the broken fingers, Riley was told to get clearance from the team doctor before he could return to the line-up.

"Jeremiah told me to see Dr. Pollard, remembers Riley. "But I knew if I saw him, he wouldn't let me play. So I never saw him and just suited up. By the time Jerry figured it out, and Doc Pollard saw me, it was too late to change."

Jack had a goal (the game-winner) and an assist in that game, a 4-3 win over Boston University, and would contribute nine goals and 10 assists in the next seven wins, bringing the streak to 12. That's when Jack was informed that the home game against Clarkson would be his last.

"All of a sudden, somebody was afraid I was going to get hurt and told me I couldn't play in the last six games," says Riley. "So I went out and got eight points against Clarkson."

The three sophomore stars — Riley, Rondeau and Harrison — combined for 101 goals and 83 assists for an amazing 184 points. The goal production accounted for nearly 70% of Dartmouth's team output for the season. While the three stars would each wear the Dartmouth jersey in other campaigns, they would never play together again.

The War Intervenes

It its June 3, 1942, edition, *The Boston Globe* reported that 31 Dartmouth students would be reporting the next day to the Naval Air Station in Squantum. "They will become student flyers immediately," it said.

The group included Bob McLaughrey, the son of Dartmouth football coach "Tuss" McLaughrey, Johnny Krol of Waltham, MA, and, of course, Jack Riley of Medford, MA.

Jack Riley's training as a Navy pilot, the training that would prepare him for more than 20 wartime missions over the Pacific in the latter stages of World War II, began at the Squantum Naval Air Station just south of Boston. But it didn't always presage the skill and competence he came to possess.

"In Squantum, when we soloed, we had to go to an outlying field. You either went to Plymouth or Mansfield. Well, this one day, I go to Mansfield.

"We are stunting all the time. Doing what they called aerobatics. Immelmans. Wingovers. Spins, loops, slow rolls. All this stuff. At first, I thought to myself, 'Hey, I'm not going to get killed doing this stuff. I'm going to climb to 5,000 feet, go north for a half hour, go south, and then land. I eventually changed my mind and spent a hell of a lot of time practicing those things, and I swear to God, it saved my life when I got in trouble later in my training.

"So, I was doing that one night and I forgot one thing. There are a lot of lakes and I didn't know where Mansfield was on the ground. It started to get dark. So they told us early, 'If you ever get lost, never follow the railroad tracks because there could be an Army pilot coming the other way.'

"I followed the tracks and ended up in Providence. I knew this was not Mansfield. So I turn around and I follow the main road back to Boston and I get to South Station. Now I realize, I'm either going to have to bail out or land on the highway. Just then, I saw a field, which turned out to be in Walpole, the next town over from Mansfield. Now remember, I was about 21 at this time. When I made this unscheduled landing, people came running out at me like I was Lindbergh.

"I said to them, 'Can you show me where Mansfield is?' I was so happy to get back that I came in low and almost hit a tower. This poor guy fell and broke his leg."

His superiors had mixed feelings for the young pilot's performance. "You stupid bastard," said one officer. "The guy that got lost yesterday never got the plane back. At least you got the plane back."

The Makings of a Hero

Dartmouth hockey's winning streak reached 28 games by the end of an abbreviated 1942-43 season. Meanwhile, the military education of 22-year-old

Jack Riley moved from Squantum to Jacksonville to Atlanta by the spring of 1943. He had now logged upwards of 600 hours of flight time and served as a flight instructor in Atlanta. He was flying bigger planes now. He was learning new skills. His fame as an athlete out of Greater Boston led to a chance meeting with another Boston sports star.

"Sportswriter Bill Cunningham, who knew me from home, told me to look up Johnny Pesky, who was also stationed in Atlanta," says Riley. "We hooked up and became good friends."

Pesky, the shortstop for the Boston Red Sox, was coming off a terrific rookie season in 1942 where he batted .331 and led the American League with 205 hits. He would top 200 hits in each of his first three seasons with the BoSox.

"John used to complain that no matter what he did, Ted Williams got all the headlines," recalls Riley. "He'd say, 'I would go 8 for 10 in a double-header, Ted would get one hit, a home run, and the headline the next day would be, "Ted Hits Another!"'"

The Riley sense of humor could not let this opportunity pass by. Finding a place in downtown Atlanta that made mock newspapers with fake headlines, Riley had some fun with his new friend.

"Pesky had a date with this WAVE named Ruth Hickey," says Riley. "So I went out and had this headline made that said, 'Pesky Sox Ace to Marry WAVE.' Now I see him the next day and I say to him, 'Hey, John, you know how you are always complaining that you don't get enough attention? Well, did you see today's *Atlanta Constitution*? You are all over it.' Well, when he saw it, he chased me halfway around the barracks. But you know, he married Ruth Hickey and they're still together today."

Pesky, whose long affiliation with the Boston Red Sox included eight seasons as a player and decades more as manager, broadcaster and special assistant, lives in Swampscott, MA, on Boston's North Shore. He recalls Riley with fondness.

"Jack was a great guy," says the 82-year old Pesky. "I know he likes to tell that story about me and Ruth. Jack tells me he made money off me when he went back to Dartmouth. Something about betting fifty cents or something on which ballplayers would get the most hits in a certain game or games. I don't know why he didn't pick Williams or Georgie Kell or somebody. I was just a Punch and Judy hitter. I guess he thought I'd come through with a bunch of singles for him. Says he made a lot of walking around money."

Later, when Riley was finishing up at Dartmouth after the war, he would pal around with Pesky, who returned to the Sox.

"I'd go to games and other functions with John and I'd be introduced as Ben Steiner or Clem Dreiswerd, or some other ballplayer," Riley recalls with a smile. "We were at a Lithuanian Night in New Jersey and they had these milk cartons you were supposed to throw at and knock down. Well, those things were always rigged. Pesky tried it and couldn't do it. So they asked me. Well, I hit the thing perfectly and knocked them all over. But since I had checked in as Clem Dreiswerd, relief pitcher, they wouldn't give me the prize. Said I was a professional ballplayer and couldn't win the damn thing."

While Riley, Pesky and others found time to enjoy themselves in Atlanta, their reason for being there remained serious business. Before becoming an instructor, Riley had to successfully complete his instrument training and when he did in early 1943, he was slated to ship out to California for carrier duty. Through the good fortune of bad weather, he missed that assignment and many who weren't as fortunate lost their lives.

"I honestly believe that it was pretty good to be an instrument instructor because I got to be a pretty safe pilot as a result."

Preparing for War

In January 1945, Lt. Jack Riley picked up his crew of two co-pilots and nine other men at NAS Banana River in Cape Canaveral, FL. Here Riley experienced his final training before shipping out to the South Pacific by way of California. He would practice night flying and he would make longer trips. This would be direct preparation for much of what he would experience in the war itself.

By late spring, he was in California, his last stop before the Pacific Theater. Amidst the seriousness, Jack Riley was still the mischievous hockey player. He brought his skates along and had a chance to play for a semiprofessional team in San Diego under the name of Jack Maguire, a friend from Dartmouth. He figured he had a 50 percent chance of getting back to school and didn't want to risk his eligibility.

Finally, on May 1, 1945, it was his time to join the action. And the confident jock from Medford was anxious to go.

"My time comes and there is a question about weather," recalls Riley. "I'm given the option of waiting a day. The trip would be from Almeida Naval Air Station to Kanoehe, about 12 hours. And I'm thinking to myself, 'What am I doing here?' You get your wings one day in some kiddie car and then they give you a dive bomber and you say to yourself, 'How'd I get to be so good overnight?'"

Jack couldn't wait that extra day. He wanted to get moving and so his other option was to go at night by way of a jet-assisted take-off.

"I made the first night-time jet-assisted take-off. They put these four big cartridges that look like missiles and it's connected to the flight deck. And those things pop us right up and we are gone."

Bad weather forced Riley to nine hours of flying by instruments on that 12-hour flight but he arrived safely at Kanoehe. From there it was off to Johnson Island. Then Kwajalein Island. Saipan. Nine-hour flights. Twelve-hour flights. All his flying at night.

Riley's assignments varied. There was air-sea rescue. There were anti-sub missions, trying to locate Japanese submarines. There were bombing raids. By this time in the war, the United States had pretty much established air superiority, but there was risk every time up in the air, if not from the enemy from the weather.

"One time we are up there and my co-pilot says, 'Look at all the birds.'

(Photo courtesy of the Riley Family)

Hell, they weren't birds. They were trying to shoot us down," recalls Riley.

Eventually, there would be a routine of fly one day, day off, and then "stand by."

"If you had a day off and they needed five planes to stop a Japanese task force, and you're in the next five, you're going. If you're going to go, you want to go first, before they know."

Riley's eagerness to tell the story of his preparation for war stands in contrast to his reluctance to play up his wartime accomplishments. Says his fellow Indian Squadron member Bob Laughrey, "I'm sure Jack downplays all that he did. And perhaps there wasn't anything spectacular or headline grabbing. But he was reliable and if he went on a mission, he was going to do it right. He was in a number of roles that carried great responsibility with them and he did those well. And that's why many commanders wanted athletes for so many assignments that required discipline."

While the war ended in August, Riley stayed in the South Pacific for another six months. One story he delights in telling captures both the impish and competitive sides of Jack Riley. It took place on the day his crew was notified that the war had ended.

A superior officer was going to check Riley out on a jet-assisted take-off and having already mastered this, Riley was none too pleased at the assignment. Riley adds that some of the pilots were also in the habit of running small betting pools, to see who could come closest to some landmark on a carrier or some other ship.

"Well, we're out there and we get the message that the war is over and we should come back. Well, I'm thinking, 'I'm going to show this guy a thing or two and I want to win that pool,'" recalls Riley. "There's this boom that hangs out over the end of the ship and there are little boats tied to it. Well, I come in and miss the thing by inches. The ship disappears in smoke. My pontoon hits a radio antenna and knocks off about five feet of it.

"They are calling me to come back. The guys says, 'You crazy bastard. What do you think you're doing?' I just tell him I'm celebrating the end of the war. And I won the pool.'"

The Streak Ends

On the first week of January in 1946, Eddie Jeremiah was preparing for his first game behind the Dartmouth bench since March 1942. Jack Riley was being discharged from the Navy on the West Coast and working his way back to New England. And in New Haven, Yale's hockey team was on a mission. No school had been victimized more than Yale in what was now a 45-game unbeaten streak for Dartmouth.

Fred Pearson was born in Pennsylvania, raised in Massachusetts, schooled in Canada and prepared for a Yale hockey career at Hotchkiss. His uncle was Lester B. Pearson, the former Prime Minister of Canada. Each year the NHL Players' Association bestows the Lester B. Pearson Award to the most outstanding player of the professional season. In the first week of 1946, Fred Pearson and his Yale teammates set out to make history. They intended to put an end to the Dartmouth unbeaten streak and pulled out all the stops to do it.

"Our coach, Murray Murdoch, emphasized defense and he was well aware of what Dartmouth's forwards liked to do," recalls Pearson, still playing the game three nights a week in a suburb north of Boston.

But before strategy could play a role, Yale had to get past the Dartmouth reputation. For this, the Elis sought two remedies.

"The week before the game, Murray arranged for us to scrimmage the New York Rangers' minor league team that also played its games at the New Haven Arena, where we played. We scrimmaged them twice that week," says Pearson.

"I think that playing against those guys that week slowed down the Dartmouth team, psychologically, for us," says Pearson. "They didn't seem quite so intimidating when we got out there with them."

That was Remedy No. 1. As for No. 2?

"A couple of us paid our first visit to Harkness Chapel that week," recalls Pearson. "For the first time in my life, I prayed for victory."

The practice and the prayers paid off in a 6-4 Yale victory that launched the 1945-46 season on January 5, 1946. Fred Pearson scored twice.

The First Olympic Experience

After Dartmouth, Jack Riley began a transition from player to coach, starting with his last assignment as purely a player. Jack, along with Dartmouth nemesis Fred Pearson, played on the 1948 U.S. Olympic Hockey Team that participated in St. Moritz, Switzerland. It was at these games that the United States actually sent two teams, one sponsored by the Amateur Athletic Union (AAU) and the other by the fledgling Amateur Hockey Association of the United States (AHAUS), precursor of today's national governing body, USA Hockey.

Jack Riley had asked Dartmouth coach Eddie Jeremiah to enter a Dartmouth team into the national AAU Tournament held in the spring of 1947, the winner of which was supposed to be the U.S. entrant in the 1948 Olympics. When Jeremiah declined, Riley put together his own team, dubbed the "Hanover Indians," and proceeded to win the event.

However, the AAU announced it would hold tryouts for the 1948 squad. Riley then turned to Walter Brown, owner of the Boston Bruins, Boston Celtics and Boston Garden. Through his mother's prominence in Boston, Riley had met Brown, who once offered his mother a significant share of ownership in the Celtics in return for writing off a debt. (She declined.) Brown, who also served as vice-president of AHAUS, told Riley to put together an AHAUS team and guaranteed it would represent the United States at St. Moritz.

And so it was that two teams arrived in St. Moritz for the 1948 Olympics, one from the AAU and one representing AHAUS. Together, there were seven former Dartmouth players split among these squads, including a Riley on each. (Brother Joe was on the AAU team.) Avery Brundage, the powerful curmudgeon who served as International Olympic Committee President, intended to break AHAUS by allowing the AAU entry to represent the U.S. He did not count on Walter Brown's clout extending overseas, primarily due to his relationship with rink owners throughout Europe.

"Walter Brown put together tours of Europe and had built strong relationships with rink owners in many countries," recalled Riley. "The stalemate went right up to midnight the night before the games began and in the end, Walter won."

The U.S. compiled a record of 5-3 but failed to win a medal. Said Dartmouth's Whitey Campbell, a member of the AAU squad, "If we had put all the Dartmouth players on one team, I think we would have brought home a medal." Riley would have another crack at Olympic success with more dramatic results.

The Rileys of West Point

After serving as the player-coach of the 1949 U.S. National Team that competed in Stockholm, Jack Riley accepted the position of head coach at the U.S. Military Academy in 1950. As of this writing, two other Rileys

Some of the Riley clan in Naples: from left, Billy, his son Bill, Brian, Jay, Rob and Mark. (Jennifer Ziegelmaier Photo)

have assumed that position covering 54+ seasons of college hockey.*

Jack won 542 games in 36 seasons, and for more than 25 years, served as the Congressional liaison for all athletes seeking entrance into West Point. Among his friends were legions of officers and coaches who passed through West Point during his time, the famous including but not limited to Vince Lombardi and Bobby Knight.

In 1986, Jack handed the reins over to son Rob, a former Boston College hockey captain who, at that time, was head coach at Babson College. After 18 seasons and 257 Army wins, Rob retired in the summer of 2004 and handed the job to brother Brian, a former Brown University skater. Not included on the West Point payroll was son Jay (who played at Harvard and was an assistant at Cornell), son Mark (who played at Boston College and was a long-time hockey equipment sales rep), and daughter Mary Beth (a pioneer with St. Lawrence University's women's program).

For all the wins and losses and every day lessons passed along at West Point, it took a series of games played in California, of all places, in February 1960 to bestow hero status to Jack Riley once more.

Olympic Gold

There was no dispute surrounding which team would represent the U.S. at Squaw Valley, CA, in 1960. But there was a mini-controversy surrounding head coach Jack Riley's final roster. It became apparent to those close to

As of this re-packaging, Brian has run the streak to 63 years.

the team that the U.S. chances of success would be dramatically improved if former Harvard star Bill Cleary could be a late addition to the roster. Cleary, a former All-American at Harvard who won a silver medal in Cortina d'Ampezzo in 1956, was home in Boston, starting an insurance business. He let it be known that he wanted to play, but he tied his availability to an invitation also being extended to his brother Bob, also a former Harvard All-American.

Jack Riley consulted with his old friend, Walter Brown, and made it clear that if he wanted the U.S. to win, both Clearys had to be brought in. Brown's response? "Do it."

It was, to no surprise, an unpopular decision among the team. Players who had sacrificed two months of work were going to be dropped in favor of two players brought in for two weeks. One of those players turned out to be Herb Brooks, the future coach of the 1980 gold medal U.S. team.

Riley and the players eventually made it work and the team won all seven games, including the first U.S. win ever against the defending champions from the Soviet Union. To put it in perspective, the Soviets won every gold medal from 1956 to 1992, with two exceptions: 1960 and 1980. Given that the Canadian team was even better than the Soviets in 1960, that gold medal was truly a miracle on ice.

Epilogue

Jack Riley lives on Cape Cod now, in a tidy home filled with mementos of a very full life. His fraying scrapbook follows his exploits from Medford High

Jack Riley returns home to a hero's welcome after coaching the 1960 U.S. Olympic Team to a gold medal at the Squaw Valley Games. Picture above are his wife, Maureen, and sons Mark, Jay and Rob. (Photo courtesy of the Riley Family)

School to the Clark School in Hanover to Dartmouth. There are accounts of his playing and coaching in the Olympics. There are West Point mementos. And there are log books and photographs from his years of military service.

He stays in touch with hockey by attending West Point games, eager to see his youngest son, Brian, get his Army career off to a good start. Even at the age of 83, he is still the imp of the many stories related here, as evidenced by his answering a recent phone call, "Colonel Riley of the Salvation Army here." And he remains competitive by nature, whether on the golf course at Hyannisport or in making sure this story pointed out that while he had not yet graduated from Dartmouth in January 1946, he definitely did not take part in that 6-4 loss to Yale.

His temper surfaces from time to time. A publication produced by the U.S. Hockey Hall of Fame, of which Jack and his brothers Joe and Bill are members, mistakenly identified Minnesota's John Mariucci as head coach of the 1960 Olympic Team. (He coached in 1956.) Jack was ready to make someone pay.

In recent months, a group of former players from Jack's early West Point teams have been discussing a book project on Jack. Their time with him was special nearly 50 years ago. As society has changed, they now see Jack Riley as more than their old coach.

Says Ed Hickey, a career military man who played for Jack in the late 1950s and who returned to West Point as an assistant coach, "He stood for all the right values. He was tough, but he was fair. He was as competitive as anyone I ever met. He served his country, in war, at West Point and in the Olympics. And first and foremost, he was a good family man. If his life was a movie, he'd be played by John Wayne."

Jack Parker: An Appreciation
("Stops & Starts," AHCA, April 2013)

In my tribute to Jack Parker, I tried to mix the professional with the personal, my relationship with Jack being both.

At this year's Hockey East Tournament banquet, Jack Parker, whose work behind a podium has always been the equal of his work behind a bench, got off one more memorable line. He said, "I just saw Toot Cahoon. Ever since he retired last year, he looks happier and more relaxed than I've ever seen him. And ever since I announced my retirement last week, Joe Bertagna has looked happier and more relaxed than I've ever seen him."

It was well delivered, like only Jack can, but it didn't capture the truth. And I'm somewhat surprised to admit that. There was a time, many times in fact, that I found myself looking forward to his retirement. But when it actually happened, I was anything but giddy.

I go back over 40 years with Jack Parker. I remember Jack the Player, when street hockey games in my neighborhood found us playing as our favorite Terriers and Eagles and Huskies and Crimson.

And I also have early memories of Jack the Coach, when I was playing high school hockey and he was an assistant coach to George Boudreau at Medford (MA) High School. In losing two games to Medford in 1969, by scores of 1-0 and 2-1, we became the first Arlington High School team coached by the legendary Eddie Burns to lose twice to the same opponent in the same season. Nice to be in the record book.

But I really came to know Jack when I began working in college hockey for the ECAC in the mid-1980s. We had a good relationship. In fact, he was influential in my landing the current positions I hold with the AHCA and with Hockey East.

But from the time I began as Hockey East commissioner, I had to balance the personal and professional relationships I had with Jack.

Personally, it's easy to like and admire Jack. He is as entertaining a person as I have ever met in this game. Intelligent, witty, a master story teller, Jack is a lot of fun to be around. He is good to his friends, and he is particularly good to friends in times of need. Stories abound of Jack reaching out to someone going through hard times, offering assistance or just letting a guy know that he is thinking of him.

Professionally, his record is one that may never be matched. Who among today's active coaches projects to be at one institution for 40 years, winning nearly 900 games in one place, not to mention all the championships?

Of course, there was also that public side of Jack that fans saw in the arenas or on television, the side that the cameras loved, when he set his sights on a referee or linesman and let him have it. As commissioner, I had to deal with these moments, and the record shows I had mixed results. I never enjoyed the confrontations. But they came with the job.

A variety of friends and observers have chimed in with opinions on this side of Jack. It was his competitiveness. His always looking for an edge. It was consistent with his attention to detail in his own life. And that he couldn't accept the sloppiness he saw from some officials on some nights.

We had many conversations about officials in general, specific officials, the standard of play in college vs. the NHL, the rise of embellishment and how best to deal with it, and so on. We agreed on some things but not all. And no matter the subject, I can say this with certainty: If you decided to take him up on a debate, you had better have done your homework. Because if you couldn't make your point, he'd eat you up. What a great trial lawyer he could have been.

For all the wins and accolades and all the visual images and the one-liners, I think what distinguished Jack from the rest was his interest in not just doing his job for Boston University, but also for his conference and his sport. Anyone who saw him at work in a coaches meeting, whether

Jack Parker was equally skilled on the bench and at a microphone. (Top: Photo courtesy of the Boston Red Sox and Hockey East. Bottom: Steve Babineau Photo courtesy of Hockey East)

a league meeting or a national meeting, saw an active participant always trying to make things better for the group as a whole.

We will all remember Jack in Naples, standing up in one national meeting after another, making points as only he could. Verbal commitments. The visor. USA Hockey. The NCAA, one of his favorites. He never lost sight of the fact that he had a responsibility to not only attend meetings but to participate and contribute. Now maybe his presence and style intimidated younger coaches who stayed on the sideline in some of these meetings. If so, that's too bad. I choose to see his example of getting involved hitting just the right note for other coaches.

He made us better at what we did. Whether we were hockey players, opposing coaches, referees or commissioners, he pushed and pushed and we all responded for the better.

At the press conference in which he announced his plans to retire, I approached him afterwards and said, "Congratulations. But to be honest, I actually came down here just to make sure you don't change your mind."

He smiled briefly and responded, "Oscar Wilde said that some people are happy wherever you go and some are happy whenever you go."

Amid the flurry of interviews that followed Jack's announcement, I told someone that the seven words I wouldn't miss at all next year are, "Joe, Jack Parker is on the phone." It got a laugh from a reporter. But, of course, that's not true.

I was one of the people Jack pushed to be better. And I was one he entertained. And, in the end, I appreciated what he has meant to our game. Best to you, Jack.

Remembering Tim Taylor
("Stops & Starts," AHCA, June 2013)

I knew most of the people I wrote about. Few were as important to me as Tim Taylor. He was one of a handful of people I could call a mentor in my life. My first memory of Tim was his being on the staff of Cooney Weiland's hockey school in the early to mid-1960s, when I attended as a middle school defenseman. Then he was a Harvard assistant when I played there. Then I lived in his house for two summers when he got me started in the hockey school business. Then he was an ECAC coach (Yale) when I worked for the ECAC. And, finally, we worked together on two U.S. teams: the 1991 Canada Cup squad and the 1994 U.S. Olympic Team. Tim died on April 27, 2013. This was written shortly after his memorial service.

Saturday, June 1, was, as Bob Johnson might have observed, another great day for hockey. In Chicago, the Black Hawks were preparing to open the Western Conference Finals of the Stanley Cup playoffs against the defending champion Los Angeles Kings. Their team having come back from a three games-to-one deficit to the Detroit Red Wings in the previous round, Hawks fans were brimming with confidence that this was their year.

In Boston, the forecast called for 90+ degrees and uncomfortable humidity, but the beloved Bruins were going to open the Eastern Conference Finals against the powerful Pittsburgh Penguins and all of New England had appointment television set for 8:00 p.m.

And a slapshot away in Cambridge, at the venerable Memorial Church nestled in the middle of Harvard Yard, this great day for hockey was launched with a memorial service for Tim Taylor, the former Harvard University captain who went on to coaching glory at Yale, of all places, and with USA Hockey. Taylor, who passed away on April 27 after a four-year struggle with cancer, was a beloved figure in hockey circles that spread from his hometown of Natick, MA, across the United States and across the Atlantic Ocean as well.

Despite the heat, and the competing events that an early June calendar can hold, more than 700 hockey people braved the weather to pay tribute to this humble yet accomplished coach and mentor. It was a response that must have pleased Tim's wife, Diana, and Tim's children, Leah and Justin.

If the late Herb Brooks and the aforementioned Bob Johnson vied for the label of "America's Coach," perhaps Tim was "America's Teacher." Surely no one had as great an impact on a combined legion of players and coaches alike as did Taylor.

The gathering heard three wonderful speakers describe Tim's life from three unique perspectives. Younger brother Ben Taylor painted a picture of life in the Taylor household, where four brothers, all separated by six years, competed in a variety of games, inside and outside the family household in their formative years. He recalled the impact his older brother had on him and the family.

"Like most families, my parents would never tell us who their favorite was when we asked the question," said Ben. "But we couldn't help but notice that there were three pictures hanging in our kitchen. One was a drawing of Abraham Lincoln. One was a photo of John F. Kennedy. And the third was a photo of Tim in his USA Hockey uniform. That's pretty good company."

John Gummere was next. A standout defenseman at St. Lawrence University, and roommate of coaching legend Ron Mason, Gummere recalled first meeting Taylor as a high school hockey player, in the days before summer festivals and prospect camps, when a group of future college standouts competed in Lynn, MA, on summer nights.

Of his early meetings with this guy Tim Taylor, Gummere recalled, "My first summer at Lynn, it seemed to me that if I played one game, 'Tayla' would play two, and if I played two games, he would play three. Finally I said, 'Hey Timmy, why don't you stay in Marblehead?' By the end of the summer, my mother is announcing that we are not to mess up Timmy's room."

Jack Parker was last. Parker and Taylor competed as Division I coaches for three decades. Invariably, when the fates of Parker's Terriers and Taylor's Bulldogs are discussed, Yale's improbable 7-5 win over what would be the 1978 NCAA champion Terriers is brought up. Almost always by the Yalies. That win at Yale's Ingalls Rink on February 18, 1978, came against a BU team that was 21-0 at the time and would finish 30-2 with that national title.

But Jack Parker's memory of Tim Taylor went back well beyond that great Taylor moment.

"I can remember the very first time I met Tim Taylor," recalled Parker with a grin. "It was exactly 50 years ago, in the spring of 1963. At that time, we all played in the Mayflower League at the Boston Skating Club. High school guys played in the Junior Mayflower League and older guys in the Senior Mayflower League.

"I was in high school, playing in the junior league, but this one week I got the call to play with the big guys. And I got to play with Tim Taylor, who was just out of Harvard. I can't remember much about the game, but I do remember that when it was over, Tim came up to me and said he wanted to show me a few things about taking face-offs.

"So there we are, out on the ice, with the Zamboni trying to make its rounds, and Tim is showing me a few things that can help me win face-offs. And that's Tim Taylor. A teacher. And a coach."

And so the afternoon went. Not only in the formality of the speakers rising to the podium but also in so many private conversations outside the church. Former players and coaching colleagues not even getting to the brilliance of his coaching mind, but focusing, more often than not, on the kindness and inclusiveness that was Tim Taylor.

His impact on hockey in the United States was difficult to quantify. But if someone could have developed an application that could have produced a hockey genealogy from the attendees on June 1 in Harvard Yard, the resulting "six degrees of Tim Taylor" would have provided a pretty good history of late 20th century amateur hockey in America.

There, under the shade trees were coaches from Tim's West Suburban Hockey Camp, a wonderful laboratory for players and coaches alike, that made an impact on so many players and coaches in the 1970s, before the promoters took over off-season hockey.

There, by the lemonade, and scattered about, so many Harvard hockey players. Household names like Bill Cleary, Joe Cavanagh Mark Fusco and

At left, Tim Taylor gives instruction from the Yale bench. At right, a portrait of Tim by artist Kelly Clark that was unveiled in 2017. It hangs in Ingalls Rink. (Top: Diane Wobolewski Photo courtesy of Yale University)

Ted Donato. And so many others spanning five-plus decades.

Some, like Bob Goodenow, Harvard '74, the former head of the NHL Players Association, flew in just for the event. He had spent the night before dining at the Newtowne Grille, a restaurant where Tim Taylor had taken him so many times. Taylor was not only one of Goodenow's coaches at Harvard, he also helped launch Goodenow in the hockey school business, where thousands more learned the game. (Tim did the same for this writer.)

Goodenow's dining partner on Friday night was Jim Thomson, who first met Tim while a youth hockey player in Waterloo, Iowa. Not only did Taylor play four years of senior hockey for the Waterloo Blackhawks following graduation, he also helped establish Waterloo's youth hockey program. Thomson, who played hockey while at Harvard, would himself get involved in youth hockey and the building of a rink. The Taylor legacy at work.

Matching all those Crimson were scores of Elis who played for Tim during his 28 seasons in New Haven. You could have suited up a few pretty good squads if there was a sheet of ice nearby. My ability to recognize them in suits was not as precise as it was with the Harvards but in addition to the likes of Jon Ormiston, Randy Wood and Dave Basseggio, I did spot five pretty good Yale goalies in the crowd: Todd Sullivan, Mike O'Neill, Dan Lombard, Alex Westlund and Keith Allain, the latter Tim's first goalie and current Yale head coach.

The college coaching fraternity was represented with some of the game's most successful and long standing coaches. In addition to the likes of Jack Parker, Ted Donato and Keith Allain mentioned above, there was Jerry York, Toot Cahoon, Bill Cleary, Dick Umile, Jim Higgins, Billy O'Neill, Jimmy Madigan, Ben Smith, C.J. Marottolo, Mike Cavanaugh, David Quinn, Red Gendron, Joe Marsh, Mike Gilligan and many more I am sure I have missed.

Brian Burke was on hand. So was Ron Rolston, recently named head coach of the Buffalo Sabres. Garry Eggleston, late of NHL Central Scouting, and Mike Smith, a former NHL general manager and Clarkson hockey player, also attended.

And finally, there, reflecting as much sadness as any constituency save Tim's family were players, coaches, and administrators from USA Hockey. Tim had been an assistant coach to Lou Vairo on the 1984 U.S. Olympic squad and had assumed head coaching duties for Team USA in the 1991 Canada Cup after Bob Johnson took ill. He led that squad to a silver medal. He was the head coach of our last pre-NHL Olympic Team in 1994 in Lillehammer, Norway.

Saturday's gathering was dotted with players from these stops. Mark Fusco and Mark Kumpel from the 1984 Olympic squad; Mike Richter and Brian Leetch from the 1991 Canada Cup team; John Lilley and Ted Crowley from the 1994 Olympic roster.

The last stop on Tim's phenomenal hockey resume was as the primary talent evaluator for Team USA's 2013 gold medal-winning junior team. For many of us, our last image of Tim was watching him on television on January 5 following Team USA's 3-1 win over Sweden in the final held in Ufa, Russia. There he was at game's end, singing the national anthem, arm in arm with the young American players. It was a sight to hold in our hearts for an eternity.

Tim's genius played a major role in this particular U.S. success, as he was the major architect of the U.S. roster, just as he had done in 2010, the last time Team USA took World Junior gold.

The night before the memorial service, USA Hockey hosted a private dinner for a cross section of Tim's hockey friends. There were contemporaries who once played with Tim. There were coaches who competed with or against him in college hockey. And there were current USA Hockey staffers — like Ron DeGregorio, Dave Ogrean, Paul George, Keith Blase, Art Berglund, Lou Vairo, Ben Smith and Jimmy Johannson — who had front row seats for so many of Tim's great international moments going back to the 1980s.

While much of the Friday night discourse was personal and private, there was a theme that ran throughout so many conversations that took place during the two-day celebration. And it was that Tim Taylor lived the life he wanted to live, and he lived it very well.

He could have returned home after being cut from the 1964 Olympic Team and pursued any number of vocations, the most likely option being

The Boston Globe, which was owned by his family at the time. But it was clear to all who knew him then that he had identified the one passion that he wanted to pursue and that was ice hockey.

And as this singular life in hockey was remembered nearly 50 years later, it became clear that beyond the satisfaction this gentle teacher and coach must have taken from so many stops along the way, the number of us whose lives were impacted in profound ways surely reached the thousands. Thousands whom he touched directly, and thousands more that those of us who stayed in hockey have had the opportunity to reach as well.

And in the end, for most of us, the sadness with which we began that hot afternoon in Cambridge gave way to an appreciation of all that Tim Taylor had accomplished in serving the game he loved so much.

Catching Up: Al Renfrew
("Stops & Starts," AHCA, 2014)

There was a time when the agenda for the annual AHCA Convention in Naples would regularly feature a "Retired Coaches Panel," often comprised of many of the same coaches. In fact, there existed a somewhat informal Retired Coaches Committee, led by the late Charles "Lefty" Smith, the former Notre Dame coach, who took the lead in this area.

Not only would the group assemble in Naples, but they also created the Lou Lamoriello Award, recognizing a former college hockey player or coach for their post-college achievement. This gesture was in appreciation for the many times Lou would fly in the likes of Ferny Flaman, Amo Bessone, Lefty and others to see a New Jersey Devils practice and a game and generally treat them to a first-class hockey weekend.

Another of these regular retirees was Al Renfrew, the former head coach at Michigan Tech, North Dakota and Michigan, the final stop being Al's alma mater and where he had the distinction of winning NCAA championships as both a player (1948) and as a head coach (1964).

In the 50th anniversary season of that 1964 championship, I had the pleasure of sitting down with Al in his Ann Arbor home, one block from "The Big House," and catching up with him. If you have had the pleasure of spending any time with the 89-year-old Renfrew, you undoubtedly come away hoping to have his sense of humor and mental acuity ... tomorrow ... let alone when you are 89.

The visit began with a phone call a month prior, as I reconnected with him and told him I'd like to come out and pay a visit. When I inquired about his health and he responded with, "Well, the doctor told me I had two weeks to live," I wasn't concerned because I knew a punch line would follow.

"Really, Al?"

"Yeah. So I told him I'd take the first week of December and the last week of January."

Al Renfrew grew up in Toronto and found his way to the University of Michigan in the fall of 1945. His path to Ann Arbor was not the result of any sophisticated recruiting campaign. No showcase tournament. No breakdown of a recruit on video.

"There was a guy a couple of streets over that said they're looking for hockey players down in Michigan. So we wrote to Vic (Heyliger) and he wrote back and said come on down. 'The streets are paved with gold' and all that," he recalled with a laugh.

"We landed in Detroit. On the train. And the first guy we saw was a about a 5´5´´ cop, smoking a cigarette. Up in Canada, you had to be 6´0´´ and you couldn't smoke on the job. We thought, 'Where the hell are we?'"

Renfrew had been playing junior hockey and his goaltender was John MacInnes, who would accompany him to Michigan and would later become the legendary coach at Michigan Tech. They won a Junior B championship and Renfrew served two years in the service before heading off to college. Michigan was the only school to which he applied.

A talented left wing, Renfrew once scored two goals seven seconds apart as a freshman. As a junior, Michigan competed in the first NCAA Championship, held for the first 10 years at the Broadmoor in Colorado Springs, and the Wolverines took home the first of their nine NCAA titles

This is a familiar scene. Al Renfrew, at left, is enjoying a Retired Coaches Panel in Naples, cracking up Amo Bessone, Lefty Smith and Bob Peters in the process. (Jennifer Ziegelmaier Photo)

with an 8-4 win over Dartmouth in the championship game.

Renfrew enjoyed his playing days at Michigan and credited Heyliger for keeping things fun.

"We had good teams," he said. "Hockey is a great sport when you can enjoy practice. And he made it fun."

In four years as a strong left wing, Renfrew scored 91 goals and added 81 assists for 172 points, finishing his career as captain of the team and second all time in Michigan scoring. Even 50 years after his graduation, he remained among the school's top 20 scorers.

In 1951, Renfrew became the head coach at Michigan Tech, starting an interesting intertwining of Amo Bessone, Vic Heyliger, John MacInnes and Renfrew. Bessone, who had played for Heyliger at the University of Illinois, left Michigan Tech after the 1950-51 season to take the head coach position at Michigan State, opening the door for Renfrew's introduction to coaching. Bessone stayed at Michigan State through the 1978-79 season, winning the NCAA title in 1966.

Renfrew coached five seasons at Tech, leaving at the end of the 1955-56 season to coach at North Dakota, where he stayed for one year before replacing Heyliger at Michigan in 1957. John MacInnes, Al's former teammate at Michigan, took over at Michigan Tech in 1957 and stayed through the 1981-82 season.

The Wolverines went 222-207-11 during Al Renfrew's 16 seasons, the highlight being the 1964 NCAA championship, the school's seventh following the six won by Heyliger from 1948-56. Surviving members from that 1964 squad will be getting together with their coach later this year.

In all, Renfrew coached for 16 seasons and compiled a winning mark of 288-286-13. A look at the years he began his stints at both Michigan Tech and Michigan shows how he improved each year, increasing win totals in each of his first five years and reaching the 20+ win mark in year five at both campuses.

Following his retirement in 1973, Renfrew went to work in the Michigan athletic ticket office, along side his wife, Marguerite, who was the sister-in-law of Vic Heyliger. Together, Al and Marguerite are given credit for starting the tradition that continues to this day whereby Michigan football players enter the field on game day and touch the "M" banner that is stretched above them. Initially, these were homemade flags and they were featured at Friday pep rallies before returning to the Renfrew home. Later, the large banner was created for Michigan Stadium on game day and that is what is seen each home weekend today.

Al was also involved with the AHCA, serving as vice-president from 1959-61 and as president from 1961-63. He marvels at how the organization has grown.

"It was fun back then because it was small. Probably no more than 50 people in the room. Always at the Kenmore Hotel in Boston," he recalled. "The guy who was in charge of the whole thing was (Eddie) Jeremiah. He always had everything written out. When you became president, you just read what he wrote. What a super guy.

"We had an agenda. (Jack) Riley took the roll. Everybody thought he took the roll and gave it to the school so they knew you went to the meeting. We always had a direct influence on the rules, just like you do today. Bill Stewart was a referee from Boston and deserves a lot of credit for what went on at these meetings."

Al still attends quite a few Michigan games and, when pressed, will offer his thoughts on today's game. In no particular order:

On four officials on the ice: "Too many refs now, too many guys on the ice. Maybe if the rinks were bigger it would be alright. We had a rule in our league. We always took the referees out. But you couldn't take them unless both coaches were there."

On relationships of coaches: "I don't think they have the fun we had. When Amo (Bessone) was at Michigan State and I was at Michigan, we would attend football games together. Mary, his wife, would come down and help babysit the kids and we'd go to the football game together."

When asked if he ever scouted opponents: "Question: Did you know anything about your opponents before you played them?" Answer: "Hell no. All you knew was that you'd beat them if you got more goals than they did."

As you can tell, a sense of humor has served Al well over his nine decades. I happened to mention Bobby Orr during our conversation. Al recalled meeting him at a Hall of Fame event up in Orr's hometown of Parry Sound.

"Well, he was leaning on me," recalled Al. "You know, he's only got one good leg. So I said to him, 'You know, Bobby, outside of Bobby Baun, you were my favorite player.' Well, he got a good laugh out of that."

And so, too, does anyone who spends time with Al Renfrew. The 1964 NCAA championship team will be getting together during this 50th anniversary season and Al is sure to keep the guys laughing. A few days after returning home from my Ann Arbor visit, I received a handwritten note from Al. He told me how much he enjoyed our visit. And he finished with a reminder of something he had said while I enjoyed our time in his home.

"Remember, the good thing about old age is that it doesn't last that long."

What is it About Hands?
(Personal essay written on Facebook: 2016)

I wrote this after two legends of sports died in 2016, Muhammad Ali and Gordie Howe. Without a place to get it published, I just posted it on Facebook for my friends.

Two of my sports heroes died during the first week of June and when I heard of their passing, I immediately thought of their hands.

In 1975, Muhammed Ali was scheduled to speak at Harvard University's Sanders Theater and I, idling around Harvard Square in those years between graduation and steady employment, heard that he would be giving a pre-speech press briefing at a common room in Kirkland House.

A few of us decided to attend and then found it surprisingly easy to gain access to the event, arriving shortly before Ali and his entourage entered the room. For all that has been written about his athletic prowess and his unique humanity, he was quite spectacularly a beautiful man, stunningly so in the proximity we enjoyed that afternoon so many years ago.

I don't remember a single question or answer, but I clearly recall a moment when, to punctuate whatever point he was making, he produced three quick three jabs into an open palm, the raw speed of his hands making all of us in the room suddenly stand a little taller in response.

About a decade later, I was employed as the goaltending coach for the Boston Bruins. Part of the preseason ritual then was an exhibition game featuring first-year players, the annual "Rookie Game." One I remember was between the Bruins' rookies and those of the Hartford Whalers, played at the Avon Old Farms School rink in Connecticut. The Whalers had recently financed the facility on the Avon grounds for the mutual benefit of the two organizations.

I actually remember two things about that day. First, rookie games are interminable affairs, characterized by one on-ice skirmish after another as the young aspirants drop their gloves upon the slightest provocation. God forbid that coaches and scouts would question their toughness.

The other memory involves my getting a tour of the new facility between periods of the scrimmage and, upon entering the training room, seeing a familiar figure clad in a gray sweat suit, sitting on a stationary bicycle.

"Joe, I'd like you to meet Gordie Howe," said my host. And so I did.

Not unlike my brush with Ali in 1975, I remember little about my introduction to Mr. Hockey other than his hands. When I shook his hand, I recall this large and beefy mitt that swallowed up my own. It was not particularly surprising because I had read much about him over the years and it was consistent with what I had learned and observed.

What is it about hands? I know that more often than not, when we think of someone from our past, we first recall their face, their smile, their gaze. But hands have a special power, too.

When we want to offer modest praise, we give a pat on the back. When we are fair, we are said to be even-handed. When we need to show strength, we may rule with an iron fist. When we seek to help the less fortunate, we lend a hand.

When my own father died in September 2000, I wrote the eulogy and was designated to deliver it at St. Eulalia's Church in Winchester. Confident that I could complete the task, I took the podium and was moving deliberately through the prepared remarks when I reached the section in which I referenced my father's hands.

The trouble began as I was transitioning from thanking the congregation for their support to defining what made my father who he was.

"A hockey friend of mine, upon meeting my brother for the first time, said to me, 'I see your brother does things with his hands; you do things with your head,' he observed.

"Putting aside, for the moment, the merits of that observation, I'd like to think my father was one who did things with both his hands and his head. Certainly, we can all picture those big hands," I said.

The typed script actually said more simply, "Certainly we can all

My father, Bob Bertagna (left), speaking with my Harvard coach Bill Cleary.

picture him doing things with his hands." Looking at the tattered page from 2000, I see a hand-written note in the margin suggesting I use "those big hands." And that's when I lost it.

He had large, strong hands. I had vivid memories of him pounding nails during household projects. One, two, done. One, two, done. But they were skilled hands in other ways, too. They painted seascapes. They carved decoys. They chopped and diced in the kitchen. And they held me, so many years ago, across my mid-section as the young father hoisted the young son onto his lap at dinner time.

Sensing the attendees were willing me to get through that personal challenge 16 years ago, I eventually found my composure and completed my father's eulogy. And today, a father of three teenagers myself, when I think of my father, I picture his face, but I see his large hands as well.

I don't know what my children will see when they remember me. I am not my father. I don't have his strong hands. But mine have tried to lift them, perhaps shape them. And if nothing else, point the way forward. That would be enough for me.

Acknowledgments

*"And I want to thank the little people. You know, little people.
Mickey Rooney, Albie Pearson ... "*
— Unknown 1960s stand-up comic

Putting this book together has been a wonderful experience. And I had a lot of help along the way. I have to start with John Veneziano, who did much of the hard work. He was my copy editor who provided so many missing commas, and he also took away many more that were deemed unnecessary.

A handful of people read chapters along the way, but I leaned heavily on input from Tim Rappleye and Steve Hardy. They knew me, they knew the subject matter and they were published authors themselves.

Attorney Maura Sheehan and her daughter, Megan, provided advice as I navigated the more sensitive matters from my conference days, steering me clear of anything that could be deemed a breach of confidentiality. Maura also made sure I considered softer ways to vent some of my feelings.

Alicia Zampitella designed the cover and gave the book the feel that I was looking for. Jerry DiFazio was the calming voice in the actual printing process. Dan Parkhurst, as he has done so often, helped me set up a website.

Finally, there were the providers of so many wonderful photographs. I have acknowledged the source of them all in the next few pages, but special thanks must go out to Harvard University, the Eastern College Athletic Conference, Hockey East, the Boston Red Sox, the Boston Bruins, Robert Fitzpatrick and the Odyssey Trust of Belfast, TD Garden, the American Hockey Coaches Association and USA Hockey.

While the primary purpose of this section is to address those who helped with the production of this book, I want to devote some space to acknowledge the people in my life who either made a lot of this possible or simply helped me get to a good place at a given moment.

I opened this effort with some love for my hometown of Arlington, MA. Three of my special friends from so many years ago — Brian Dacey, Bernie Quinlan and Rick Rigazio — remain just as close today. Until Covid-19 emerged, we would dine every two months, along with my brother Bob and (until his passing in 2014) my Harvard roommate Joe Walker. This went on for 15 years, and I hope we can renew the tradition soon.

Todd Lampert is my go-to guy when I want to discuss all things goaltending. Maybe it's a comment on one of his Northeastern University netminders or perhaps to seek his take on the latest bad goal we saw on televison the night before. But more than that, it's to stop by his sporting goods store to continue a five-decade friendship.

When I need advice on a commissioner-related matter, Steve Hagwell of ECAC Hockey is my sounding board. He is knowledgeable, but beyond that, he does things the right way. He has also become a travel buddy, the two of us having enjoyed a couple of trips to Italy with, I hope, many more to be planned.

While we don't share as many lunches as we used to, Steve Nazro and I have maintained a special friendship that was born of a work relationship so many years ago. Steve has always had a gift of being supportive when I needed it but honest at the same time. And I could say the same thing about my old boss at Harvard, Dave Matthews.

Once a week, weather and schedules permitting, I enjoy a three-mile walk around a lake near my old Hockey East office with Bob Conceison. Bob and I are both former college goalies who are finishing our seventh decade on this planet. He is a highly successful high school head coach, and when we started these walks, he would share with me his world of high school hockey and I would counter with the latest in the college game. But in recent years, the talk has been focused on family matters and the aging process. Lots on the aging process.

Then, of course, there is my family. I have referenced my siblings in the body of the book. And there are my wonderful kids. I have always loved them. Now they are adults and I find that I like the people they have grown to be. When I was a young adult and would call my mother, she always picked up the phone and acted like we hadn't spoken in years. There was always this pure joy in her voice. I hope I show that joy when I hear from my kids.

Finally there is my partner. She would hate any special attention. So I will just make sure she gets the last word. Thanks, Kath.

The real athlete in the Bertagna family (at left), with Rick Middleton.

Photo Credits

When a photograph required a specific credit, it was provided with the caption. What follows is a comprehensive documentation of the source of all images used in this book listed by chapter and source.

Front Cover
Boston Bruins

Chapter One: Arlington, Massachusetts
Pages 7, 10, 13, 15, 17, 22 (top): Bertagna Collection;
Page 18: Boston Garden;
Page 21-22 (bottom): Boston Globe;
Page 23: Boston Red Sox

Chapter Two: Harvard University
Pages 26: Tim Morse/Harvard Varsity Club;
Page 29: Gary Waleik/WBUR;
Page 31: Bertagna Collection (top);
Pages 33, 37, 43, 45, 48: Harvard University;
Page 31 (bottom), Page 36: Mel Hookailo/Harvard University;
Page 35: Dick Raphael/Harvard University

Chapter Three: Coaching Goalies
Pages 50: Paul Chalue;
Pages 51, 53, 59, 61, 63, 66 (right), 68: Bertagna Collection;
Page 56: USA Hockey;
Page 60 (left): Jennifer Ziegelmaier;
Page 66 (left): John Aiken Sr.;
Page 69: Larry Bella

Chapter Four: Adult Hockey
Pages 75, 82, 84, 90 (top), 91: Bertagna Collection;
Page 87: *Gloucester Daily Times*;
Page 90 (bottom): JAS International

Chapter Five: The ECAC Years
Page 95: Patriot League, West Coast Conference, University of Vermont; American Athletic Conference;
Page 99: John Garner;
Page 100: Dave Matthews (left) and Northeastern University (right);
Page 103: Boston Red Sox:
Page 106: Rich Gagnon;
Page 107: Rudy Winston/ECAC Hockey;
Page 109: Tim Morse/ECAC;
Page 112: Dave Smallwood;
Pages 114, 115: ECAC

Chapter Six: Hockey East Calls
Pages 122, 161 (top), 163: Hockey East;
Pages 132, 134: Boston Red Sox;
Pages 142, 143 (top): The Odyssey Trust;
Pages 143 (bottom) and 161 (bottom): William Cherry/The Odyssey Trust;
Page 149: Jennifer Ziegelmaier;
Page 159: University of Vermont;
Page 166: Steve Babineau/Hockey East;
Page 167: Boston College

Chapter Seven: Alphabet Soup
Pages 175, 186 (top left), 187, 189, 192 and 195 (bottom): Jennifer Ziegelmaier;
Page 176: Brian Blanco/Hobey Baker Foundation;
Page 186 (top right): Bowdoin College;
Pages 186 (bottom) and 195 (top): Bertagna Collection;
Page 190: University of Maine

Chapter Eight: Starting Over
Page 205: *Yale Daily News*:
Page 207: Dan Hickling/Eastern Hockey League;
Pages 212, 215, 221: USA Hockey;
Page 203, 217: Bertagna Collection

Chapter Nine: Tributes
Page 224: Charles Carey/Harvard University;
Page 227: Harvard University;
Pages 230, 231 and 233: TD Garden;
Pages 238, 243 and 247: The Riley Family;
Pages 246 and 257: Jennifer Ziegelmaier;
Page 250 (top): Boston Red Sox;
Page 250 (bottom): Steve Babineau/Hockey East;
Page 254: Diane Wobolewski/Yale University;
Page 261: Bertagna Collection

Back Cover
Jennifer Ziegelmaier

Color Centerspread
Family at Fenway Park and Ceremonial Pitch: Boston Red Sox; Depot Cafe Bombers: Elz Spofford; Boston Bruins Team Picture: Al Ruelle/Boston Bruins; Goalie Camp Staff: John Giammatteo; All Others: Bertagna Collection

About the Author

Joe Bertagna has spent a half century as a player, coach, administrator and journalist in the sport of ice hockey. A college hockey commissioner for 38 years, he remains active as a goalie coach and commissioner of the Eastern Hockey League, a junior hockey league in the eastern United States. He has also served as the first and, to date, only Executive Director of the American Hockey Coaches Association, a position he began in 1991.

A graduate of Harvard University, he played goal at Harvard and briefly as a professional. He also coached for a short time at Harvard, most notably as its first women's hockey coach. His goalie coaching has taken him to the National Hockey League and the Olympics.

Joe and his wife, Kathy, reside in Gloucester, MA.